Crafting Society

LEA'S COMMUNICATION SERIES
Jennings Bryant/Dolf Zillmann, General Editors

Selected titles in the Communication Theory and Methodology subseries (Jennings Bryant, series advisor) include:

Berger • *Planning Strategic Interaction: Attaining Goals Through Communicative Action*

Dennis/Wartella • *American Communication Research: The Remembered History*

Greene • *Message Production: Advances in Communication Theory*

Heath/Bryant • *Human Communication Theory and Research: Concepts, Contexts, and Challenges*

Jensen • *Ethical Issues in the Communication Process*

Riffe/Lacy/Fico • *Analyzing Media Messages: Using Quantitative Content Analysis in Research*

Salwen/Stacks • *An Integrated Approach to Communication Theory and Research*

For a complete list of other titles in LEA's Communication Series, please contact Lawrence Erlbaum Associates, Publishers

Crafting Society

Ethnicity, Class, and Communication Theory

Donald G. Ellis
University of Hartford

LEA

LAWRENCE ERLBAUM ASSOCIATES, PUBLISHERS

1999   Mahwah, New Jersey   London

P 91
. E377
1999

Lawrence Erlbaum Associates, Inc., Publishers
10 Industrial Avenue
Mahwah, NJ 07430

Cover design by Kathryn Houghtaling Lacey

Library of Congress Cataloging-in-Publication Data

Ellis, Donald G.
Crafting society : ethnicity, class, and communication theory / by
Donald G. Ellis
    p. cm. — (LEA's communication series)
  Includes bibliographical references and index.
ISBN 0-8058-3273-4 (cloth : alk. paper)
1. Communication. 2. Social classes. 3. Ethnicity. I. Title.
II. Series
P91.E377 1999
  302.2 —dc21   98-54947
                                                      CIP

Books published by Lawrence Erlbaum Associates are printed on
acid-free paper, and their bindings are chosen for strength and dura-
bility.

Printed in the United States of America
10 9 8 7 6 5 4 3 2 1

For my son, David

Contents

Preface

The ideas in this book have been bubbling around in my head for the past few years. I started to make notes and gather materials in 1995, but was only able to write in the small crevices of my time. I proceeded slowly because I wanted to be as clear as possible about things. The study of communication, language, and discourse continues to excite me. These topics have, at the same time, a simplicity, elegance, and complexity. They are informed by both the microsubjective experiences of individuals, and the macroprocesses in a culture. The questions and concerns of communication are very modern, but seek anchorage in the traditions of the humanities and social sciences. All of these make for a challenge that I cannot ignore.

I take some risks in this book. I patrol some theoretical borders that have been pretty heavily armed, and set up some defenses that have yet to be tested. But I am searching for new strategic communication positions, and some risks are necessary. It is not enough to hold the old lines.

A few of these issues appear in earlier publications. Some of the ideas about meaning and coherentism that appear in sections of chapter 3 were first published in Ellis (1995).

This book could not have been completed had I not had a sabbatical leave, graciously granted by the University of Hartford, in the spring of 1998. During this sabbatical I spent 3 months in Israel finishing the book. I was in contact with colleagues at Hebrew University and had the opportunity to use their facilities. To write and think in that context was a privilege.

I also benefited from the New York University (NYU) Faculty Associates program. This program provided time and money for travel to NYU to use their library and facilities. I am indebted to the Faculty Associates program and my university for allowing me to participate and helping me complete this project.

Susan Coleman of the International Center at the University of Hartford pitched in when I was short of money needed to complete certain work. Her generosity and understanding are particularly noteworthy because Professor Coleman simply volunteered to help after sensing my frustration in a conversation.

Linda Bathgate and Lawrence Erlbaum Associates have provided wonderful support for this project. Linda's professionalism and talents for working with authors are refreshing.

My friends and colleagues in the School of Communication at the University of Hartford are always there to explore, criticize, and discuss ideas. There remains a bond between many of us that makes it a joy to dwell in a community of people that unite work and friendship.

My family's love and affection, which is a reservoir of strength and energy from which I can draw, are something for which I am always grateful.

—*Donald G. Ellis*
West Hartford, Connecticut

Introduction

There is a sense of common terrain with respect to future issues in communication. These are the issues I grapple with in this book. Scholars generally agree on three things:

1. There is a growing emphasis on meaning and the role of human agency in constructing messages and discourse.
2. The importance of mediated experience and the post-mass media.
3. Continuing efforts to link microcommunication activities (e.g., language, interaction) with macrosocial categories such as ethnicity and social class. In other words, how social categories such as class and ethnicity are "coded" into everyday interactions. In this introduction, I briefly explain each of these and then detail how they fit into this book.

The first issue—meaning and human agency—is essentially concerned with the way people construct their social worlds through communication. As language users confront and produce oral and written texts, they represent these texts cognitively in particular ways. These representations are not pure; they are influenced by an individual's attitudes, ideologies, biases, and so on. For example, in news reports about ethnic affairs, a journalist will favor a particular interpretation by how a story is written. In a sentence such as, "Because of their lower levels of education, African Americans have a higher unemployment rate," a psychological explanation of unemployment is privileged over a structural or political one. In short, everyday interaction is the edifice on which other social issues (e.g., ethnicity, class, and gender) are erected.

It is also true that social structure is made of networks of contacts and the communication that takes place within these networks. What people talk about and how they talk to each other determines their relationships, and these relationships make up the various social stratifications of society. This book includes analyses of types of communication, their meanings, and how these types are associated with social categories of ethnicity and class.

The second issue is the very important and modern concern of the media and how consciousness and social structures are influenced by modern forms of electronic media in particular. Although individuals create subjective meanings in their conversations, the nature of modern media is probably equally influential. "Medium" theory is not concerned with content—for example, what is "on" television—but with the impact of the medium on consciousness in general and society in particular. The work of McLuhan, Ong, and Havelock is all relevant here. All messages are filtered through a medium (e.g., oral language, printed words, or electronic messages), and each of these media have characteristics of speed, personal involvement, and information load that ultimately influence consciousness, expectations, and social order. For example, modern issues of global democracy and culture were not possible until the advent of high-speed electronic information transmission.

In keeping with my focus on communication and social theory, I extend the work of McLuhan and Ong by showing how modern media are responsible for some of the fault lines in society. I argue that media, including their resources and touch points, are the crucial dividing lines in social structure. For example, it is commonly understood that the development of writing, and later the printing press, changed the entire nature of information dissemination, and created an elite literate class. This resulted in democratization of information and significant power changes.

I explore modern electronic media that makes for dramatic increases in speed, information transmission, and storage, and the distances among users. Modern electronic media create a powerful sense of verisimilitude, such that we experience what is called the *distant present;* that is, even though messages are complex, sophisticated results of high technology and planning, they appear to be natural, real, and occurring in real time. Feelings, identifications, images, empathic rapport, and emotional responses are all heightened because of the ability to create isolated senses of reality. One need only turn to television and computers for examples.

The third main theme of this book is more theoretical in nature. It is concerned with the connections between specific communication patterns and more general social conditions. The focus is on the nature of these links. I do this by extending the work of theorists such as Goffman, Anthony Giddens, Karl Weick, and Randall Collins, and using the concept of interaction chains. This concept is concerned with the micro–macro link, or the grounding of nonempirical social categories, such as class or ethnicity, to concrete empirical communicative events.

The essential argument is that macrotopics of sociology (e.g., ethnicity) are never actually seen but exist in and through the activities of individuals in microsituations; that is, individuals communicating in situations. These

macrotopics are idealizations or typifications that are documented and continually reproduced through microexamples. This is how the "realities" of issues
such as ethnicity and class change. As interactions and their assigned meanings
change, so do the macroconcepts.

OVERVIEW OF THE BOOK

The plan of this book is to begin with some comment about the status of communication theory, and then move to the explanatory core of communication,
namely, medium theory, discourse, and structuring processes. Chapter 1 is a review and critique of trends in communication theory. It criticizes strong social
constructionism and establishes media, discourse, structuration, as central tenets in a workable scientific theory of communication. Media theory, discourse,
and structuring are detailed in chapters 2, 3, and 4. Chapter 2 addresses a neglect in social theory with respect to communication, and "mediation" in general. True, Marx made mention of the printing press and its role in the
breakdown of certain class structures, Parsons made scant referral to the media,
and the concept of communication is understood by Giddens in his
structuration process. Moreover, medium theorists such as Innis, McLuhan,
and Ong successfully built a theoretical model of how media are responsible for
fault lines in society. Communication is an important theme in much social theory, but is rarely an endurable part of the theory. This chapter argues that media, including their resources and touch points, are the key dividing lines in
social structure and identity. Consistent with my primary concern of linking the
macro and the micro—or structural and interactional elements—I work in
chapter 2 to identify relations between media and interactive experiences, to
show how media constrain human experiences and then how human agency in
turn constrains media.

The fundamentals of the theoretical reconstruction are continued in chapter 3, but from the more micro-analytic perspective of discourse analysis. Here
the focus is on everyday talk. The first part of the chapter is a brief review of
these issues leading to the argument that everyday interaction is responsible for
shaping social reality, and forms the empirics of sociology. The remainder of the
chapter develops principles of conversational interaction drawing on discourse
and conversational analytic assumptions. The chapter argues that everyday interaction, including the technical details of language and discourse structure, is
the edifice on which macrostructures are erected. The chapter also attempts to
demonstrate that detailed interaction is where to look to find out how social
identification, such as class and ethnicity, is negotiated, constructed, and reproduced. The concepts of meaning and code are particulary important to the issues in chapter 3, because we must demonstrate their authenticity for a viable
communication theory.

Chapter 4 takes up the issue of organization and structuration, because these
are the interactional processes that establish organized relations and are consti-

tutive of social structures. This is essentially an inquiry into interdependence, or how things connect and hang together to bind elements into a whole. The chapter includes a brief characterization of two important statements on interdependence, beginning with Weick (1979), but mostly focusing on Giddens (1979, 1984). This chapter continues an emphasis on a microlevel, but is removed from the issues in language and discourse discussed in chapter 3. Thus, it presents a more metatheoretical framework that has reflexivity at its center. The terms *structure* and *action* are central to communication theory. It is not possible to understand organizational interdependence and its various forms without understanding these concepts. Essentially, scholars have failed to remain faithful to metatheoretical perspectives that are interdependent, processual, and action oriented. Chapter 4 is an effort to regain this focus, to return to a concept of structure based on a network of actions, not entities, that include recurring patterns that renew themselves.

The next two chapters elaborate on the basic premises of the first four chapters and move to a more abstract sociological level. Both chapters consider a sociological term—each the subject of much opinion and confusion—and discuss it according to the central explanatory issues in this book. Chapter 5 addresses the issue of ethnicity. The term *ethnicity* is damnably convoluted and filled with difficulties. It was once a term roughly coterminous with land space, common culture, and shared values. In the modern era, it is more associated with race and national origin, that is, where your ancestors were from, not where you currently live. I pose no conclusive definition in chapter 5, but risk an attempt to show that ethnicity can also be grounded in the empirics of reconstructed theory; in other words, the chapter illustrates the structuring processes for ethnicity associated with media, language use, ritualized encounters, and discourse forms. In chapter 6, I attempt the same for *social class*. Although sociology is fundamentally concerned with stratification and social class, communication scholars have essentially neglected the subject. The chapter begins with some brief history and explication leading to current thinking on class in the postindustrial age. In this chapter, I use the tenets of restated theory, combined with a Weberian notion of class as opposed to a Marxian one, to show how social class is both subjective and objective. Class is the result of a particular organization of income, behavior, authority, and literacy practices, and is reproduced and sustained in daily interaction and interpersonal organization. The labels *middle class, working class,* and so on must be grounded in the empirics of microlevel processes if these terms are to have scientific standing.

I experiment in chapter 2 by summarizing basic causal statements and propositions in the theory. I do this in chapter 2 only because the issues are most appropriate. Sometimes the statements reflect the tentative nature of the theory, but are still included for heuristic reasons. I chose this device to underscore that the goal of a scientific theory of communication is to come to grips with testable statements. Some of the statements end up as inadequate, but it is still preferable to have some formulations to be attacked, clarified, and refined than it is to have an imprecise collection of issues. I want to strive for explicitness and direction, even if these goals are elusive. The study of communication remains unfocused and scattered, and I wish to take steps, modest as they might be, to increase resolution and order. Some will find this technique of stating causal statements and propositions pedantic, premature, inappropriate, or perhaps a rather pathetic attempt at rigor. But theories advance through argument, discussion, and research; it seemed important to me to set into motion some engine that would help find out which statements were important and which might be altered or discarded. I have no problem with being proved wrong.

Length considerations, and my own scholarly proclivities, prevented me from writing an additional chapter on gender, but future analyses that draw on the theoretical underpinnings of this volume should deal with the matter of gender. Gender is usually added to race and class to form a trinity of injustices in America. Even though all three are important and interesting, they are never treated equally. Class is always easily ignored, perhaps because it remains so macro in nature. Some sociologists collect data on social class, but most of the public are quite confused about the concept, and care little about it. Interestingly, race and ethnicity are more micro in nature. There is much data and little theory about race and ethnicity. This is probably because the immorality of racism and rigid ethnic categorizing is so clear to most people that they do not need to theorize about it.

Gender strikes a balance between the micro and the macro. There are many descriptions of the microlinguistic and communicative differences between men and women. Historical inequalities faced by women have become increasingly apparent, especially since the publication of *The Feminine Mystique* by Betty Friedan in 1963. There are many detailed social scientific analyses of the lives of women. But modern feminists, by contrast, theorize heavily about gender. They are very influenced by the speculative and imaginative tenets of postmodernism. In the true sense of being "macro," they describe society as inescapably gendered.

A naive utopianism is one of the problems that results from the highly theorized statements about gender. The goals of much gender research are political, so these authors offer radical solutions that lack the empirical micro link that would relate their work to normative concerns. This book traffics in the dialectical relationship between microinteractional reality and macroconcepts, but it is thoroughly realistic at its core. Realism (see chapter 3) assumes that people live a relatively coherent boundary- defined world that constitutes a reality for them. Realistic social science tries to paint as accurate a picture as possible of the human world. Realistic social science collects data, makes arguments, and continually works the relationship between microdata levels (e.g., "female" speech) and macrocategories of understanding (e.g., "gendered" inequality).

The more abstract and macroconceptions of gender consider it only a metaphor for inequality and power differences between men and women. From this perspective (cf. Lorber, 1994), there are only minor biological differences between men and women, and the history of the world is a catalogue of misery enumerating the ways women have been discriminated against. But others argue with equal force and conviction (e.g., Gilligan, 1982) that there are gender differences. Women are different and have different "ways of knowing" and doing things.

So which is true? Are women and men the same or fundamentally different? This is an important question that must be grappled with. This literature very easily vacillates between the idea of gender as artificial and socially constructed, and gender differences as clear and essential. The ease with which these authors do this, and the unresolved tension between these two positions, should be troublesome for theorists of all types. This theoretical problem with feminism is also the result of the extreme social constructionism that I criticize in chapter 1. A majority of feminists are social constructionists who argue that differences between genders are constructed socially. These unresolved theoretical problems are the result of an undisciplined social constructionism. They also result from being influenced more by ideological considerations than empirical ones.

Gender studies seem to have their share of successes with the micro; that is, there is research that describes or illuminates concrete empirical findings pertaining to attitudes, socialization, differential treatment, discrimination, and linguistic patterns. But as we have seen here, there is considerable confusion over the macro. Gender studies need to continue going nose to nose with the empirical status of women, but need to be guided more by a micro–macro logic than by ideology.

The primary criterion for any workable theory is coherence (Ellis, 1995; Rescher, 1973), in terms of evidence, intersubjective acceptance, and relations among propositions. Our confidence in the theory increases as statements in the theory become tighter and more apparent. Networks of causal and propositional statements are systems for organizing knowledge and determining what we know. We want the networks to be coherent, and coherentism requires intelligibility, order, and verification (Rescher, 1979). A theory is a road map that makes connections and helps us get from one place to another. And of course, theories must be verified, they must be subject to empirical tests of consistency, completeness, and consonance. I try to make some progress toward these goals in this volume. I try to increase the symbolic richness of the theoretical road map. To be sure, it is an effort at synthesis, and one that is mixed and incomplete. Working out just the issues in this volume has been a large enough task for now. I have pushed the boundaries of my contested territory far enough. I leave it to others to renegotiate the space.

❖ 1 ❖

Constructing
Communication Theory

A statement is like a check drawn on a bank. Its value depends on what is there to meet it.
—Ezra Pound

The goal of this volume is to continually patrol the boundary between more microindividual processes and macrosocial processes. Human communication is at the root of social categories and structures. The experiences humans have in their past contacts with one another become the subjective attitudes and intentions of the future. As people talk, argue, and persuade one another, they realign resources and thereby restructure their relationships so that social groups and processes get renegotiated and reformed. This is the basis for social change and reality. This chapter demonstrates that language cannot be separated from social life, and is logically connected to it. It is critical of constructionist tendencies in communication and suggests a realist science of communication.

Since the Enlightenment, understanding, both lay and scientific, has been a process occurring in the mental world. This perspective surfaces in present times as logical empiricism. Interestingly, social scientists have been so quick to hinge their theories to observables that a language of mental representational states has not been forthcoming, and what is postulated is quite hypothetical. Although theorists such as Piaget and Chomsky are associated with the cognitive revolution, their constructs and assumptions about cognition are easily reduced to a computational metaphor.

The traditional "mental world" position has three assumptions, each of which is problematic. There is the *correspondence* assumption that the active cognitive agent reflects and corresponds to the external world in some substan-

1

tial way. Knowledge is carried around in the cognitive system, and understanding is more or less "correct" to the extent that it matches the objective world. Next is the *generative* assumption. This is the notion that cognition directs behavior. Learning is very important because as you increase the quantity and quality of your cognitive content, your behavior becomes "better" or more "correct." The third assumption is the *linguistic representation* assumption. This is the implication that language is directed by cognition and therefore reflects the external world. Correct, true, and accurate communication is possible.

It is certainly the case that simplistic traditionalist views of cognition and reality have been supplanted by more sophisticated theories that account for the development of "subjective" reality. In Groeben (1990), for example, the argument is made that the cognitive structure of a scientist is the same as a lay person. Language is seen as a guide to knowledge such that it is possible to make accurate inferences *from* language *to* cognitive structure and content. Everyone must make everyday assumptions about understanding, and some are better at it than others. The traditional relationship between language and cognition assumes pictures of reality that are more accurate than others. This leads to the obvious conclusion that one view of the world (e.g., a scientific view, or the view of a "smarter" person) is better than another and should be privileged by being accepted or taught in the schools. Those claiming a superior picture of reality are obligated to defend and articulate that picture, thereby continually testing it, and rendering it yet again more accurate and legitimate.

It is not much of a leap to conclude that one's picture of artistic, cultural, educational, and creative reality are also better and more deserving. Certainly, technical language and the cognitions it points to are subject to measures of accuracy, predictability, and explanatory power. But the domains of art, education, and government also have fields of language that "point" to certain realities that are predominant and "first among others." Such fields of language become "capital," in the Bourdieu sense, and therefore have power.

The title of this book and the first chapter draw on some active verbs, namely, to "craft" and to "construct." A key argument throughout this volume is that communication is a constructive process, but that construction relies on a public accessible reality. This reality is independent of representation but influenced by it. In the following sections I critique a "strong" constructionism, which holds that language is the only reality, and therefore, all of our conceptions about the world are completely discursively created subject to all linguistic limitations, even unstable and variable meaning. I elaborate on this issue in more detail in chapter 3. Searle, in his book *The Construction of Social Reality* (1995) offered the clearest and most eloquent defense of how I am using the notion of communication as constructive. When people encounter one another, or text, they assemble or "construct" meaning, but they do not do this out of thin air. They do not do it casually. They do it on the basis of rules (e.g., "Statement X counts as Y"), and background, or sets of preintentional capacities, strategies, tendencies, or cultural predispositons. (see Searle, 1995, chap. 6). These assumptions form the foundation of the issues on which I try to build in this volume.

A *field of language* is a structured space whereby positions in the structure (e.g., language) are determined by a set of relationships. A field of language under the management and control of an individual acts as a resource or *capital*, in the Bourdieu sense of the term. It is a form of cultural capital (knowledge, skills, technical qualifications). What is interesting about cultural capital is that it can be cashed in for other forms of capital, such as symbolic capital (status and prestige). These all, of course, convert to employment and financial resources.

These types of capital form fields of thought and emotion and they are developed and sustained in interaction. This chapter and the remainder of this volume are devoted to detailing this perspective with respect to a number of sociological levels of structure and interaction phenomenon. We will see that it is possible to ground social structure in the linguistic experiences of humans. The only way that "structure" can be empirically meaningful and explanatory is if it bubbles up from the real experiences of humans. This experience cannot be separated from the linguistic system, although it is not isomorphic with it. I take the special symbol using capacity of humans as a given. Humans are animals, like so many others, but they are a special eruption on the evolutionary scene because of their linguistic ability to transcend the here and now. That language can be considered capital—either cultural or symbolic—and used in power relationships is fundamental to how language bisects structure. The language-as-"capital" metaphor is important because it draws attention to how symbolic forms are practical and conspicuous displays of actions and interests. This economic metaphor is not, of course, used in the narrow reductionist sense of material gain, but to show how there is an economic logic between language and structure. If a teenager speaks and dresses in a certain way to increase the chances of attracting the opposite sex, then he or she is using a symbolic capital to negotiate an outcome.

It is equally important to underscore the limitations of an "economic" metaphor. It in no way implies that human communication is the result of conscious calculation and deliberation: a result of a cost–benefit analysis. If we are going to correlate communication patterns with social structure, then it is certainly the case that some people have undesirable linguistic deficits and positions in the social structure. Their access to and use of cultural capital cannot be premeditated and calculated, otherwise they would not choose their current station. No, a theory of communicative practice that accounts for the vacillation between structure and action must result from an encounter between one's communication code (see Ellis, 1992b) and a context or field that intersects with that code in some way. For example, an African American who finds himself in a White suburb. Or an educated professional who must manage poorly educated and unskilled workers. As communication codes develop—including their experiential and stylistic peculiarities—along with the individual, they become habitual and naturalized. Of course, linguistic capital is distributed in a related manner to economic and cultural capital (Bourdieu, 1991), so all aspects of language, from the technical details of structure (e.g., phonetic form, syntax) to the subtleties of meaning, announce social position.

LANGUAGE AND PRESENCE

To make clear the sinews that connect communication with social structure, we must demonstrate how language and communication are social in nature and cannot be definitionally removed from social life. For some people, this is an obvious enough point and does not require restatement. But there remains disagreement and interesting controversy over some fundamental assumptions about the relationship between humans and nature.

At the core of this problem is the question of whether or not human cognition is detached from objective reality. In some theoretically ideal scientific domain, there is an objective world and a human processor that maps that world. The closer the fit between cognition and reality, the more accurate and better our understanding. Science is pitted against common sense, and ultimately science wins. Although science can claim a privileged understanding of certain phenomena, it is increasingly difficult to defend the separation of cognition from reality. Skinner (1957), of course, represented such a position by arguing that learning language was a simple modeling and learning process whereby the environment was copied onto the cognitive system. But Chomsky (1959) convincingly and compellingly demonstrated that inputs from the empirical world could not adequately explain language. The great complexity and productivity of language is dependent on congenital cognitive apparatus.

This line of thinking—that people bring dispositions and strategies to the linguistic process—was important and inviting because it meant that we have the ability to organize, select, and act on the environment. Therefore, the environment did not determine meanings and understandings, but the penchant of the individual. Chomsky, and this general line of reasoning, put to rest the dream that there is an empirical world that could perfectly match the cognitive dispositions of human organisms. Still, the problem of the relationship between language and the social world remained. Certainly human consciousness did not "build up" from minuscule empirical stimuli, but neither was consciousness "given" by cognitive predispositions. An overreliance on a pure "cognitive" perspective makes communication little more than matching up cognitive systems. Moreover, it leads to the extreme solipsistic position that some idealized cognitive world is predominant. Such a perspective is also inconsistent with evolutionary theorizing that would predict that human organisms must respond to environmental variations.

There is also the interesting question of the relationship between language and mind. Chomsky (1968) maintained that language was the mirror of the mind, and that structure could be revealed through language (the "presence" of language). The larger question here is simply how informative and reliable language is. On the one hand, we must assume that ideas, thoughts, and values are present in language and recoverable from language. A theory of language and social stratification requires such an assumption because the theory must have language anticipating stratification, and stratification anticipating language. We must be confident that language use carries reference. Yet these presumptions are not without problems. It is certainly not easy to determine whether a speaker understands his or her own mental state and whether he or she can explain it. And it is perhaps impossible to establish standards of interpretation for first-, second-, or third-person observers of communication.

I do not concern myself here with the philosophical debates about the independent existence of mind and nature (see Rorty, 1979). Rather, I work with an alternative explanation of understanding that is a modification of the cognitive view, a social cognition perspective, but one that is critical of the extreme social constructionism of Gergen and Semin (e.g., Gergen & Davis, 1985; Semin & Gergen, 1990). This perspective, on the one hand, does not view humans as socially-disembodied cognitive organisms that are essentially universal and transhistorical. On the other hand, I do not make the argument that cognitive categories are only social and created by sociocultural circumstances. As one might imagine, it is not possible to suggest that class, ethnic, or gender consciousness is possible without sociocultural processes being fundamental to everyday understanding. I take it as evolutionarily determined that humans must orient themselves to a particular material world, and moreover, develop a rigorously ratifiable communication code that facilitates naming, classifying, and understanding objects and processes in the world. This communication code is only possible because of the biologically evolved cognitive capabilities of the human organism. Pure cognition is the structural process that accounts for the executive management of consciousness and understanding (e.g., recall, memory, organization), but everyday meanings and understandings are grafted onto cognition. It is important to state a position on these issues because my coherency and code theory of interaction depends on it.

Extreme constructionists (Miller & Holstein, 1993; Semin & Gergen, 1990) never leave language. For them, this automatically implies a reality that is limited, conditioned, fashioned, and subjective. The role of the scientist loses its privileged status as the keeper of reality, and putative, scientific knowledge presumably only reifies cultural understanding. For the constructionist, all social problems and conditions are a matter of definition. Constructionists draw from the intellectual traditions of Husserl, Heidegger, and Merleau-Ponty to suggest that separating the individual experiencer from the object of experience is impossible or artificial, at best. This means that there is no understanding of reality that is not conditioned by the human experiencer. Communication problems, then (e.g., confusion, misunderstanding, power, conflict, information quality) are in no way distinctive and have no inherent conditions; rather, they are problems only of definition and orientation that respond to *supposed* situations that are rhetorically constructed. In sociology, Spector and Kitsuse (1987) argued that social problems (e.g., alcoholism, violence, poverty, class consciousness) result from the "politics of claims making," and forms, letters of complaint, political speeches, press conferences, editorials, advertisements, and government policies are all responsible for the "construction" (in the strong sense) of social problems.

This strong sense of constructionism has been appealing in the social sciences and communication (Deetz, 1994; Schneider, 1985; Shotter & Gergen, 1994). Yet, many still feel that the question of the relationship between language and mind is unresolved. Certain cognitive activities and structures are at the essence of humanness, and although much concept formation is surely sociocultural and therefore interesting and important, others are endemic to the species. Certain problems persist. For example, if the mind is purely social in origin, then how do initial inputs from the environment get processed and categorized in the first place? If the mind and consciousness are purely social, how does an infant learn language at all, because he is not taught, and there are no known social categories to produce this learning? There must be some congenital conditions.

Still, many scholars insist that understanding truly human communication means that only the reality of the experiencing agent is important. This has stimulated the phenomenological perspective in which the subject and object are fused and the scientist must gain access to the lived experience of the individual. But again, this phenomenological tradition of blending the subject and object fails. There has yet to be an acceptable explanation of how a scientist, or anyone for that matter, proceeds once his identity is inseparable from another's. Just what can you conclude about the other person when you finish? What has a scientist accomplished if he assumes there is no reality outside his own? You might say the scientist brings his unique representations to the situation, but then he could not communicate them.

One problem with strong constructionists' accounts of reality and scholarship is that few people take them seriously. That is, they may claim that all reality is discursively created, but they do not behave that way. This is because it is possible to have a strong reading or a weak reading of constructionism. A strong reading of constructionism means that any knowledge claim is inextricably mired in language and socially embedded. But this amounts to programmatic relativism that leaves any analyst in the untenable position of the hermeneutic circle. We are left in the trap of recognizing that knowledge claims are socially embedded, and if we ignore this, then we are taking this social embeddedness for granted, and thus granting it ontological status. Arguing that social problems such as AIDS or the existence of cults, and interpersonal terminology such as meaning, understanding, or intimacy are socially constructed (Shotter &

Gergen, 1994), leaves these concepts to the whims of culture and a historical period. A strong reading of social constructionism leaves no criteria for recovering meaning or adjudicating knowledge claims. An analyst ends up trapped in his own self-contained theoretical system.

Strong social constructionism cannot provide any justification for how any claim to understanding, knowledge, or praxis is defensible beyond the confines of a self-defined theoretical system that makes it all a tautology. Shotter and Gergen (1994) tried to patch up this problem by suggesting that understanding is contested but negotiable. They tried to have it both ways. They wrote:

> Further, such contests and negotiations are not of an "anything goes" kind, but they are not grounded in any predetermined, outside, systematic standards either. They are "rooted" in the developed and developing conversational contexts within which the practical negotiations take place (p. 28)

This passage suggests some of the problems that plague a constructionist analysis. Constructionists try to describe what they do as empirically based ("rooted") in interaction, but they actually push analysts away from empirical research. Instead of studying how communication constructs emerge, which might provide an empirical foundation, they offer up their own analysis of "conversational context" and "practical negotiations" without explaining how they were derived. Moreover, even when derivative explanations are proffered, they are subject to the same limitations of time, space, individual, and culture. Constructionists make statements denouncing unwarranted assumptions about the world, but one finds evidence of such assumptions having been made. Ironically, when the implications of constructionism are pushed, one ends up in a mess of abstractions about humanness, language, and dialogue. The study of communication began with the assumption that it could help people and improve the world; constructionism peddles this dream for epistemology.

LANGUAGE AND EXPERIENCE

Strong social constructionism is too much of a language game that removes agency from communication (Pearce, 1994). Communication is a practical activity that accomplishes something as well as creates something. The constructionist tradition replaces God with conversation. Even though it claims to move beyond the models of unified knowledge that came with the Enlightenment to account for diversity and alternative epistemologies, constructionism ends up replacing one master narrative with another. They are actually trying to create a "pure" theory, and in the process, neglect the gritty role of political, economic, ethnic, and moral assumptions in real communication (Schudson, 1997). Moreover, a communicator's assumptions, desires, concerns, and influences are so fundamental that individuals do not recognize them as anything other than facts. These conditions, then, are not matters of reflection and debate.

We will leave the airy realm of strong constructionism's epistemological abstractions and proceed in the tradition of quantitative researchers by staying close to data, evidence, and argument (cf. Glaser & Strauss, 1967). The role of language will remain central and we will build a theory of language and communication. But the linguistic symbol will be neither godlike in its ability to "construct" reality, nor mistaken for the fundamentals of experience that language both captures and influences. We will focus on a world of social action that leads to sociological theories that are empirically grounded. The lives, interactions, and class experiences of people are related to *real* social conditions that are reflexively related to *real* communication. The rest of this chapter is devoted briefly to our experiences as animals in the evolutionary scheme, and then to the relationship between language and experience. This provides the groundwork for a theory of communication that is consistent with a coherentist epistemology. Such an epistemology avoids the problems of foundationalism, but allows for progress in communication science. I use a "weaker" sense of the verb "to construct" to describe the linguistic and cognitive assembly process that occurs during communication. The meaning of an interaction is discursively created, but it is not a substitute for reality.

Pragmatics and Biology

That humans are biologically endowed with language capabilities is not controversial (Chomsky, 1968). But the relationship between pragmatics and biology needs to be reestablished. Context or situation is at the core of pragmatics. Pragmatics comes from the relationship between language and its users. Where a linguist would note the phonetic or grammatical structure of an utterance, a pragmatist would note how and why that person or group uses the utterance. What function does the utterance or word serve? How is it meaningful to them at that time? Pragmatism is analogical and context dependent. The traditional distinction between biology and culture is misguided. There is not opposition between them; culture is an expression of biology, and different cultures are different expressions of the same biology. Culture is a form that biology takes. How could it be anything else?

Pragmatics is a "variationist" way of thinking that is in opposition to an "essentialist" way of thinking. Early intellectual history was essentialist and described humans in a Platonic, philosophical, rationalist tradition in which human mental categories were immutable and preordained by either nature or some higher intelligence. Later advances in evolution recognized variations in human functioning that were distributed along a curve. Biological thinking was transformed from a Platonic to a pragmatic approach, an approach that emphasized variability, adaptability, and purposive behavior. This opportunity for variability is evident in our diverse languages, cultures, and behaviors. But all of these diversities rest on top of the foundational human capacities for social attachments. Most animals are social, so this is not a unique human phenomenon. What is, however, is our capacity for symbolism.

We make symbols by endowing signals of various types with signification. We can use words, our bodies, behaviors, objects, and visual signs to signify power, submission, play, love, sex, family, or any of a host of human emotions and concepts. Complex human language is a powerful expression of the human ability to symbolize, but it developed in the service of our biological needs to associate and communicate. Human association and the resultant coordination of activities requires communication. All animals that group together have evolved some sort of communication system that might be simple and routinized (e.g., instinctual olfactory signals) or complex and variable (e.g., human language). Complex human language is a highly refined outcome of the evolutionary advantages that accrue from socialization and coordination with other members of the species (Cappella, 1991). The obscure and imperceptible worlds of governments, cultures, and organizations are fixed in the real communicative behavior of people in existent contexts, which is where a theory of society and communication must begin. These existent contexts are the causal center of propositions about communication and society.

The value of biology here is at the microlevel (see Collins, 1975; Durkheim, 1954). Basic issues in communication explain social phenomena. Here lies the important work of Durkheim. He showed how a group of people focused attention on one another and generated shared thought. This shared thought was suffused with emotions, ideas, and symbols, and gained fixity and strength. In *The Elementary Forms of Religious Life*, Durkheim explained how the bonds that unite animals are the same in men, the only difference being that humans attach these bonds to emotional symbols that carry meaning and significance. Durkheim's explanations of ritual behavior are very powerful and provide insights into how human cognition arises out of our biological heritage, and does not represent a radical evolutionary break with the animal world.

The basis for communication is fundamental in the manner just described. It requires at least two people and involves focused attention and formalized exchanges. Communication has evolved a common perceptual and experiential state that serves to frame our attention, and, most importantly, to transcend the present. In other words, our symbols can be stored and recalled at later times and in other situations. So human communication was aroused by animal social necessities and strengthened by routinization and our capacity for symbolization.

The submissive, acquiescent patterns of animals that form the basis of asymmetrical relationships can be seen in the power relationships in organizations as workers do what they are told, in church members invoking God, and in compliant and deferential interpersonal relationships. "Polite society" associated with the upper classes has evolved an entire system of mutual deference that is defined as "respectful" and "proper" and is rooted in the survival advantages of deference. Of course, raw power has been tamed by the internalization of social language. Power is now symbolized and unseen. Leaders rarely resort to raw co-ercion when "symbolized" threat and punishment is available.

The underlying structural foundation for human language and animal sig-naling is quite similar. Other animals make noises and gestures that become rit-ualistic and stereotyped. Human communication is more automated and innate than we usually think, and animal signaling systems are more responsive than typically imagined. Human smiling, saluting, crying, and bowing are easily asso-ciated with biological functions (Lorenz, 1966), and many animals use observa-tion and detection to learn about play, mating, hunting, dancing, and other rituals (cf. Hauser, 1996).

Nevertheless, we should not minimize the differences. Animals do not read philosophy, write poetry, or send rockets to the moon. Humans have *symbolic* capabilities that enable them to name things, endow those names with signifi-cance, and move meaning beyond immediate experience. We will examine these qualities in more detail in the ensuing chapters, but for now, our essential concern is with establishing the biological foundations of language so we can begin to build a theory of communication and society that is grounded in indi-viduals. Even granting that humans and other animals have some elemental foundations in common, we must underscore that humans have a biological language capacity that is unlike any other. The argument that human language is only possible because of linguistic structures that derive from the human ge-nome is well enough established (Chomsky, 1968; Pinker, 1994).

Pragmatics and Consciousness

We do not want to accept insights from animal ethology as constitutive of the essence of social science. We have to consider a complicated relationship among people, language, and the world. There is something that makes humans a special case; something that separates us from others on the evolutionary stage. That something is consciousness that allows symbols to carve up the world and transcend the here and now. Some anthropologists argue that the physical world to a child was an undifferentiated continuum where nothing was really "separate." Human consciousness, at the service of language, imposes a grid on the world and sorts things into categories with labels and meanings. Our understanding of the world is a re"presentation" of these language categories. A strong version of this point would be that there is no natural or intrinsic nature in the world and everything exists in a language game. The "other side" of this argument would be that the world has a set of elemental characteristics and nat-ural distinctions, and language passively draws meanings from it. The important point is to recognize the interaction between language and the world. Language does chop up and influence our concept of reality, but it does not create it out of airy nothingness.

The communicative phenomena that we are usually interested in—things such as emotions, attitudes, beliefs, and feelings—are real. Our perceptual experiences are always mediated by brain processes (How could they not be?), but it does not follow that we do not really engage the world, and that our meanings and understandings are "only" symbolic interpretations. If I look at my refrigerator, I see a real refrigerator, not an interpretation of one, even if I am processing information through photoreceptor cells in the retina that set off neuronal processes. Consciousness is a natural biological process on the same level as digestion, hearing, and eating. We will not accept the dualist insistence that there is a world "out there" and a world "in here" (the mind). Consciousness is a natural property of humans in the same way that weight is a natural property of physical objects. Just as my refrigerator is real, so too are my conclusions that you are nice, friendly, crude, aesthetic, or bright. The human communication system is part of consciousness that has evolved like all evolutionary processes evolve; that is, as a result of interaction between organism and environment. And the guiding principle of evolutionary interaction is always a functional adaptive one.

This is also true for the communicative endowment in humans. It has evolved in relationship to preexisting neural processes in a long biological scenario (cf. Givón, 1989). The current complexity and abstractness of language and communication is a natural adaptive extension of humans as biological organisms. There is no strong reason to believe that the abstractions and conventions of language and communication are not part and parcel of function-based evolutionary principles. Simple vocabulary-driven languages evolve into more complex syntactically governed languages in the same way that early childhood pragmatics gives way to adult versions. Human development, in general, moves from global to specific just as cognitive structure moves from simple to complex. These are evolutionary and developmental principles that are important because they form the foundation of arguments supporting the natural relationship between humans and the material world, and the universal cognitive constraints that underlie human sensory apparatus.

The process of symbolizing and categorizing the world is not determinate of reality, but a natural strategy of order and simplification. Humans have the advantages and satisfactions that come with complexity, but at the price of a world that can be overwhelming. That is why we understand the many events and moments of our daily lives as types of categories. Communication is a pragmatic activity; that is, one that must include context, change, adaptation, and functional requirements. And this is not because the system is weak, but because it is natural to the human organism.

The tendency in communication and consciousness to categorize allows variety to be simplified and irrelevancies to be ignored. We all know what a door or a friend is. When we encounter an instance of one of these categories, we assume some fundamental defining characteristics and ignore those that are insignificant. For example, just as a door allows for the separation, and ultimately transition, from one space to another regardless of the door's size, design, shape, or construction material; a friend is the object of certain privileges and affections, whether the person is young or old, African American or White, male or female, close or far. The economies of this partitioning and classifying disposition are clear. If someone is introduced to you as a doctor or professional athlete, you will begin to formulate speculative ideas and impressions on the basis of your experiences with these categories. These formulations influence your understanding and communication even before you acquire additional details. If somebody informs you that they have recently purchased a car, you will not ask if it has a front lawn. We understand that this economy of classifications brings liabilities: a cognitive organizational scheme, rather than initiating understanding, may produce stereotypes that hinder understanding; thinking can become routine, uncritical, and artificial, even if your categories are "warranted" by experience. This sort of thing is apparent in the example about being introduced to a doctor or professional athlete. Both of these examples easily assume certain genders (male in these cases), income, and behavior standards. And these assumptions may even be warranted by our mediated and nonmediated experiences with people in these professions, but they are, of course, also incomplete.

It is true that humans use language to classify the world in order to simplify and manage the world. And human classifications seem natural; members of a language community regard their interpretations as "common sense." But we do not want to consider these interpretations to be merely ideology or world views. Human sense making is natural and helps represent and control the world. The "truth value," in the rigorous scientific sense of the term, of these interpretations is not the issue. The pragmatics are the issue. The actual practices, beliefs, language, and behaviors humans employ to "get by" in the world are most important. Surely these practices and beliefs have ideological implications, but the term "ideology" is reserved for the uncritical and routinized versions of reality imposed on others rather than to signify one's everyday reality as "false" or controlled by unseen forces.

Fitch (1994) described ideology about people communicating as established premises about individuals and relationships that determine meanings in a speech community. These issues are cognitive and can be observed in actualized language. Certainly ideological systems related to power, class, and economics influence language and communication. In fact, this volume is about how social categories of this type and others inform and are informed by language and communication. But too often ideologies are considered synonymous with consciousness. Lannamann (1991), for example, suggested that interpersonal communication reflects the hegemony of one class over another, and power is played out in discourse. Class consciousness is certainly pervasive in communication, and it is explored in chapter 6. But critical theorists of Lannamann's ilk replace one ideology with another. They are wed to a single account of communication and are blind to contrary data. This is no different than assuming that all knowledge must pass some statistical test before it is acceptable.

It is more sensible to argue that concept formation is responsive to the material circumstances of life and is social in nature. The cognitive categories that make up common sense arise in an individual naturally and are a result of biological imperatives. Categories pertaining to color, geometrical relationships, spatial arrangements, and logical relationships are easy enough to demonstrate. The fact that *all* languages and cultures categorize colors and space in some way is evidence of their universality. All languages recognize nouns and verbs and have methods of expressing them. But many of the ideas and beliefs that we hold are not so natural. And these are the ones that are most interesting and important. For example, my definition or idea of edible food is cultural in origin. All groups divide food up into categories of "edible" and "inedible," but what counts as an instance of each category is subject to negotiation. "Food" cannot be defined simply by listing different things to eat. Plants and animals exist in the environment, but what is "edible" is a cultural category. Logical relations and certain scientific methods and facts are natural categories.

This question about what "counts" as an instance of a category and what does not is an axis around which many issues in this volume are organized. And it is language that plays the major part in establishing these categories that we use to organize the world. Language is not the only system of coding the world, but it is probably the most important. But language does more than simply characterize; language stabilizes and crystallizes concepts. When a concept has a linguistic expression attached to it, that concept takes on an independence and a specificity. It becomes something that we control—and, in turn, controls us—and allows us to make distinctions and see relationships. These are not trivial. Words such as "freedom," "democracy," or "beauty" carry great potency within us. People die for such words. They give the impression of being singular entities, when in fact, the words only make the ideas plausible and orderly, but this does not make them any less central to our existence.

This symbolizing capacity of man, his ability to use language to transcend the here and now, has been the 20th-century answer to the question of human biological distinctiveness. The significance of this peculiarity has been fueled by German idealism and the appealing distinction between the cultural sciences and the natural sciences. Cassirer, Langer, and Whorf have strengthened this position by their concern with evolving human consciousness, and the easy acceptance of the influence of language on perception. Communication scholars have drawn on Peirce and George Herbert Mead's innovations about the *social* nature of consciousness. Others before Mead wrote about the social nature of humans and how cultures drew from long traditions of language and practice, but Mead grounded this in his argument about how thought was social. He explained how humans internalized communications by adopting the roles of others, which meant that behavior was determined by the social reality of a situation. Mead's work was perhaps the earliest application of modern philosophy to social science.

Symbolic interactionism—and other macro- and microsocial theories as developed by Schutz, Weber, Parsons, and Garfinkel—is a response to established social theories that drew their impetus from the natural sciences and logical empiricism. Accordingly, language was considered a one-to-one mapping between words and the world. In early Wittgenstein, before he rejected such arguments, language was considered a pure picture of reality. But logical empiricism was thoroughly preoccupied with the descriptive qualities of language. Description is a highly circumscribed function of language. Of course, many rigorous studies of natural and social scientific phenomena seek as precise a language as possible to describe various portions of reality. But language is also a medium of social *practice*. It is a part of all human activity and even "brings reality into existence," to use an awkward phrase. If I yell, "I hate you" to my wife in a moment of anger, then I have used language to "bring into existence" a certain reality that is no less important or "real" than any other. Ordinary communicative language is a focal point for communication theory and it cannot be treated as simply a degraded form of more precise scientific language because it is principal to the very constitution of social activity.

But theories such as Mead's symbolic interactionism have become increasingly unsatisfying. Mead's ideas about internalizing "symbolic" interactions, and the importance of symbols, are tantalizing, but they are based on undeveloped ideas about society and relationships. In particular, Mead failed to engage society as a highly differentiated system that does not lend itself well to understanding terms such as *generalized other*. It is true that reflexivity in Mead is important and continues to be a process that is necessary for understanding social and human development, but his explanations of social or individual categories (e.g., the "I" and the "me") remain cryptic. Moreover, Mead's discussions about institutions and how they change are undeveloped. But as Giddens (1979) maintained, this now leaves the way open for some useful conjoining of symbolic interactionism (a microcommunicative level) with functionalism (a macrosocietal level).

In *Central Problems in Social Theory*, Giddens reserved the notion of duality of structure as a primary theme. He recognized that ordinary language and social theory are reflexively related such that social organization shapes and is shaped by human interaction. This is his improvement, and an attempt to extend and clarify weaknesses in Mead. In other words, we cannot have a theory of society without a theory of communication, and vice versa. It has been commonplace to assume that communicative activity was a reasonably deliberative and conscious activity, whereas the influences of macro structures in society (e.g., economics, class) are unseen and unconscious. Giddens successfully reinterpreted this conscious–unconscious dualism as the duality of structure or the essential recursiveness of social life. This simply means that social structure *enters into* the creation of the individual, and the individual, in turn, *enters into* the creation of social structure. Both are dependent on one another and part of an ongoing process of personal and social change. This relationship forms the basis of the empirics of stratification. Much of what I want to do in the pages that follow is to restore the individual to the social world. Orthodox functionalism in sociology always seems to have the cards stacked against the individual. Roles, scripts, and institutional power always seem to end up as the systemic forces that direct behavior. And, on the other hand, communication theorists must confront the questions about how differences, diversity, and individuality all somehow make up a collective.

EVERYDAY LANGUAGE AND COMMUNICATION THEORY

If we labeled someone as a member of the *underclass,* we would be using a term to identify a consistent series of characteristics that presumably apply to this person. Interestingly, the term *underclass* might be an apt description of the person and his position in society, but not a word he would use or perhaps even understand. The relationship between everyday communication and these social categories (e.g. *underclass*) is problematic. There must be a logic that connects one set of terms to the other. This logic does not need to be precisely determined, but it must be rational and empirically based. Early social science conceptions of language were naive in that language was considered simply a neutral instrument for tagging the world. But in the wake of later Wittgenstein and hermeneutics, it is now understood that language is more than a medium of description. Language is also a social practice; that is, it brings ideas, beliefs, and realities into existence. If I yell "you idiot" at someone in a moment of anger, I am doing far more than simply describing the state of the other person. I am creating new understandings, implications, and of course, problems.

When language is considered simply an instrument for mapping reality, then one set of terms is as good as the next. There is no need to fret over the language used by everyday speakers and that used by theorists, except to say that the language of the theorist is "better," that is, a more accurate and rectified language. But if the linguistic system is vital; if it changes, shifts, and enters into the creation of the social world, then the language of everyday users becomes a significant social phenomenon unto itself. If the language of the theorist is fundamentally different, with different purposes and goals, then we need to establish the quality of the theorist's language by grounding it in the language of everyday speakers. One strand of phenomenology requires that the language of the theorist must be understandable to the everyday user. It poses that theorist language must be easily and obviously converted into the language of the practitioner. The theorist was "wrong" to the extent that he could not make his language easily understood by the lay person. This argument is weak. There is no reason in science that a term must be understood by the lay person. And even though this is clearly distinguishing the human sciences from the natural sciences, and arguing that a human science must be grounded in human consciousness, the requirement that a term be translatable has nothing to do with the usefulness of the term. We would not require a child to understand that he or she was "autistic"; we would not make it necessary that a schizophrenic understand that he or she is "schizophrenic"; and a member of the underclass does not need to understand *class consciousness* for the term to be theoretically useful.

Although the requirement that a social scientific term be understood by the lay person is untenable, there is an alternative that is desirable. This is that there should be at least a logical or sensible tie between the language of the lay person and the language of the theorist. Calling someone a member of the underclass is appropriate when the term applies to their behaviors and the consequences of behavior. Given a certain economic and occupational standing, as well as patterns of behavior, certain people group together and share commonalties. These commonalties may have terms associated with them, albeit never perfectly, that make for an acceptable metalanguage. The chapters that follow strengthen the tie between lay communication patterns and the theorists' language. These chapters examine the practical nature of this tie. This tie between communication patterns—including language, attitudes, and message characteristics—and the mutual knowledge that theorists try to develop, forms the basis of the field of communication and its relationship to social order. This tie between concrete interactions and macro social categories is certainly indebted to Goffman, who was concerned with how reality was socially constructed in actual communicative circumstances. The perspective here is on actual talk, language, and messages that make up the whole of communication and the socially constructed categories that represent mutual knowledge treated as real. In this perspective, "social class" or an "organization" (macro theoretical terms) are things that construct and are constructed by people in everyday interaction. I hope to pose a restatement of communication theory to provide a more satisfactory ground for discussion of central issues in communication and the new social world.

The Established Harmony

The origins of the current state of communication theory are reasonably discernible, but that does not mean they sprung from some simple coherent source. There is plenty of explanatory confusion to go around. In the past few years, communication scholars have spent more time reconstructing their history, usually because they found themselves in the embarrassing position of being popular in universities, but without the requisite intellectual and historical roots. These historical narrations are interesting reading, but solve no problems (cf. Anderson, Birkhead, Eason & Strine, 1988; Delia, 1987; Peters, 1986). Yet, there remains something like a consensus; a middle ground of communication theory. It is not, to be sure, unchallenged, but, does offer a focus of debate. This consensus includes two connected circuits: ideas whose roots can be traced to antiquity, but with elaborated and fresh contemporary forms. The first begins with a step into the 19th-century parlors filled with rhetoricians and elocutionists and what can be generically referred to as theories of rhetoric. Those who contributed to theories of rhetoric—scholars such as Aristotle, Cicero, St. Augustine, Campbell, and Blair, as well as I. A. Richards, Toulmin, Burke, and Habermas—have held a broadly similar view. By stressing *spoken messages in contexts designed to produce some effect*, they were able to distinguish themselves from consideration of the various literary forms. These authors held the view that the spoken word was distinct from the written, and was a teachable skill. Rhetorical moments, in an era when live speech making created the greatest sense of immediacy, were assumed to have significant impact on politics, policy, and the public. Early rhetorical theorists held that messages could be manipulated and sorted into modus operandi that appeal to particular human faculties. They agreed that the proper tactic could achieve the desired effect. They recognized that speaking was a performance, and were therefore equally preoccupied with its expressive qualities (e.g., elocution). Public speaking, debate, competitive group discussion, business and professional speaking, and rhetorical criticism helped institutionalize rhetorical theory in universities and establish departments of *speech*.

In 1914, a group of elocutionists and rhetoricians severed ties with the National Council of Teachers of English and formed the National Association of Academic Teachers of Public Speaking, now the National Communication Association (see Cohen, 1994). Although *rhetoric* has often been defined broadly to include any symbol exchange, and it embraces some lively and interesting emphases such as rhetoric and epistemology (Croasmun & Cherwitz, 1982; Scott, 1967), argument (Brockriede, 1983), performance (Conquergood, 1992), and narration (Fisher, 1984), "The paradigm case of rhetoric is the use of the spoken word to persuade an audience." (Foss, Foss, & Trapp, 1985, p. 12).

The second historical strand of communication theory that fits into the established harmony is the "communication research" tradition, founded by Schramm (1948, 1949) and Lazarsfeld (1941), that dates from the 1940s. As Delia (1987) explained, this tradition incorporated the basic rhetorical model of speakers, messages, audiences, and effects into an emphasis on (a) mass communication, (b) social science methods, (c) U.S. culture, and (d) retaining the emphasis on messages influencing receivers. Until recently, this communication tradition was mostly an empirical social science. Both of these strands share an emphasis on the pragmatics of everyday communication; an emphasis or perhaps even a fetishlike belief in the power of messages to have effects, whether those messages are uttered by politicians, lovers, or newscasters. Foss, Foss, and Trapp (1985) recognized this consensus or established harmony, when they wrote that the terms *rhetoric* and *communication* are "essentially synonymous terms" (p. 11n). From this central core, the discipline fragments into various research practices, contexts, problems, and media. What is most important (what passes for consensus) is the acceptance of teaching and research on anything that passes for purposeful communication. Arnold and Frandsen (1984) presented an encyclopedic survey of the then state of knowledge about communication and conclude that rhetoric and communication are concerned with "interactions in which some meanings are intended and interpreted by at least some of the parties involved" (p. 3).

The early traditional views of rhetoric as public speaking for persuasive effect, as well as the more recent communication tradition, developed in a historical context of progressive liberalism and stable economic growth. They now appear simplistic in an era of increased economic and cultural confusion and upheaval. Indeed, a belief in the directional efficacy of messages, especially within the communication research tradition, can be considered a warning as to the liabilities of easy confidence in research methods and facile generalizations about "communication." It was not long ago that generalizations about rhetorical tactics and media effects were considered stable conclusions about the social and communicative world. In the late 1960s these traditions hardened into academic camps with standard bearers that placed you in either the "rhetoric" or "communication" side, the primary difference typically being one of methodology (cf. Miller, 1966).

Rifts in the accepted harmony have been succeeded by a cacophony of voices trying to be heard. There have been essentially three responses to the accepted harmony. The first is a wail of disillusionment. This comes from those who say that rhetoric and communication have no basic and agreed on theoretical assumptions of their own, and these problems should be ignored. Most of the issues in "communication" theory, it is argued, are really philosophical or general philosophy of social science issues and may be ignored in favor of applied problem-oriented work. These authors (e.g., Streeter, 1995; Beniger, 1993; Swanson, 1993) typically argue that excessive debate about the disciplinary standing of communication, including a search for foundations and basic assumptions, is wasted energy. When Beniger (1993) entreated us to "embrace the subject of communication, not the field," it was essentially an act of despair, a statement that communication has no coherence and its subject is at once a text, a practice, a structure, and an effect. Our methodologies are borrowed reworkings from other theories, so why even pretend to disciplinarity. But this first response will not stand serious analysis. On the one hand, it is based on a rather naive positivistic notion that separates theory from data. The scholarly and research enterprise that is the field of communication, as opposed to the discipline, is always driven by philosophical assumptions, even if some are ignorant of them. Moreover, we must insist that theoretical notions have an important bearing on empirical work.

A second reaction might be considered a craving for safety and confidence. It is a grasp at scholarly trust in grand schema and reliable narratives (e.g., media effects, see Lowery & DeFleur, 1988). One example is the easy reversion to cognitivism and its logical empiricism philosophy (Berger, 1986; Berger & Calabrese, 1975). Here, the individual is assumed to be a cognizer who is in some way correspondent to an objective empirical world. Language is guided by cognition and if it is tied in some way to the real world, then we can say that knowledge or understanding is the result. A return to orthodox Marxism is another example. Although the political economy approach (Golding & Murdock, 1991) to media research is mostly a modern "critical" phenomena, it draws its entire intellectual history from classical economics and the Marxist concern with macroquestions about the production, distribution, and consumption of resources. Its central tenets are moral philosophy, the whole of social relations, and historical transformation, which are all elementary Marxist principles.

The other reaction to the established harmony has been to import a medley of perspectives, approaches, topics, opinions, politics, and research methods, and celebrate the confusion. It embraces the despair of the first reaction and becomes the opposite of the second by rejoicing in difference, diversity, and fragmentation. These scholars (e.g., Sholle, 1995; Streeter, 1995) question the existence of any accepted harmony, or claim that such pretenses are wrongheaded and oppressive. That the state of communication theory is in disarray (e.g., "Ferment," 1983; "Future," 1993a, 1983b) is taken to be more than an unsettling periodic state and granted epistemic status. We should not even attempt to solve these problems, the argument goes, because this diversity is testimony to a productive theoretical umbrella that can accommodate many. This reaction has a powerful natural appeal as an easy justification for many scholarly questions, activities, and assumptions. Even though this view is a potent concoction, it should not be used to slake the thirst of those who advocate and justify any abstract perspective. We may certainly engage in continuing disagreements about theory and research, but this should not prevent us from finding defensible connections between various perspectives and trying to transcend them.

A SCIENTIFIC COMMUNICATION THEORY

If we try to build an explanatory science of communication, rather than an ideological or aesthetic one, how do we know we will succeed? I am not asking a procedural question. There have been advances in theory and research, and the task of putting them together has been held back by nonscientific orientations. Specifically, we know a fair amount about *medium theory* and *discourse analysis*, and these provide the core of a general communication theory. Also, we have made considerable advances in *organizational theory*. I refer here to "organization" as a verb, not a noun; I refer to the "process" of organization that produces patterns, collectivities, and grounds for interpretation.

Medium theory is clearly of central importance to research in communication. The numerous electronic forms of media (e.g., television, radio, computers, and papers), as well as people talking, have all revealed influences. Moreover, families, organizations, political institutions, ethnic groups, consumers, and members of social classes are all significantly impacted by media. Sometimes the theoretical importance of medium theory is lost on the content of media messages. Scholars are often engaged in questions that concern the effects of messages or the interpretations of messages by different audiences. But a concern only with what content flows through various media will not advance us in stating precise social influences and implications of a medium. A more fruitful approach for communication theory qua theory will be to identify content, uses, and social implications that are subsumed by the term *medium*. After all, medium theory simply centers on the representative features of particular media. As Meyrowitz wrote: "Broadly speaking, medium theorists ask: What are the relatively fixed features of each means of communication and how do these features make the medium physically, psychologically, and socially different from other media and from face-to-face interaction" (1994 p. 50).

One important set of relationships, for example, is between the political economy and the media. The political economy is concerned with the power relations that constitute the production, distribution, and consumption of products (cf. Golding & Murdock, 1991). We know that the visual mass media are responsible for the creation of consumer desire and the products that satisfy such desires. The concentration of power in book publishing, radio, and television is associated with the cultural imperialism that forms many conflicts among nations (Murdock & Golding, 1995). The task for the future will be to show how the movement from differentiation to concentration in various media dominates cultural material, news flow, and economic opportunities.

The effects tradition is another important media influence. Probably the most frequently cited reason for even studying the media is because we believe that a medium of communication has a significant effect. Effects theories are rooted in strict behaviorism—now clearly a limited and misleading set of assumptions—where media messages were thought to produce short-term measurable effects on an audience. The purpose was to generate predictive theories about responses that served some administrative point of view. The term *administrative* refers to Lazarsfeld's (1941) concept of a taken-for-granted rational society in which the existing social order represents a consensual social justice, as opposed to a critical perspective that problematizes the current social order. As Gitlin (1978) argued, this behaviorism in the service of administrative interests relied on discredited assumptions about power and how it works, the private and public spheres, meaning, audiences, and attitudes. That effects research is now more interested in the media as an "intervening" variable influencing an individual in a social and cultural context means that understanding unique medium qualities is even more important. In the future, the various strands of effects theory that are audiences, cultures, institutions, and messages, will inter-twine and give way to a more precise medium theory.

There are other characteristics and driving forces in media research that have been responsive to problems in effects assumptions. First, we now have a more sophisticated notion of ideology and are able to decode mediated messages for political and cultural assumptions, and the extent to which these assumptions nurture conformity and disperse opposition to the dominant culture. Second, the notion of meaning is more clearly understood as a pragmatic construction process (Ellis, 1995) rather than as simple transition. Audiences are more active or "obstinate" than originally believed, and play a more forceful role with respect to how they will "allow" the media to influence them.

There is a good deal of evidence that the contemporary "postindustrial" world (Bell, 1973) will be defined by symbolic work that develops new patterns of information traffic. Information is the primary economic resource of the postindustrial era, and this resource is created by communication media that make information production, transmission, and storage fast and inexpensive. Mass communication (a centralized message distributed simultaneously to many receivers) is now less important than simply mediated communication (a message that is made possible by the existence of some conduit). And the control of messages and information is shifting from the sender to the receiver. The new types of information traffic vary with respect to interactivity and control of time and place (cf Bordewijk & van Kaam, 1986), but they are mostly available from the same communication technology. In other words, the electronic infrastructure that makes television possible can also connect a user to libraries, the Internet, E-mail, your bank, and other machines.

We have the elements of a theory of social behavior based on media theory and its multiple implications. Technology, information patterns, control of time and place of information, cultures, psychological and ideological effects, and media structures and institutions—these are the pieces of the puzzle to be assembled; these are the issues that must produce generalizations, including multiple effects. Other issues and variables may certainly be fitted into this framework of media and social theory.

A second area of central import, which, of course, is intertwined with medium theory, is *discourse analysis*. A unifying theory is emerging around themes of text, context, and society. The components of this theory have been developed in numerous areas, many of which have not converged because of local research practices and overspecialization. The link between discourse and society is social cognition (van Dijk, 1994). Social cognition is the shared representations of groups and the mental strategies that group members use to produce, represent, and understand situations, people, and institutions (Farr & Moscovici, 1984). These cognitive categories and models are pragmatic in nature and the crucial link in the interface between macrosocial structures and microdiscourse (i.e., communicative) features. Discourse theory complements medium theory in a unifying theory of communication. Medium theories that describe the various mechanisms of information flow must ultimately be related to social representations of knowledge and ideology. Analysis must be one of medium-discourse society where discourse and cognition are not linguistic and "cognitive," but social; that is, mental models and meanings that are acquired in social relations.

Research on discourse (van Dijk, 1990), cognitive sociology (Cicourel, 1973), social action (Atkinson & Heritage, 1984), and talk (Boden & Zimmerman, 1991) have extended the picture of the reflexive relationship between media, discourse, and society. Out of these projects, authors have formulated principles of a general theory of language and society that is more than correlational in the traditional sociolinguistic sense. More specifically, it is commonly understood that discourse as a social practice is inseparable from society and its institutions. But as of now, much of this relationship is imprecise. Much more work is necessary to specify the reciprocal relationship between features of discourse (e.g., syntax, lexical choice, structure, rhetoric) and characteristics of culture, relationships, politics, and organizations. Communication, in the form of discourses, presupposes, reflects, and legitimizes organizational arrangements in society.

Historically, in the field of communication, the relationship between discourse and society has been couched in the relationship between speakers and hearers communicating in contexts. In recent years, there has been more attention and borrowing from microsociology (e.g., Atkinson & Heritage, 1984; Boden & Zimmerman, 1991) with an emphasis on human "methods" for making sense of the world. This strand of work has been productive, but limited to observable properties of shared knowledge and understanding. Macrolevel social categories and the rules that characterize the relationship between speaker "methods" and these categories continue to be essentially ignored.

In the approach taken in chapter 3, I take seriously the relationship between language use, a particular form of interaction, and social categories. Even with all the nuances of meanings for the term *discourse*, it still predominately refers to phenomena beyond the sentence level. That is, not only observable verbal and nonverbal features, but also cognitive representations and social forces. Understanding situated language (communication) is not merely a matter of explaining observable language that is logically related to mental structures. Rather, all communicative activities are viewed as social, and therefore actual communicative utterances are explained by the social representations that produce them. The psychological in this perspective is not limited to the individual or some concern with universal psychological structures and processes. On the contrary, the focus is on the production and effects of shared representations (van Dijk, 1990) that result in class, ethnic, and other sociological forces. This approach is intended to augment both psycholinguistics and sociology by incorporating the double analysis of observable language and social structures. It is based on principles of "code."

Finally, communication has a solid explanatory framework in *organization theory*. Some unifying principles are emerging around a communicational basis of organizations (e.g., Giddens, 1984; Taylor, Cooren, Giroux, & Robichaud, 1996; Weick, 1985), including principles of conversations, meanings, speech acts, reflexivity, text, and social action. These elements have been developed in a number of separate disciplines, and their convergence is not yet widely understood, or even accepted, partly because of fragmented specialization and the highly practical concerns of much organizational communication research. Employers, employees, and researchers have long known about informal groups within organizations, struggles for control over working conditions and forms of dominance, loosely coupled and intractable networks and patterns of command, as well as the symbols, confusions, errors, and multiple meanings inherent in all social collectivities. Many have struggled to tame these beasts, but to no avail. Out of these subjects, Hawes (1974), Weick (1979), Taylor (1993), and others have begun to formulate principles of a general theory of communication and organization.

Interestingly, organizations have been conceptualized as entities that contain activities, and this may have been the impetus for the study of communication as an organizational process. A focus on the activity of organizing is responsible for advances in organizational communication, and is beginning to state a set of conditions for theorizing. The work of Weick (1979) and Taylor (1993) on complex organizations and the translation of text into organizational action is most striking; classic work by Weber (1946) and Taylor (1967) can be incorporated. Giddens' (1984) thinking is very important here as an exemplar of how interdependence and structure can work. I show here that current thinking in organizational processes meshes with other social processes because the "process" of organizing necessarily involves the resultant rule structure that emerges from the interaction of microcommunication processes and macrosocial processes.

Communication, then, has a strong explanatory framework in media theory, discourse, and organization, all of which are related. Cultural differences, including stratification, ethnic identification, and communication skills, are crucially related to the explanatory framework. The shaping of modern individual behavior is explained in particular by media and discourse. The wider questions of power, information, and class are essentially enumerated by the struggle over wealth and resources, and these are increasingly influenced by media, discourse, and organizational patterns in networks of personal association.

What about the rest of communication? Media, discourse, and organization are the exegetic heart of the field. The rest are empirical applications. Media structures, institutions, and effects are but particular types and consequences of media theory and forms of discourse. Interpersonal and group interaction—including writing, public speaking, and all forms of "applied" communication—result from the discourse structures that facilitate the particular messages and social representations preferred by originators of communication.

Almost every aspect of communication now separated out for study as an applied problem can be seen as an application of discourse theory or media theoretic principles, or both. Institutional applications of communication principles to professions, communities, industry, and the family all draw on contemporary conceptions of media, discourse, and organization. Particular problem contexts, such as health communication, political communication, therapeutic contexts, public relations, interpersonal intimacy, and decision making, are subsumed by a general theory of discourse and social interaction. Broader social categories of class, ethnicity, gender, and social change require applying communication theory to historical and social conditions. This represents a change from the search for laws of history to a more concrete level where discourse forms and structures, including close language analyses and descriptions of causal concatenations, become more of what we include in explanation. In other words, these macrocategories are reproduced, sustained, and explained by more microcategories.

2

Medium Theory

There are no plain women on television.

—John Ford

The camera makes everyone a tourist in other people's reality, and eventually its own.

—Susan Sontag

A coherent theory of media would be an accomplishment indeed. The nature and structure of media impacts so many features of social life—language, cognition, information, politics, culture, intimacy, identity—that a model or framework that tied these things together would occupy a prominent place in communication theory. Interestingly, this would be true even if the theory were incomplete and flawed, because communication is too multifaceted and complex to be reduced to a few simple propositions. There are a great many models and theories of communication (e.g., see McQuail), some of them quite limited or minimally useful, but their carcasses remain, too unmanageable to be hauled away, and too substantial to be ignored.

Two rival concerns in communication theory, medium theory and the content of media, have been articulated for some time now. For the longest time, most of the questions that busied communication theorists were preoccupied with the content of messages and the role of some medium in delivering that content. Research has mostly been influenced by the Shannon and Weaver model of information transmission and therefore concerned with reactions or effects of media, and mass media in particular (e.g., DeFleur, 1970; McQuail, 1994), or, with how mass media messages "interacted" with the personal mean-

25

ing structures of audiences (Gamson & Modigliani, 1989). Other theoretically consistent related issues are how political and economic institutions influence what the media conveys (e.g., Gans, 1979); the degree of correspondence between the media and the modernistic assumption of reality (e.g., Shoemaker & Reese, 1991); or the critical studies tradition of decoding messages (Jensen & Rosengren, 1990). All of these are content preoccupied. A related effects tradition is dominant in other media as well. Chapter 1 highlights this preoccupation with content effects in the oral medium of the rhetorical tradition, and the same may be said for the interpersonal communication medium (also oral, but in a different context).

All of these are interesting and important subjects, but these questions still leave us at something of an impasse in developing a more comprehensive and powerful explanatory system. For all the importance of the content of media, it still assumes pretty simple causality in a complex causal world. The result has been the awkward position of concluding that message content is the only important effect of media, and the rather embarrassing one of leaving other things unexplained entirely. The content and standard effects tradition of communication theory (by communication theory, I include mass media effects, speech effects, interpersonal effects, etc.) stumbles in the face of new electronic media, multimedia, changing forms of access to media, new forms of discourse, more active audiences, and changing ethnic and social divisions.

Communication effects emanate from a variable analytic theory that strives for intellectual symmetry by arranging a tidy collection of concepts into a causal order. The inadequacies of this have been apparent for some time. Presumed effects of messages do not always line up with people, institutions, or strategies. As variables and issues of scholarly concern become smaller and more technically defined, we begin to learn more and more about less and less. Some people regard these problems as methodological impurities, and others try to salvage these causal models by insisting that they are one perspective, albeit a quite circumscribed use.

Finding the right images and metaphors is one of the main problems of theory building. The complexities of the world simply cannot be grasped all at once, and we require some device that suggests a location for order. We need a clear vision that can elucidate complexities, but not overwhelm us; a vision that directs us to important processes and principles without obscuring them. Many communication theories confuse us; they might look like hierarchies, ladders, layers, causal chains, or pyramids, but they do not look much like the communication around us. They do not look much like people watching television, reading, chatting at work or in the living room, giving or taking orders, listening, and so on. There isn't anything necessarily wrong with many of our theoretical images, it is just that they do not always lead us forward because they cast our thoughts in terms of hierarchies or causal models, when the goal is to understand human communicative relationships and how these relationships enter into social structures. I try here to avoid an image of theory as a ghostly machine of clanging parts in favor of one that privileges connectedness among people and communication technologies.

We can also take some clues from a phenomenological perspective that tries to ground everything in daily life. We must work hard to achieve a sort of radical empiricism in which we assume that humans construct meaning and reality from everyday life. And these constructions are rule governed, and not an anarchistic subjective creation. Social "structure" in terms of class and ethnicity is one of our theoretical metaphors that seeks to reify repetitive encounters and the consequences of certain types of encounters. To say that a particular social class exists means that people must be interacting and using communication in some consistent way that warrants the class label. *I am proposing to treat the interactions of everyday life, and the nature of human media, as the subject matter for a theory of social structure and reality.* I do not label people as exhibiting certain characteristics or being members of certain groups, but look for influences from fundamental communication principles. In this way, I identify the more basic influences on behavior that are responsible for labeling people and determining how they associate. It would be silly and unworkable to try to identify all influences on behavior and cognition, so a few issues should provide a sufficient approximation. "Society" and its various structures is just a way of talking about how people behave, and human behavior is inextricably interwoven with mechanisms and habits of communication. We are animals capable of appropriating the world through symbols and constructing an invisible world in our heads. Our forms of contact determine symbol systems and discursively shape subsequent thoughts, images, and contacts.

THE BASICS OF MEDIUM THEORY

One of the most fruitful traditions of explanatory theory for society is medium theory, running from Innis (1964, 1972) and McLuhan (1962, 1964), through Ong (1982), Havelock (1963), Goody and Watt (1963), to Chaytor (1966), Boorstin (1978), and Meyrowitz (1985, 1994). If we extract the main issues and causal processes from extraneous matters, medium theory can be described as follows:

Innis and McLuhan initiated the basic argument that the characteristic features and epistemologies of ancient cultures and civilizations were attributable to the dominant "media" of communication, each with its own strengths, weaknesses, and biases that determined the social form. We do not experience the world directly, but through different media of communication. There is no machine-like correspondence between what is "out there" and our encounter with it. We experience reality through the filters of media—either oral, typographic, or electronic—and these filters determine what we know and how we know it, and our relationships to social power structures. McLuhan and Innis, unlike most communication theorists, were more concerned with *how* we experience than what we experience. Therefore, the emphasis is not on the content of media, but on the nature and structure of media. Ong and Meyrowitz added additional insights and specifics to how media have altered thinking and social organization. Ong's distinction between primary and secondary orality is important for modern electronic media, and Meyrowitz added a theory of social interaction and role theory, which begins to sketch a relationship between micro and macro levels.

good history

McLuhan was a literate, classically educated man whose ideas regarding influences on perceptual and sensory functions were drawn essentially from Aristotelian and Thomistic philosophy (see Bross, 1992). Where some early philosophers (e.g., Plato) maintained a mind–body dualism such that the body was an unreliable source of information about the mind, others (e.g., Aristotle, Thomas Aquinas) blurred this distinction. Here, the senses played a central role in philosophy because *all knowledge was assumed to be based on sensory information*. Aquinas inaugurated British empiricism, which extends to modern times. McLuhan (1964) was very influenced by this line of thinking and suggested that (a) there was a hierarchy of senses with respect to dominance and control of information, (b) the experience of one-sense modality can be translated to the other, and (c) it is possible to determine the contribution of each sense to the total sensory experience. This line of thinking led McLuhan to his well-known equation of media as extensions of the senses. Information processing is mediation; it is extending yourself to interaction with the particular medium of information. As these media change, so does your information processing.

This blurring of the mind–body dualism, and the attendant argument that the mind, including thoughts and images, is fashioned and formulated via the senses, and is fundamental to the work and theorizing of medium theorists. It is what allows for the arguments about the relationships between media technologies and individuals and societies, as well as what as what has come to be known as media epistemology (see Gozzi & Haynes, 1992; Postman, 1985). Modern cyber-ideology and language is probably the most dramatic example of this fusion of media and the nervous system. In Gibson's *Neuromancer* (1984), computer users directly connect their nervous systems to a computer system. They literally "jack in" and negotiate virtual space. Gibson wrote that cyberspace was a "simplification of the human sensorium … " (p. 55). Even less imaginative writing (e.g., Stenger, 1991) argues that technology is corporal and the physicality of the computing experience is responsible for alterations in the sense of time and reality. But McLuhan's thinking is mostly metaphoric and heuristic. Modern science would not support any of the three aforementioned issues. There is no sense that would be considered dominant, nor is there a central modality that translates one sense into another (although senses are related), and the suggestion that the excessive stimulation of one sense alters sense ratios—the notion that overstimulation of one sense causes the body to amputate or modify that sense—is not supported by data of any sort (see Bross, 1992). Nevertheless, McLuhan was highly innovative and insightful with respect to the psychological and perceptual reactions of human organisms to sensory information from various modalities. He was correct that humans participate in the sensory strengths and weaknesses of various media, and this participation is very influential with respect to the experiential and social structure of life.

So the essential argument that the form of media is the chief ingredient of an individual's experience and social structure is a sound one. Others (e.g., Wiener, 1948) have advanced the thesis that communication and messages are important for understanding society, but it was McLuhan who forced the relationship between media and sense perceptions. Individuals develop expectations about their own needs with respect to sensory and perceptual information. They internalize these expectations, but these internalizations are subject to modification from outside sources. The typographic medium, for example, is fixed and processed aurally. It makes for a slow, deliberate, and orderly processing of information (Ong, 1982). In the early days of typography, the rate of change in individuals and society was slow. Politics, fashions, and values were relatively constant for long periods of time. But the electronic media have radically altered the reference signals and changed the way we think, act, and perceive the world. McLuhan coined the term *outering*, or the notion that internal neuronal processes have external manifestations. Just as a wheel is an extension of the foot and clothes an extension of the skin, media are extensions of the senses (Murphy, 1971). The telephone and television allow us to hear and see in ways that we cannot naturally. These technologies form a loop between humans and the world, and we are changed for the experience. In McLuhan's (1962) terms, our "sense ratios" are changed and "We no longer feel the same, nor do our eyes and ears and other senses remain the same .... The result is a break in the ratio among the senses, a kind of loss of identity" (p. 24).

McLuhan may be seen as developing this line of analysis, adding complexity to earlier thinking, and showing that medium conditions involved in communication are analytically distinct from content transmission, thereby revising some fundamentals of communication. We can summarize McLuhan as showing that technologized material media are extensions of natural human senses, and these technologies have their own patterns of dominance and influence that feed back to humans and reorganize the sensory balance and the structure of culture. By implication, the three dominant forms of media (oral, typographic, and electronic) correspond to periods in human history and behavior. Other authors (e.g., Goody & Watt, 1963; Havelock, 1963; Meyrowitz, 1985, 1994; Ong, 1982) extend this spectrum by suggesting that different media foster different modes of human consciousness. Medium theory opens up another area that might be called the "means of consciousness production." This medium power that influences consciousness underlies and undergirds the interaction patterns that produce and reproduce macro social structures; it sustains social classes and ethnic groups; it transforms communities into status groups (e.g., Internet users); and it becomes a legitimate concentration of power. So McLuhan's claim is on par with Durkheim and Freud, such that the human animal is not only composed of strong emotional and psychic desires that form the basis of society (e.g., Collins, 1975), but also forms of interaction, stirred by media, that provoke patterns of thinking and expectations about information. These form the empirics of culture.

Medium theorists such as McLuhan and Meyrowitz have amplified knowledge about the means of consciousness production within a classical framework of knowledge. Medium-fashioned information does not supplant consciousness, but is a main ingredient in the consciousness mix that cooks up interaction patterns. We will see that this mediated consciousness can be used as a vehicle to form alliances in struggles against other groups, and can impose status and prestige hierarchies that are the archetype of stratification. From this analytical stance, we can move into an explicit theory of society and stratification. My emphasis is not on the types of stratified societies, but on the essential communication causal principles that are the shearing tools of theory.

For medium theory the basic insight is that all human beings are influenced by the media from which they process information. Add this to the sociable nature of human beings, in that they attempt to maximize their subjective experience through communication with others according to the resources available to them (real or imaginary), and we see that the key to individual and group identity is held by other people. This, of course, is no surprise to Mead or Goffman. So forms of mediated information influence how we self-construct subjective worlds; these subjective worlds are the resources we use in the struggle for status and economic resources, and therefore become the location and guiding principle for making sense out of social arrangements. A reconstructed communication theory, beginning with medium theory and its influence on consciousness, can be applied to any empirical context, as illustrated in the following statements:

1. Begin with the assumption that humans are essentially self-interested and maneuver for gain. Although they are leaning toward satisfaction and away from dissatisfaction, they require symbolic resources and are susceptible to the structure, forms, and patterns of the media that supply those symbolic resources. These symbolic resources are signs and texts that bring a self into focus.

2. Look for the particular availability and arrangements of interaction. Examine modes of communication, physical places, and linguistic devices for staging oneself. Assess the dominant forms of media that determine each interactant and the potential of these media to produce an individual consciousness that positions a person in a dominance network.

3. Apply the general principle that individuals will then work from their position in the dominance network as they try to gain rewards. Social structures can be explained by the communicative behaviors that follow from the interactions produced by these individuals in their positions.

4. Ideology will also follow because it will develop in accordance with the interests of the individuals located in the various places in the dominance hierarchy, and the potential for the ideology to serve the consciousness needs of the individual.

5. Compare empirical contexts; establish and test hypotheses by looking for individuals with different mediated experiences and who live according to different social arrangements. Always be on the lookout for complexity and mutually causal loops.

These principles are best exemplified in social differentiation and stratification. We must separate particular spheres of social interaction. As we continue to examine medium theory, we turn to the details of language and discourse (chap. 3), and to principles of organization (chap. 4). We can posit a decent explanation and make useful predictions about individuals' behavior and social grouping if we know how they use media and discourse, and how they interact. These things are related to conventional sociological variables such as occupation, education, age, and sex, but in a reciprocally influential way rather than a directly causal one. In later chapters on ethnicity and social class, where these principles are demonstrated, I look for media resources and patterns of interaction, and how these culminate in ideas and beliefs that help the individual establish a line of attack for managing various interests.

Media Epistemology

Medium theory begs an epistemological question. We must ask how media and knowledge are linked and what forms and methods media knowledge takes. Innis and McLuhan, of course, were fundamentally media epistemologists, and others have contributed to this connection (e.g., Gozzi & Haynes, 1992; Postman, 1985) as well as the insights from those analyzing oral and literate traditions. My purpose here is not to rehash discussions of orality and literacy—although these will play an important role in my analysis—but to continue to explore and unearth insights from various lines of scholarship about modern electronic mediated interaction and then summarize these into causal principles.

Real-time, face-to-face interaction is the most organic form of communication. It is unmediated and thoroughly human. The single power of mediated communication is the power to transcend contexts and carry messages to new and unexpected ones. These mediated messages, as with all messages, influence our cognitive organization and make claims on our consciousness and culture.

Modern electronic media, just as more elemental typographic media before it, is absorbed into our concepts of truth and governs the flow of information as well as the form of information. The evolution of truths that cultures lay claim to is directly correlated with the dominant medium of communication at the time (Innis, 1972). Messages only make "sense" when connected to their appropriate medium. This point was demonstrated interestingly at an art opening I attended some time ago. In the main gallery, halfway up the wall was an electronic sign with repeating messages moving across from right to left. These electronic signs are used for quick general public announcements, upcoming events, starting times for theatrical performances, or the like. The message quickly slides by with red bulbs going on and off to form the letters. But the messages moving by on this particular sign were as follows:

"Any man's death diminishes me, because I am involved in mankind."

"Fame is the thirst of youth."

"Let us not doubt in philosophy what we do not doubt in our hearts."

The incongruity between the medium and the message was striking. A medium used for brief and commonplace messages was pressed into service for more serious philosophical matters. The result was to diminish the gravity and the sharpness of these quotations. Displayed in this way, they became trite and platitudinous. The medium drained the content of its significance.

The meaning and significance of a message is fundamentally related to its medium of communication. Ong (1982) pointed out that in oral cultures, clichés and proverbs are not cute, irregular sayings that are trotted out to add significance to special occasions. On the contrary, they are constant and the very stuff of the mind. It is how knowledge is stored and organized. Formulaic statements, aphorisms, platitudes, dictums, and rhymes contained the collected truths of a culture. But imagine today if an employee went to his employer requesting a raise and the employer responded with "Honest labor is its own reward." The employee might be amused only for a moment.

A medium privileges certain assumptions about people and warrants for knowledge. Media are even contextual. Communicators establish expectations about the appropriateness and importance of messages given their medium of communication. One does not "expect" the aforementioned wisdom from John Donne, Byron, or Peirce on an electronic sign. It is impossible to separate the medium from the full significance of a message. The printed word is still considered a formal and sometimes sacred act in our culture, where the electronic word is not. That is why in a court of law, a witness places his or her hand on the Bible, not a CD-ROM of the Bible. Brummett and Duncan (1992) offered one of the better explications of a medium:

A medium is a form immanent in recurring, similar experiences that provides a discursive structure in which the self is extended as a subject position and within which the subject position orders and unifies the experience in ways that are empowering or disempowering. The medium, in this sense, is the *means* by which the bricolage of experience is pulled together, the logic in which subject positions are formed, and the parameters set for struggles over how signs are organized and unified in empowering and disempowering ways. (pp. 232–233)

From this definition, it is important to consider the available means of extension that make for an epistemological system. Gozzi and Haynes (1992) referred to "zones of epistemology" (p. 217) that structure ways of knowing. These zones of epistemology are well enough known, and put schematically, they are:

1. The dominant medium of communication produces sets of assumptions about the knower and the known. This medium foregrounds certain types of knowledge and reorganizes patterns of power in a culture. A medium makes certain types of discourse possible, and reorients thought and sensibilities. The media make it possible to form, break, and recreate information monopolies.

2. *Orality* is the most basic and natural medium of communication. Here, the human communicator is a natural part of the production, maintenance, and storage of knowledge. The world and reality are "semantically ratified" every time a human in an oral culture speaks. All knowledge is produced and interpreted through the direct experience of people. The grounds and warrants for knowledge come from group oral traditions and rituals. Language and discourse are organizationally and syntactically simpler in oral media. Memory, and all its strengths and weaknesses, is the primary mechanism of information storage and reliability.

3. Print and *typographically* based media make for more permanent and objectified knowledge. The "known" is documented and subject to complex symbol manipulation. Human knowers may easily engage in this symbol manipulation and use it as a foundation of authority and knowledge. Memory is now freed from much of its labor in oral cultures and available for innovation, scientific or otherwise. Print systems are fixed and subject to more rigorous rules of usage and interpretation.

4. The *electronic* media makes for dramatic increases in speed, information transmission and storage, and the distances among users. There is a very powerful sense of verisimilitude such that we experience what is called the distant present; that is, even though messages are complex, sophisticated results of high technology and planning, they appear to be natural, real, and occurring in real time. Knowledge and understanding come from a manipulated and aroused identification that is easy to create because there is no natural context. Feelings, identifications, images, empathic rapport, and emotional responses are all heightened and predominant because of the ability to create isolated senses of reality. The "distant pres-

ence" can combine oral and written forms of mediation instantaneously to produce powerful facsimiles of primary sensory encounters.

"Knowledge" is information that can be used for perception and action. It is organized and linked together to form cognitive programs, schedules, and patterns that give sense to the world. All cultures in any stage of development have something they call knowledge. Moreover, all knowledge is able to be stored, conveyed, and archived. The difficulty, speed, and logic in accessing or carrying out these functions is related directly to the nature of the medium. Some media time-bind knowledge and privilege tradition by making knowledge permanent and difficult to change. Cultures bound in tradition are more narrow and conservative. Stone tablets, for example, became sacred and the information they contained was pure and inviolate for generations. Other media make transcending space easier. Computer networks, and paper before them, make it easier to move knowledge from one person to another, but do not necessarily promote permanence. On the contrary, modern computers make information and the knowledge it produces available, cheap, disposable, manipulable, and easily reproducible. A knowledge medium also produces an affective component. Because of its fundamental participation in the human senses, it is impossible to separate a medium from affect. We come to enjoy or appreciate the printed word, computers, or an oral performance. We develop positive or negative emotions and attitudes about media.

All information is selected, transmitted, and received through some structure that renders it intelligible. But the essence of mediated information involves the use of technology (paper, electricity, machinery) that transmits to individuals who are inaccessible in immediate time, space, or both. Information can reach across time and space, and thereby takes on some special characteristics. This reaching across time and distance is the foundational quality of media that alters the nature and form of information so profoundly. This reach creates a new reality termed the *distant present*.

Some Formal Principles

There are a number of different implications of media. They are often lumped together with other social and economic variables, which is frequently confusing. In the interest of clarity, I state them here as postulates and propositions that mostly organize extant knowledge, but also serve an heuristic function. I do this not because I am convinced that all the propositions are complete or even necessary, but simply as an attempt to make progress in that direction. This enables us to work at theory building and make some decisions about the quality and quantity of evidence. The goal, after all, is to improve the confidence with which we argue that particular formulations are correct and powerful. Consider the following postulates:

Postulate 1:   With the *Innis Media Principle*, we do not experience reality directly, but through media of communication (Innis, 1964).

Postulate 2:   In the *McLuhan Sense Extension Principle*, media are extensions of our senses and influence information processing by changing sense ratios (Postulate from 1).

Postulate 3:   The nature of knowledge in a culture is attributable to the dominant medium of communication. Because media participate in the senses they also have an affective component (from Postulates 1 and 2; Gozzi & Haynes, 1992; Postman, 1985).

Postulate 4:   The most basic media types are oral, typographic, and electronic, and each has its own strengths, weaknesses, and biases that determine the nature of knowledge in a culture (Ong, 1982; Postman, 1985).

Postulate 5:   The types of mediated information are resources in the struggle for status and economic resources, and each results in dominant historical periods, social structures, and ideology (from Postulates 3 and 4; Brummett & Duncan, 1992; Meyrowitz, 1985).

Oral Medium (Primary Orality).   The following postulate concerns the oral medium.

Postulate 1.0:   The oral medium is organic. Messages are experienced instantly and subject to the qualities and organizational forms of direct semantic experience. Structure is paratactic. Memory is the primary mechanism for storage and reliability, and warrants for knowledge come from the lived traditions, rituals, and information stored in memory.

The oral medium depends on the active living memory of people in a culture. It relies on mechanisms that assist memory such as recitation, rhythmic qualities of language, narrative, and memorization. This active reliance on real-time language and memory ties people to one another. The repository of information in a culture, its history and traditions, lies in the minds of others. It is necessary that this information be easily communicated through engaging narratives with stock phrases and memorable passages of wisdom. The knower of such information makes no distinction between himself and his knowledge; there is no separation of people from their knowledge, culture, and reality (see Havelock, 1963; Luria, 1967; Ong, 1962). Oral cultures are more confined and circumscribed, in that members are always physically present and have very little contact with other groups. Moreover, the notion of "self" and individuality are limited because of the importance of the community in ratifying knowledge. Change and innovation are very slow because knowledge and how reality is perceived are so intimately connected with the being and presence of members of the community. Finally, all the senses—but particularly touch, sight, and sound—are richly implicated in the communicative and aesthetic experience of oral media. Consider the following:

Postulate 1.1: Memory and group identity are the most important determinants of primary oral medium effects and influence consciousness, speech, and knowledge.

Postulate 1.2: As a group, culture, or institution increases its reliance on orality, it converges on a collectivist consciousness or frame of reference that assigns meaning to actions based on accumulated experience.

Postulate 1.21: The more a group converges on a collectivist consciousness, the more individual identities are diffused and associated with group values and beliefs.

Postulate 1.22: The stronger the collectivist consciousness, the more attenuated are power differences.

Postulate 1.23: As the strength of the collectivist consciousness increases, so does the emotional attachment to group values.

Postulate 1.24: As the strength of emotional attachment to group values increases, so does cohesion, thereby exerting a conservative force on the group.

collective consciousness

The statements in Postulate 1.2 speak to basic issues in collective consciousness that describe close groups and cultures, especially those that rely on orality. These groups are keenly aware of their culture and common experiences, and these experiences are incorporated into their stories, language, and patterns of behavior. The sense of reality in these groups is accepted uncritically and it is easier to communicate without misunderstanding because the common fund of knowledge is so readily available and understood by participants.

We do not even need the traditional and antediluvian concept of intact oral cultures to see this phenomenon at work. These propositions apply equally well to qualities of modern groups that are based on close interpersonal relations and seek to establish group consciousness. Families, religious groups, and organizational cultures, as well as societies, may depend on mutual interaction that makes for the acquisition of similar concepts; that is, it facilitates the convergence of perspectives among individuals. Individuals convert their experiences into "shared knowledge," which is the result of mutual interaction. The oral medium is qualitatively different with respect to the centrality of mutual interaction and the importance of reference persons. It creates this shared perspective or collective consciousness that is designed to narrow the gaps between communicators. General support for these propositions is easy enough. Wittgenstein's metaphor of the language game is necessarily social and reliant on convergence, and from a phenomenological perspective, Merleau-Ponty (1962) explains that a concept is the result of previous experience resting on acts of personal commitment:

Postulate 1.3:   As groups establish this collectivist consciousness, the importance of verbal performance increases.

Postulate 1.31:   As orality becomes increasingly the predominant medium of communication, messages become more high context. That is, the information is either in a context or internalized in a person, and very little is coded explicitly in the message.

Postulate 1.32:   The more a culture is oral and high context, the more language functions to stimulate existing meaning carried in the consciousness of individuals and groups.

Postulate 1.321:   The more language functions to stimulate existing meaning, the more it relies on clusters of clichés, epithets, and sayings.

Postulate 1.322:   The more language relies on clichés, epithets, and saying, the looser its internal structure.

Postulate 1.33:   The more high-context a group or culture, the more information resides in group memory, and this increases the importance of conversation to access the information.

Consciousness and the reality it spawns are what people negotiate a belief in, and the foundation for oral consciousness is conversation. The next chapter shows that even in a modern electronic culture, where the centrality of oral media are diminished somewhat, conversation is the foundation of social organization (see Collins, 1975, chap. 3). The symbolic interactionists have made this argument for some, but have not been very successful at going beyond this abstraction to a classification of conversational situations or an analysis of the medium of communication. Oral communication determines a large part of our social experience. Our mind is, as the symbolic interactionists maintain, a sort of internalized conversation among generalized others. If this is true, then our content and knowledge comes from our vivid experience of reality enacted in the transaction of words. This leads to special characteristics of knowledge in the oral medium.

Postulate 1.4:   The form and nature of knowledge in the primary oral medium is communal and holistic. Knowledge is subjective, organic, and there is little difference between the knower and his knowledge (Havelock, 1963).

Postulate 1.41:   As the type of knowledge is derived more from an oral me-
                   dium, the more it is embedded in praxis and the human life
                   world than deduced propositionally.

Postulate 1.42:   The more a group or culture is dependent on orality and
                   praxis, the less distinction there is between opinion and
                   fact.

Postulate 1.421:   As the distinction between fact and opinion blurs, the
                   more warrants for knowledge come from group traditions.

Postulate 1.422:   As distinctions between fact and opinion blur, knowledge
                   becomes less systematic and organized.

In the oral medium of either primary oral cultures, or contemporary families
and groups, it is important to underscore that the relations between humans
and the world are active and practical. There is greater emphasis on the type of
knowledge that results from situational realities rather than abstract ones.
Counting, in the marketplace, is more important than mathematics. And there
are totalizing effects of situational knowledge because as humans encounter
new situations, they are understood as experientially homologous to previous
situations. Children, whose language development is pregrammatical and oral
(Givón, 1995), data from nonliterates (e.g., Luria, 1967), and studies of families
and close groups (e.g., Kreckel, 1981), cite the consequences of knowledge being "lorish" and the result of mutual interaction rather than individual attain-
ment. These groups are predisposed to cooperate through shared application of
communal knowledge.

The social character of knowledge is apparent. Language serves a characteristic functional orientation rather than a referential one. For example, in groups
where certain concepts are overlexicalized, such as when criminals have multiple terms for the police, or drug users for drug paraphernalia, they are focusing
on individuals and interaction and "realizing" a subjective reality, not merely
expressing it. There is this special conception of the information that emanates
from the primary group, and this information is organized by principles that reflect the group's value system, and it is expressed according to group-specific
conventions (cf. Halliday, 1978; Kreckel, 1981). Knowledge that is oral based
remains tacit unless it is objectified in some way. This is one reason why there is
little distinction between opinion and fact. Objectified knowledge frees the in-
tellect to tease out such distinctions. It technologizes knowledge. The first and
most elemental communication technology is typography.

Typographic Medium (Writing).   The following postulate concerns the
typographic medium.

Postulate 2.0:   The typographic medium is not "natural" and stimulates
                  consciousness through technological means. It is visual, se-

quential, and fixed such that information is more deliberate and orderly (McLuhan, 1962; Ong, 1982).

The introduction of technology is perhaps the most important impact of typographic media. Whether that technology is simple (a stick making marks in
the mud) or sophisticated (computers), writing was the first technology of communication. The technological logic proposition foreshadows the history of
writing and print along with epistemological implications of the typographic
medium. It is also the foundation of the organizational and economic consequences of typography that began to fully advance after the invention of the
printing press. Postulate 2.11 divides the essential McLuhan insights into sev-
eral variables. They have ramifications from differences in experiencing reality
to how information is represented. The following issues crosscut all the subsequent issues in Postulates 2.2 and 2.3, as well as issues in Postulate 3.0:

Postulate 2.1:   Technology is an important determinant of medium effects
                 and has its own logic (Altheide & Snow, 1991; McLuhan,
                 1964).
Postulate 2.11: The term *technological logic* refers to the idea that as the
                 technology of a medium changes and becomes more so-
                 phisticated, its influences on (a) sense experience, (b) rep-
                 resentational forms, (c) subject matter, (d) patterns of use,
                 and (e) human relationships become more pronounced.

The following propositions derive some consequences of the fixity of print.
They also suggest some basic findings to be discussed in the ensuing sections.
They help explain the literacy class culture and the evolution of educational
values and literacy-based models of discourse, rather than community-based
models:

Postulate 2.2:   The more fixed the elements of a medium, the more that
                  medium is seen as separate from natural human experi-
                  ences.
Postulate 2.21:   The more separate they are from humans, the easier it is to
                  manipulate the elements of the medium.
Postulate 2.22:   The more manipulable the elements of a medium, the
                  more individuals develop differential abilities and skill
                  with the medium.
Postulate 2.221: As the members of a culture develop differential abilities
                  and skill, the more the culture is divided by a literacy-based
                  class system.
Postulate 2.23:   The more skill necessary to master a medium, the more
                  learning and practice are required.

Postulate 2.231:   As the requirement for learning and practice increases, so
digital divide or.   does the cost and the access to the opportunities for learning and skill, which further exacerbates the literacy-based
class system.

The following propositions predict epistemological assumptions, as well as
cognitive processes, forms of expression, and mastery of knowledge:

Postulate 2.3:   The more a medium is experienced as fixed and separate
from human experience, the easier it is to objectify the information from that medium.

Postulate 2.31:   The more information is objectified, the more separated
the knower is from the known.

Postulate 2.32:   As reality is objectified, it is increasingly recorded and considered permanent.

Postulate 2.33:   As reality is recorded and considered permanent, it increasingly assumes a truth that corresponds to an external
world—a world only possible with media that are not
purely oral.

Postulate 2.34:   The more information is objectified, the more it reflects
the imposed structure of the elements of the medium. This
is alphabetic in the case of writing.

Postulate 2.341:   The more the medium imposes its structure, the more it develops a grammar to assist with meaning.

Postulate 2.342:   As the acceptance and uniformity of the grammar increases, its meanings become more sacred and serve as a
conservative force.

Postulate 2.343:   The more difficult it is for the medium to transcend space
(e.g., stone tablets), the more conservative and permanent
the message is. The easier it is to transcend space (e.g., the
Internet), the more open and liberal the message.

Postulate 2.35:   As reality is objectified, the self is more distinct and constructed.

has the comparison   Mead and Ong explained how a sense of self emerges out of interaction and
the isolation that is possible when one can "separate" from the world. This is
quite distinct from the oral consciousness.

Distant Presence.   When our sense of taste, hearing, or sight is activated,
we experience flavor, sound, or vision in the immediate present. When we read,
listen, or watch visual images, we experience these in the immediate present as
well. All of these things take place in a context with relatively stable physical

objects and temporal constraints. Our families, work, politics, and communication all have a robust native presence. They take place in our living rooms, offices, and backyards. But a medium of communication makes information and experience available from other experiential contexts that are not local. The location of knowledge and experience is important because our entire sense of self is produced by symbolic exchange with the environment (Mead, 1934). Self, others, and society form a production circuit in which individuals extract experience from others in an immediate environment, and the resultant patterns form a social reality. So in an oral culture, and epistemology, individuals have direct experience with others and groups, and knowledge comes from the tradition of interaction with those others and groups. Individuals in oral traditions have directly ratified semantic experience and they come to quickly recognize situations and define them appropriately. Knowledge is not separated from the knower, and knowers are not separated from one another. Imagine, for purposes of illustration, modern teenagers whose social organization is almost tribal in nature. Their experience is communal and the overlap in shared consciousness in considerable. Members of such groups share a common frame of reference and an aggregate of experiential associations that make it easy and quick to assign meaning to actions.

This sense of the "other," this formation of meanings and the content of our consciousness, is radically unfurled by media. Meyrowitz (1989) explained how the other is related to media and community in two ways: first, the media reach into contexts so that others who become significant to us increasingly come from strange worlds. We continue to see ourselves in these others and use these worlds as reflections of reality. This, of course, debilitates the importance of the local culture. Second, we begin to change our perceptions and understanding of the local culture itself. We use these distant contexts as metrics to evaluate the one we live in. The advent of print was a first step in splitting consciousness and alienating individuals from communities (Ong, 1977). The distant other in the typographic medium was an objective entity, one that was separate from us and constructed through the fixity of the alphabet. Ideas such as logic, self concept, analysis, and science required the notion of an objective world where an individual could position himself outside of himself (cf. Cathcart & Gumpert, 1986; Luria, 1967). If there is an objective world, then the individual is "located" in it. And as he continues to relate to other objects outside of himself, he generates a sense of "individuality" and isolated personhood by contrasting himself with others. Thus, humans steeped in typographic culture experience others and objects as separate entities rather than as joint participants in a collective and concentrated mythic adventure.

Any homogenization resulting from localizing experience is dissipated in a typographic culture, but atomized in an electronic one. This atomization does not mean that members of a culture are stripped of group references, it is just that our horizons are extended electronically. These extensions result in a more expansive but superficial sense of commonalty. Even local experience with newspapers or television is less substantial. Meyrowitz (1989), in responding to Kirby (1988), described local media experiences as generic uniqueness in which most news stories, for example, and advertisements are drawn from national issues and products. Problems in families or on the job used to be personal disagreements between individuals. People had quarrels. Now, with the long reach of mediated global culture, these disagreements are social problems exacerbated by race, class, or gender. People do not have quarrels, they have legal disputes played out in a national context. The production standards for local media are the same across communities, and even local community problems are described in terms of national issues. This is certainly consistent with the globalization of experience, in which information can be quickly and widely disseminated.

The electronic media make for some interesting paradoxes: There is a lifelike sense of presence and immediacy, but the message is "at a distance." There is a vivid sense of reality, but we are not witnessing anything "real" occurring at the moment. Because of the complexity of electronically mediated messages and their ability to mine a variety of senses, the experience of involvement is much more vivid. Computer networks enhance participation with others and have the ability to imitate the orality of face-to-face interaction. Ong (1971, 1982) described this as "secondary orality," in which the electronic media return us to oral-like epistemological conditions. There is a high use of formulary devices embedded, interestingly, in a world of print and rationalism. The electronic media enforces more involvement and participation, so the high literacy and rationality of typography is countered by quick and immediate experiential communication that resembles the language and communication patterns of preliterate times. These modern patterns are both "distant" and "present" because the relationship between messages is not anchored by the fixity of text; rather, messages are fashioned and packaged at an earlier time, but designed to embody the generalized domain of knowledge held by diverse audiences. Electronic communication is an admixture of oral and written traditions, but the primacy of the aural augmented with intense visual images and delivery creates a powerful sense of the immediacy of oral epistemological conditions.

Some people have been quite critical of this transformation to secondary orality. There is no shortage of scholars from a literate tradition (e.g., Postman, 1985) decrying the irrational, incoherent (a concept from the age of literacy) "show business" epistemology of television and newspapers where titillation, lure, speed, brevity, and visual impact are privileged. And Jamieson (1988) complained bitterly about the degradation of presidential discourse and the debilitating effects of electronic media on the political process where speech making has become theater rather than thinking. Nevertheless, these new forms of communication must be understood and mastered rather than only reproached. We continue with the nature of knowledge in electronic epistemology.

Knowledge and Secondary Orality. The following proposition concerns knowledge and secondary orality.

Postulate 3.0:   The electronic medium is a synthesis of key aspects of orality (immediacy, simultaneity, perception) but not subject to the physical limitations of time and space. The senses are extended to a global scale, creating a secondary orality.

Surely the nature of knowledge—what is worth knowing and how it is known—is changing as a result of changing predominate communication media. The written word is losing its supremacy as the repository and organizer of knowledge in the modern electronic world. This is not to say that science and the humanities, given their foundations in literacy, will disappear. On the contrary, typographic principles enter into the countless details of media production—such as scripts, advertising, legal matters, and technological sciences. But the secondary oral world of radio, television, and movies promises to, at least, expose everyday viewers to the noetics of primary orality. Although electronic experience is not malleable and indefinite like primary orality, or permanent like print, it has elements of both. We will certainly not return to a time when we think in clichés, because secondary orality relies on literacy, but will become increasingly media conscious. We will have an increasing ability to extend and compress time and space to meet the needs of statistical audiences.

Knowledge in the media-conscious society is not subjective as in primary orality or objective as in typography, but intersubjective. The truth of print loses its moorings and the concept of what is true or correct changes more easily from week to week or medium to medium. As information explodes and media exposes us to more and more, we develop a realization that there are other people and different ways of knowing. Information and different truths confront one another and stimulate an awareness of knowledge as unsettled and diverse. The gap between truths increases, but this does not mean that one truth is necessarily better than the other, just that the emotional attachment to ideas is aggravated. The passion attached to a "truth" is intensified. One reason for this is that print isolates individuals. Reading is a solitary activity. But electronic media facilitate participation in the lives and activities of others.

The sheer amount of information becomes daunting. What passes for knowledge accumulates at startling rates and develops exponentially. As the amount of apparent knowledge increases, it becomes more necessary to make it attractive and usable. Thus, knowledge is sold and packaged like any commodity. Its value takes on business values of attractiveness, speed, price, and ease of use. So the "sound bite" was invented, and long discursive disquisitions become scarce. The distinction between knowledge and entertainment is blurred and words such as "infotainment" gain currency. In oral cultures, entertainment and gratification were by-products of the communication process, not endemic to it.

As knowledge becomes more widespread and easily available, it loses speci-ficity. What is gained in quantity is lost in quality. There is less time for detail and analysis, and more necessity for abstracts and executive summaries than for longer documents. The generalities and clichés that carried wisdom in oral cul-tures return as handy devices for easy storage and distribution of putative knowledge. Although social and political issues are complex, they too are re-duced to slogans and formulas.

When knowledge is easily available and smartly packaged, it is easier for indi-viduals to claim that they know all they need to know. When the commodity becomes easily available, it is devalued. The entire social distribution of knowl-edge changes when the dominant media epistemology changes. The acquisition of knowledge becomes easier, so its distribution is more peculiar because indi-viduals can serve their personal needs and interests. The Internet, for example, is available in schools and libraries, so it is easier for people to develop esoteric and obscure knowledge about narrow topics.

Other consequences of these changes are more troublesome, however. A very complex and detailed structure of knowledge is hidden behind many very simple technological appearances. For example, consider the situation when a message appears on a computer screen during the operation of a program asking the user a simple question, such as "Do you want to delete the selected item?" and display-ing two "buttons," one that says "yes" and the other "no." The user simply places a pointer in the preferred space and clicks. These buttons obscure very sophisti-cated technical, mathematical, electronic, and logical knowledge. The user of the computer needs to know none of it, but increases the distance between himself and the creators of this knowledge. Cash registers in fast food restaurants also have buttons with pictures of hamburgers, sodas, and french fries on them. The employee simply touches the picture of the items ordered and the machine sends the order to the kitchen, adjusts inventory, calculates the bill, and displays the correct change. The employee does not need to know how to add, subtract, or give change. The use of this technology contributes to the intellectual coloniza-tion of certain segments of society. It robs the users of an internalized text that is a psychosocial frame of reference and breaks the connection between themselves and the knowledge they rely on. It redistributes literacy.

In "A is for Ox," Sanders (1994) explained how new media increasingly re-duce individuals to membership in a statistical mass. They become elements of market groups and then adopt the language and symbolism of those groups to state their individuality. An inner-city teenager lusting after a pair of Nike ten-nis shoes, and a suburban yuppie coveting a new BMW are seeking the same "individual" identity, but paradoxically, with group characteristics. It is appar-ent that the secrets of complex modern media and technology are hidden to the casual user in the same way that individuality is hidden in statistical groups. The knowledge required to understand how and why things work the way they do is elusive. So, confronted by so many simple symbols that teem with so much hidden knowledge, when so many invisible forces inhabit our daily lives, we feel a void. We then try to conjure some quintessence that cannot be diminished, some invisible ghostly, godly, or spiritual reality that is more real than real and can never be destroyed. We end up with a strange state of epistemological affairs where the world is dominated by sophisticated technology, but looks to the spiritual, the arcane, and the occult.

Increasingly, knowledge is elsewhere; we look outside for knowledge to some "other," some expert or professional. This is not the competence and objective knowledge that comes from the typographic culture as much as it is the search for solutions and acquiring what we need with minimal effort. The computer helps us do things and it does not matter how it works. There is a ghost in the machine. The following propositions organize the material in the previous sections around the issues of knowledge, information, and development:

Postulate 3.1:   Knowledge and truth are subjective in primary orality, objective in print, and intersubjective in an electronic empistemology (secondary orality).

Postulate 3.11:   As knowledge becomes more intersubjective, it changes more rapidly.

Postulate 3.12:   The faster knowledge changes, the more unstable it becomes.

Postulate 3.13:   The faster knowledge changes, the more it appears to accumulate.

Postulate 3.131:   The more knowledge accumulates and changes, the more a group or culture is unsettled and confused.

Even at the risk of overstating the point and sounding unjustifiably cynical and misanthropic, Postulate 3.131 is defensible. The argument that our current culture has coarsened with continually shifting and blurred lines of morality, fairness, and justice is easy enough to make. Both liberals and conservatives are demoralized and suffer from a malaise. Certainly the everyday virtues of honesty, manners, work, and restraint are more attenuated than ever.

Postulate 3.14:   As knowledge increases, it becomes increasingly commodified and takes on economic value.

Postulate 3.141:   As knowledge becomes more commodified, it is treated more like a business product.

Even at the risk of oversimplification, we can see a change from a class-structured society to a cellular structure. Fortner (1995) speculated about a society characterized by heavy access to personalized media. In a class-based society, the differences between groups are horizontal. There might be conflict between layers, but there is solidarity within layers. Language and interaction within layers is inclusive and emphasizes the commonalties that bind people to-

cell as metaphor)
horizontal layer metaphor)
46   CHAPTER 2

gether through blood, land, kinship, neighborhood, and friendship. Communication within layers reinforces relationships and helps people maintain and repair their realities. The singularity of the type of communication within class-based structure, that is, primarily real-time, face-to-face communication, has been so effective and confirming that most of us develop a strong group identity. We more often than not take pride in this group identity, and it lasts us a lifetime and has been known to at least maintain civility in some cultures for generations.

The information society, as Fortner argues, is cellular. Economic, technological, and power interests divide cells vertically, and individual or private interests divide cells mostly horizontally, but also vertically. The distinctions between cells are pronounced by the communication medium. Some cells are defined by computer-mediated interaction (PCs and modems), some by satellite, some by cable or radio frequency, and some by human communication.

People exist within these smaller cells, these tribalized enclaves, but can move from cell to cell much easier than one moves from class to class. Communication "between" all these cells is designed to press each group's case against the other. Each cell marshals evidence and argument and challenges other cells. The cells compete for symbolic significance and value. None of this promotes civility. And because people can move so easily between cells, they do not develop the strong group commitment of a class structure. Individuals communicate anonymously, and often uncivilly, in a tight little cabal that exists in thousands of different locales, but is held together electronically. People drop in and drop out at will, pander to their own prejudices, interests, and momentary desires, and move from group to group. The question of how society is possible, when we move from a class structure to a cellular structure that is defined by one's primary "medium" of communication, remains intriguing, as illustrated by the following propositions:

Postulate 3.15:   When knowledge is commodified and easily electronically available, there is a shift in a culture or group from a class structure to a cellular structure (Fortner, 1995) organized around economic and special interests.

Postulate 3.151:   Communication in cellular structures is designed to compete more with other cells for resources and symbolic significance.

Postulate 3.152:   Cellular structures have less group commitment than class-based structures.

Emotions and feelings are an important test of knowledge in secondary orality. And it is easy to accept the fancy and sensational packagings of knowledge. This is directly related to the passivity that is associated with television. As media such as television do more of the "work" of thinking and information, there will be a premium on those who can penetrate and question such information packages. Because of the emotional and affiliative dimension of the media, this form of knowledge will continue to oscillate between the fanciful, dramatic, and emotional. This type of information is stimulating, but individuals become accustomed to its actuality. Thus, media such as television become even more high definition, and simulated presence becomes even more convincing. Of course, virtual reality experiences hold the promise of moving even closer to an indistinguishable meld of technology and senses.

New tests of the quality and authenticity of information are necessary. The ability to control and manipulate simulated electronic images means that no message is as it appears. Photographs, moving pictures, and text can all be digitalized and manipulated for effect. This results in unprecedented levels of interest and creativity (note the quality of movie special effects), but is very unsettling with respect to questions of accuracy, authenticity, and reliability. Tabloid techniques of taking words out of context, cropping photographs, and using illusory and artful visual advertising pose the problems of muddling simulations with reality and cause increased identification with the simulation. In the future, intellectuals will need to be more adept at navigating multiple epistemologies.

Media Theory and the Concept of "Public."   Consider the following postulate:

Postulate 3.2:   New media (e.g., electronic media) reorganize old publics and create new publics.

The changing mix of social life is one of the hallmarks of modernity. Individuals are more likely to acquire information and socialize in a manner other than in interpersonal contexts. New patterns of communication, traditions, and processes are a consequence of media. In fact, the entire issue of public and private and how members of a culture relate to the public domain is transformed by the extended availability of symbolic and simulated media forms.

Certainly Habermas' (1989, 1995) account of the creation of the public sphere—and the entire concept of "the public"—demands careful attention. Critical theorists have little left to say about media and social theories, primarily because they viewed the media with so such contempt (e.g., Adorno & Horkheimer, 1944). But Habermas' analysis of the critical public sphere, and the role of print media in transforming cultures into liberal democracies, is pivotal to modern societies. Habermas identified the time and circumstances that led to a practice of a freerer exchange of ideas and discussions about important political and cultural issues. These discussions and practices created the concept of "the public" as an empirical and socially embedded activity. The advent of print, and later media like radio, created new publics and changed the nature of national and cultural identity. The concept of "literature" was evolving as a consequence of advances in typography, and this literature provided more grist for communication.

Habermas explained how 18th-century *salons* and coffee houses became a forum in which social and political issues were discussed. It was a context where pamphlets, journals, and books were available and open to analysis. Before this time, the notion of a public was pretty much reserved for the nobility and elite classes who had the time and inclination to talk about the arts and literature. These gatherings were ceremonial and intimate. They were politically useless and insignificant to economic development, and the nature of the conversation was polite and artistic, driven more by the proprieties of class differences than by defensible substantive argument.

The emergence of the salons and coffee houses meant that the nobility increased their contact with the upper strata of the bourgeoisie who were more "intellectual" in temperament. These intellectuals were more verbally aggressive and demanding. Now, opinions in discussions about literature had to legitimize themselves; they were subject to more pressing analysis and standards of accuracy and completeness rather than the hierarchy of social status. Such critical discussions were then extended to other topics, such as politics and economics. Almost all writers and artists subjected their ideas to the discussions in the coffee houses and salons. The salons monopolized discussion about these ideas and set the agenda concerning which ones were legitimate and which might be discarded. These organizations took important steps toward dissolving social inequalities and establishing a mode of communication based in dialectic rather than social hierarchy. A dialectic form of interaction made "reason" more possible. The secrecy and manipulations of the nobility and upper stratum of the bourgeoisie were weakened and gave way to the early stages of public reason.

Let's be more specific about the influences of the various media of communication. As Habermas explains, it was print that gave rise to the fraternal organizations that were the incubators of reasoned public discourse. But oral communication in the native tongue was the dominant medium of communication inside the salons and coffee houses. So what communicative criteria arose as a result of these social organizations? As I mentioned previously, status was ignored. But some acceptable social lubricant is always necessary for communication. Status differences cannot be just cavalierly ignored. Therefore, deference to authority was replaced with tact. Tact allows for the appearance of social parity and preserves the priority of intellectual exchange. Tact, as a verbal strategy (e.g., diplomacy, politeness, refinement, finesse, poise, and discretion) is a micro communication behavior that is necessary for the macroconcept of "public." The jumble of ideas and temperaments that are inevitable in a collection of people (a public) require some calming organizational force. If the power to "win" arguments and let reason prevail is going to be maintained, then economic and class differences among people must be at least theoretically diminished or eliminated. Because it is impossible to eliminate such differences, and often even to ignore them, they must be mitigated in some way. Politeness and deference rituals are one solution. The obligatory verbal rituals of all societies have not disappeared; they remain perhaps less obtrusive in contemporary cultures, but they are still necessary for allowing individuals room to co-construct and uphold an idealized image (cf. Goffman, 1971).

This co-construction is central to the earlier notion of public, and the modern concept of democracy. A collegial structure of authority is the heart of democracy. The abstract idea of democracy requires the actual meeting and interaction of individuals who must assuage their economic and class differences. This process can take many different forms, ranging from mass participation to select assemblies of notables, but collegiality is central in any case. The ancient democracies of Greece and Italy began as war coalitions that eventually extended their sense of citizenship. Western European fraternal organizations were influential in the graduate decentralization of power. And modern democracies that grew out of aristocratic and representative assemblies have continually expanded to be more inclusive and participatory. Collegiality itself is most upheld when resources are reasonably equally available to separate but interdependent groups. It is communicative tact that removes some of the constraints from the communication. Tact, grace, and finesse give rise to greater equality of opportunity for all participants in the discourse, as illustrated in the following postulates:

Postulate 3.21:   As opportunities for direct contact with another increase (such as in the case of electronic media), the status differences that typically regulate relationships become less important.

Postulate 3.211:   As status differences become less important in communication, they must be replaced by collegiality (politeness, tact, and deference) to maintain a concept of citizenship in a democratic public.

Postulate 3.212:   As resources (e.g., financial, communicative) become more unequally distributed in the community, collegiality decreases.

Postulate 3.213:   As collegiality decreases, the democratic public becomes less effective and threatened.

Second, the communication in salons and coffee houses opened up new problem spaces. Taboo topics and those that had never been questioned received critical attention. The impact of this was not to simply make new subject matter available, but to create a realm of "common interest." A realm where interpretation was not controlled by the church or the state. As topics of discussion became more familiar to a greater range of individuals, there was a demand for information. This was an important moment in which information became available and more in demand, if not yet commodified. It became something that individuals valued and lent their interpretations. As the need for information grew, it stimulated the growth of media and institutions that valued and distributed information. Public education and the library system, for example, are services that emerged in the 19th and 20th centuries and are one consequence of an increased need for information.

An increasing need and availability of information always spurs development and democratization (cf. Bell, 1973; Machlup, 1980–1984). Information-propelled changes in society increase levels of participatory democracy. The early analyses by Clarke (1940) correctly explained and predicted that differences in productivity and new demands for social services (e.g., education, health) would shift the labor force away from manufacturing and toward the service sector. Historical trends confirmed this expectation. But, as Machlup demonstrated, information and knowledge are the key to understanding changes in social and economic structures. This chapter restates the liberal and Marxist views of the information society and then offers a contemporary alternative. But for now, it is important to underscore that an emerging concept of "public"—born in the interpersonal relations among social groups—was responsible for a new type of subject matter and information. This changed the diversity of communications and altered the habits of thinking in terms of "common" interests. It created a sort of cosmopolitanism, or "intellectual" discussion from the point of view of establishing what is true or correct, rather than maintaining social relations. The talk itself was important, not the appeals to solidarity. This type of talk, of course, continues to reinforce class and identity differences, but it was seminal for the evolution of society into the "information society," as illustrated in the following postulates:

Postulate 3.22:   As technology creates new publics, it stimulates interest in new information and creates new "common interests."

Postulate 3.221:   As common interests increase and develop, they increase the number of institutions devoted to information storage and dissemination.

Postulate 3.222:   The more information available in a group or society, the more pressures there are toward participatory democracy.

The third change in communication, Habermas explains, is a change in the idea of *inclusiveness*. The same process of communication that instituted a public, and one that by nature is defined by common interests, is required to be regularly inclusive. In other words, as new groups and interests develop, they must be incorporated into the "public." Their interests are necessarily part of the common interests and therefore must be consolidated. Whatever the nature of the public at a moment in time, it cannot become exclusive and remain a "public." This means that collections of particular interests or smaller publics are always assimilated within a larger inclusive public. The topics of conversation and the requirements for accessible information are even greater. And as a public institutionalizes itself, it exhorts, educates, persuades, and becomes a conscious broadcasting body. It then, of course, utilizes the available media to achieve its communicative ends.

An established public is a communication network that mobilizes itself to ensure its health, continuation, and power. It does this from three analytically distinct bases. The first is information. It establishes and advances an ongoing body of knowledge that must be deemed beneficial. The power of the public can range from one extreme, where it engages in equal exchanges of information, to the other extreme, in which the public dictates. Secondly, the public must be validated and recognized. This is accomplished through legitimate forms of knowledge and information. The resources and information of a group must be communicated to others and judged as worthy. The third way a public ensures its existence and power is through resources. Resources are always necessary for communication and for securing fiscal health.

Postulate 3.23:   As the availability of information increases, so does inclusiveness in a group or culture.

It must be noted, albeit briefly for my purposes, that Habermas' account of the public sphere has received its share of criticism (Calhoun, 1992), and Habermas himself stated that his account of the public sphere is limited. It is far too focused on the bourgeois public sphere and is neglectful of popular discourse and political movements, such as those characteristic of the French Revolution. Also, Habermas' "public" is an idealization (cf. Thompson, 1990, 1995) that does not detract from its explanatory power, but in practice, was probably more restrictive than originally conceived. Habermas was, of course, part of the Frankfort school, and therefore critical of modern society. His theory of the public sphere was in the service of his theories of liberal democracy. He posed the public sphere as an idealization that has been lost because of modern media. Habermas correctly noted how print, a distinctive medium of communication, produced new social relations and altered old ones. The medium intertwined itself with the life of local society and reconstituted itself into a macrosocial concept called "the public sphere." His theory of the liberal public sphere is essentially conceptualized and formed by face-to-face interaction.

The most serious problem for Habermas is his insistence that the public, a liberal ideal of the marketplace of ideas, is in decline. New media have fragmented the society such that collegiality and commonalty are disappearing and our democracy is threatened. In this portion of his work, he shifted from a more standard liberal theory of media and society, one that holds that media and information will be responsible for transforming social and economic structures into new opportunities for work and culture that break down differences and inequalities, to a Marxist criticism. This criticism suggests that new media create islands of riches and widen existing gaps through privatization, commercialism, and corporate exploitation (e.g., Schiller, 1985; Slack & Fejes, 1987). This is where Habermas reconnected with the Frankfort School and suggested that citizens are being replaced by consumers who are narcotized by media spectacles. He maintained that society is breaking up and becoming refeudalized. The following section presents a more balanced view of media than that offered by liberal or Marxist views is possible, a view that takes the position that the confines and terrain of public life have not been destroyed, but shuffled and recomposed.

New Media and Society

Consider the following postulate concering new media:

Postulate 3.24:   Even though information proliferation increases inclusiveness in a group or culture, it is also true that the "form" and media source of the information are important. This fractionation is defined as "media publics." These media publics shape information and adopt their own logics (Altheide & Snow, 1991).

New media has restructured and redrawn the boundaries of public life. Certainly modern media are highly commercialized and yoked to particular cultural and corporate interests and values. The highly stylized and idiosyncratic uses of the media are quite removed from the liberal communicative exchanges that supposedly took place in the coffee houses. The liberal notion of "public" has now been fractionated such that people do not share a common "sense of place," in Meyrowitz's (1985) phrase, and cannot call on a direct plurality of others. Thus, modern mass media has created "media publics" that are new and quite different from the traditional sense of public. What are the social and human consequences of these new forms of media? Following I begin an answer to this question by examining the accumulation of conclusions and theoretical developments in the political, ideological, economic, and cultural arena. The approach is one of "medium sense" that is forged from the structural nature of media; that is, its organizational and technological structure as it interacts with individuals and publics. The structure and sense-making effects of the media are far more important and extend way beyond simple content influences. Medium theory is concerned with the negotiation between audiences and media (cf. Anderson & Meyer, 1988; Fiske, 1987), and how the structure of the media influences sense making and social organization. In keeping with a theory of media epistemology, we must demonstrate how media offer people an alternative way to meaningfully construe reality through symbolic interaction. The goal is not to extract and analyze the technological and social nuances of every individual medium, but to work with the most fundamental and shared influences of various media.

The term *sense* in media sense draws some sustenance from the thinking of Karl Weick (1995). Sense making is a quasi-rational act of connecting ideas and providing warrants for claims. The present-day media utilize forms and formats that organize cultural content. The "content" of messages is increasingly shaped by the "forms" of media (Carey, 1987). These forms determine the organization, focus, and impact of messages. Human experience these days is almost always a reflection of an earlier mediated experience that relies on information and messages produced elsewhere and is subject to specific discourse formats. It is not a matter of dictatorial type control by media, but a relationship between organized media that processes and transmits information and culture. It is this relationship that is responsible for altering cultural "sense."

Much media research is not in the medium-theory tradition. There are a number of deficiencies in the media research tradition that are easy enough to identify. There has been a tremendous emphasis on content (e.g., sex, violence, family values), which is important, but does not address the way media alter sense making and social organization. Moreover, there is simply no confident understanding of how media content effects people. The collection of variables that influence human behavior are tremendously complex and there is an exception to every finding. Also, there has been a tendency to focus on individual cognitive effects (e.g., attitudes), which is probably the consequence of the field's historical association with psychology, and these studies also have unreliable findings. Communication media are an extremely powerful institution in a culture, and the form of the media cannot be separated from the form of the culture.

Consider the following: There was once a magazine cartoon that pictured a mother pushing her baby in a stroller and a passerby stops and says, "Oh, isn't she cute." The mother responds with, "Yea, but you should see her picture." Or, there is the story (see Altheide & Snow, 1991) about an expensive wedding that was videotaped, and when the mother of the bride reported how much she disliked the tape, the wedding was reenacted so that the tape would be improved. True, these are exaggerated and border on humorous, but they are perfectly good examples of the "sense" that media reality is more real than real. And they further indicate how completely and meaningfully involved audiences are in media and their modes of sense making. The mother of the baby is more excited and influenced by the hyper-reproduced image of a picture. And the mother of the bride knows that it is the videotape that will be the permanent record and image of the wedding. She wants to manipulate and manage the impressions of others and future generations in the same way as an advertiser, film producer, editorial writer, or a courtroom lawyer.

Postulate 3.241:   All media involve sense participation and therefore have entertainment value. As the number, range, and intensity of sense participation increases, so do the entertainment effects (Postman, 1985).

Although Postman (1985) was writing about a single medium, his statement that "entertainment is the supra-ideology of all discourse on television" (p. 87) is true for all media. There is the constant presumption that the media are there for one's ease and pleasure. This is equally true for film, radio, and computers, and each influences the structure and nature of discourse in the community. These literacy formats are cultural byproducts of the media.

Postulate 3.242:   The more audiences are exposed to information with entertainment value, the more these values become taken for granted, and the more they establish new forms of literacy, such as media literacy. (cf. Desmond, 1996).

Entertainment is perhaps the most elemental characteristic of media (cf. Altheide & Snow, 1991; Stephenson, 1967). Any sensory experience has a stimulating and excitatory quality, so it makes sense that these experiences should be heightened as the pervasiveness and sophistication of the media continue to evolve. All cultures have a love–hate relationship with entertainment. We are simultaneously attracted and repulsed by anything that is too pleasurable, especially in America with its Puritan work-ethic traditions. Television, for example, is typically considered either a vast wasteland or an indispensable delight. Even the early forms of print had strong emotional and aesthetic implications as they increased the range, frequency, and creativity of poetry and narrative. But as McLuhan explained, it is a mistake to think that one medium is simply an amplification of an earlier one; that a light is just a more powerful candle, or a word processor just a fancier typewriter. New media, such as television and computers, redefine entertainment and the discourse that accompanies it. There is nothing especially insightful about describing media as having entertainment values. But the fact that this impacts culture and other institutions, and replaces more traditional interpretive frameworks in audiences, is not insignificant. Moreover, the effects and implications of this are not always obvious. One of the fallacies in sense making is the "fallacy of centrality" (Weick, 1995; Westrum, 1982), or the notion that because we do not know or see something it does not exist. Writing on a computer, watching television, and electronic mail are routine and not considered mysterious. But their impact on language, cognition, literacy, family life, politics, and ideology continue to unfold.

So what does it mean to say that something is entertaining? Something is entertaining if it is absorptive of attention and attracts people for reasons of personal satisfaction (Turow, 1991). There is a performance quality to entertainment. Entertainment relaxes and diverts attention by providing amusement. It is difficult to assign entertainment value to a particular genre because anything, even news and politics, can be entertaining if presented in a particular way. A first quality of entertainment is that it is not ordinary or common. There is a continuum from ordinary to entertaining, and medium theory is not concerned with placement of a subject or content on the medium, but with how the same subject matter changes as it moves along the continuum. When a medium treats subject matter as entertaining, it changes the attitudes and meanings that audiences have for the subject matter. The creativity and "entertainment" value of "Seinfeld" lay in his ability to make everyday trivia funny. But content never remains unchanged. It is impossible to completely isolate content from how it is communicated or extract meanings from the medium by which they are communicated. That is why a decision to make the news more entertaining fundamentally alters the relationship between the subject matter and the audience. When the news becomes "quick," "breezy," and "visually appealing," viewers are lulled into experiencing excitement, tension, and personal identification. They come to expect this and they come to expect all news to be tidy, appealing drama. The news is produced to ensure entertainment values. In other words, form ordains content.

As one moves along the entertainment continuum, it becomes increasingly necessary to suspend reality and judgment. The strange and unusual are an important part of entertainment. Grizzly accidents, magic moments, and extraordinary performances can become increasingly necessary to capture attention. There is an escalating expectation of interest and attention. All media—the Internet, television, books, and so forth—have a voracious appetite. They consume content so quickly, it is difficult to keep up. The response of media institutions is to find new ways to spectacularize subject matter. The "event," or coherent narrative, is also essential to entertainment and its ability to capture listeners, viewers, or readers. This is because one of the most important ways of keeping subject matter from slipping down to the mundane side of the continuum is to make it special, unique, or a stand-alone phenomenon that is clearly distinct from the ordinary flow of life. Internet Web pages permit one to link around to other pages and databases, but each individual page is designed for coherency and attention. Narrative structures with clear sequential patterns are a traditional way of making content individualistic and whole. Clarity and formulaic organizational patterns were defining features of classical literature. But modern media allow for uniqueness and specialization to be achieved through the incoherent, strange, and bizarre (e.g., music videos, computer games). In time, audiences have come to define uniqueness by these attributes. Defenders of more traditional aesthetic values protest the easy association of uniqueness with the bizarre or fantastic.

It is difficult to confine the concept of entertainment to any genre or formula, but clearly audience involvement with content is the essential. Users of media are not as passive as traditional theorists claimed, nor are they the cultural pawns of corporations sometimes described by neo Marxists (cf. Banks, 1996). Media users are active (Biocca, 1988) and *involvement* with content is a key characteristic of audience activity. Involvement is arousal or being caught up in content and includes identification with characters and issues. It is, of course, a consequence of empathy at a distance, the ability to not feel detached from the content of the media. Soap operas, romantic fiction, and computer graphics make it possible to be vicariously (at a distance) involved in many emotions and feelings. Media values and formats increasingly work to achieve this involvement, and its vicarious nature is a powerful attractor because the experience is safe, transitory, and available again in the future.

Thus, all media develop formats and rules to ensure that entertainment criteria are met. But as Altheide and Snow (1991) explained, these formats function as sense-making devices. And as "with any language or communication system, format rules become part of the taken-for-granted character of communicating and are largely unnoticed ... in day-to-day media use" (p. 18). We form a new literacy, a media literacy that may be metaphorically compared to traditional literacy in that symbols must be recognized and decoded, and grammatical rules must be mastered. And the evidence that there is interdependence among media in constructing narrative structures is accumulating (Kinder, 1990). Each medium uses procedures to influence the way audience members interact with time, narrative, structure, and syntax, including the rhythm and tempo of sequential sounds and images. The ability of these forms to achieve the desired entertainment or advertising effect is of less concern here— although the rational dissemination of information and effects is a part of all media—than is understanding the presentation of a reality that is rendered intelligible, and the influence on audiences who must establish categories of understanding. These categories for new electronic media are different than those that developed as a response to traditional typographic media. Nevertheless, anyone exposed to an information medium (crude or sophisticated) develops levels of literacy defined as an ability to understand formats, an awareness of your relationship with the medium, and a critical function that includes understanding systematic distortion (see Desmond, 1996; Singer & Singer, 1992).

New media have reorganized the boundaries between public and private. This is most evident in the political arena and in the way political power is exercised. Publicness no longer requires co-presence. Political action is not necessarily linked to a common locale. All of this is a logical extension of the entertainment and involvement magnitude of these media. The new relationship between the citizens and their political leaders is a double-edged sword. On the one hand, there is tremendous access to political leaders who can appear before many constituencies and expose themselves to many contexts. There is also the increased level of participatory democracy so valued in western cultures, the United States in particular. Moreover, there is a vigorous openness and accessibility of political leaders. Traditional communities were kept more distant from their leaders in a way that is not possible today. Leaders are very visible, and any efforts on their part to overmanage their visibility will undermine those very efforts.

But on the other hand, the full power and force of modern media are brought to bear on the political process. Citizens, as members of audiences, develop sustained mediated quasi-relationships with political leaders that are subject to all of the emotions and feelings of any relationship, albeit one that is empathically distant and constantly managed. This creates risks and considerable opportunity for mismanagement and distortion. There is no co-presence required. And given the nature of media previously described, and their new forms of literacy, messages are fashioned and understood in ways that can be as easily controlled. Political leaders must be in a constant state of reflexivity, a constant state of monitoring their language and behavior, because their messages are not heard by unified groups, but by diverse mass audiences that employ a degree of variable interpretation. For example, the visual codes of television are more context driven and require communicators to "assume" more. This is, of course, consistent with the oral mind. But modern media signs and symbols do not have the fixity of interpretation of traditional typography. Modern political leaders know that they always run the risk of meanings that they did not intend. This seriously increases the pressure on leaders to manipulate and manage impressions, especially when events are capable of being witnessed. The Gulf War, which was controlled completely by the military and released to the public in tightly managed video packets, is an obvious example. And the tight media management of the Gulf War was a response to what was considered the damaging role of the media in the Vietnam War.

Television is most responsible for altering the sense of the public and private. Other modern media have unique characteristics, but television is the nation's medium. It is the tribal fire that we gather around in the evening. The basic theoretical functions of television, (such as surveillance, information, and socialization (see Lasswell, 1948; Wright, 1986), are conditioned by the essential characteristics of the medium. So information transmission and monitoring is a function of print, but also of visual medium such as television. But the two media differ considerably with respect to how the same information is communicated; differences such as level of detail, time, depth, argumentative structure, logical organization, and visual acuity. Even considering these differences, data clearly indicate that the judgment of voters in an election reflects a composite of media coverage, and that audiences think about what they are told, even if they do not automatically do what they are told (McCombs & Shaw, 1993). This is essentially the agenda-setting function of the media, and in combination with long-term and well-documented cultivation effects (Signorielli & Morgan, 1990), it is safe to conclude that television disciplines the symbolic environment and substitutes its contorted presentation of reality for others. Any medium has this potential, it need only dominate the consciousness of its users.

As a medium becomes intertwined with the consciousness of its users, it becomes more difficult to separate the two. And the clever human can capitalize on this difficulty whenever it suits him. This is why presidential candidates travel with movie stars and borrow catchy phrases ("where's the beef," "make my day"). Television speaks the language of wholistic emotions rather than analytical thought (cf. Hart, 1994). It must be entertaining and involving. Even new terminology designed to describe new genres of television include a blend of two genres to make a new one, such as in "infotainment," "edutainment," or "docudrama." The return to a type of orality in television means that feelings, emotions, and personal identification can all be marshaled to create pleasing or disturbing feelings.

Medium Theory and Information

Electronically mediated information, and the knowledge that is a consequence, is different in contemporary society. Individuals are no longer rational autonomous individuals. This section outlines some theoretical qualities of information, but without the accompanying hysteria about the "information revolution" and the deterministic assumptions of revolutionary change just over the horizon. Surely, new media make for important differences in information, but we will align ourselves with Rogers (1986) who calls himself a "soft technological determinist"; that is, new media technology along with other issues cause change. There are three important features of technology that are relevant to information.

The first is individuality. Technological developments have not only made information easily available to individuals, but make it possible to tailor information to individual needs. The Internet and various electronic databases make it possible for a single individual to amass, organize, and use information for various personal, business, or social reasons. Next, new technology makes for asymmetrical communication, such that individuals do not need to be co-present to communicate. Electronic information can be tapped at any time without the cumbersome, time-consuming, and expensive assistance of another human being. Third, digitalization makes two-way interaction possible among diverse networks. Communication between widespread interest groups (e.g., Internet discussion groups) is either welcomed as a powerful tool for community work, or renounced as a force of impersonal power. These technological developments have significant social structural implications, and influence some of the characteristics of information, as shown in the following postulate:

Postulate 3.25:   Advancement in technology makes information more individual, asymmetrical, and increases interaction among diverse groups.

Of course all societies are information societies, the major differences being the amount, speed, institutionalization, and dominant form of information. Traditional societies, reliant on oral discourse, kept information close to the users and primary functions. Knowledge about life and markets resided in individuals who were in proximity to the sites where information was applied. Modern information is generated, stored, and transmitted from great distances and resides in electronic space to be extracted at will. Moreover, it is commodified, that is, it has exchange value. For example, in traditional cultures, knowledge of the marketplace had intrinsic value to the source of the information. It was useful to the individual for buying, selling, and maintaining life. But commodified information, which can be bought and sold like any "commodity" (e.g., television shows, computer software, movies, Disneyland) replaces its intrinsic value with market criteria. Information takes on the commercial and entertainment values of its primary medium of communication, and becomes subject to the systematic biases of that medium.

Modern information is very heterogeneous and manifold. And as a commodity, it is subject to the marketplace. It can be bought and sold, and changes its value in accordance with market conditions. On the other hand, information is central to the goals and values of particular societies. The educational system commodifies information. It packages information and sells it. A citizenry educated in literature, logic, and science was the consequence of dominant typography, and that collective stock of knowledge had economic and social benefits. One strength of information as a commodity is that it is not destroyed on consumption, although its value will change as the number of consumers changes. Because information remains to be continually consumed, and because information has value, and because its replication and distribution is cheaper than its origination, there are more societal efforts and resources devoted to distributing, replicating, and storing information than to creating it. So spreading knowledge and information throughout society about AIDS is less expensive, faster, and more successful than creating knowledge about AIDS. This causes particular problems for cultures or segments of cultures who are trying to protect themselves from outside forces, especially the information of a dominant neighbor or an unwelcome political or cultural influence.

Still, because information is an economic commodity, its economic value is in inverse proportion to its availability. Specialized information that provides advanced knowledge is more valuable to its owners when it is scarce (Antonelli, 1991). Insider information makes for imperfect markets and strengthens the positions of individuals or institutions who have such information. This information may not even be difficult to obtain, but is valuable solely because it is scarce. Commodified information may also be purchased at a price. Modern society has seen an increase in specialized information prepared for the private consumption of select groups. Governments and corporations will commission studies and confidential reports for their own use. And they "own" the information. Ideas for movies, book outlines, and computer software are intellectual property that can be registered and protected just as manufacturing products are patented. The opportunities for market concentration and monopolies increase under these conditions because of the relatively low cost of extending services that already exist. Once an institution is established in the market, it is easier for that organization to grow than for new organizations to gain a foothold. Thus, competitive forces are weak and monopolies are likely (Schiller, 1981), as illustrated by the following postulates:

Postulate 3.251:   Commodified information has value in inverse proportion to its availability.

Postulate 3.252:   As information increases in value, there is an increase in efforts to protect it.

Postulate 3.253:   Increased efforts to protect information increases market concentration and monopolies.

Computers and telecommunications are the media most responsible for radical changes in the information society. The costs of data have been significantly reduced by computers, and telecommunications have transcended local markets and are the skeletal structure of a global information infrastructure. These markets without limits have interesting theoretical consequences. Conventional theorizing would hold that more information is better and expanded competition is desirable. Recent experience, however, suggests that increased information changes markets so they function less efficiently (Melody, 1994). Massive amounts of information make it more difficult to predict the future. It introduces uncertainty, complexity, and instability into markets. Moreover, as information, technology, and capital concentrate and markets become less competitive (e.g., Microsoft's competitive advantages) benefits are unequally distributed. The advantages of information and technology accrue disproportionately to large corporations and governments who are in the best position to take advantage of opportunities. Corporate interests are aware of these tendencies, and the surge of takeovers and mergers was the response. And new products and applications are more likely to benefit the interests of conglomerates at the expense of localized businesses with unique needs.

Medium Theory and Development

The role of communication and national development has been of interest since World War II (Rogers, 1962; Schramm, 1964). Actually, from the 18th century and the Enlightenment, the notion of society unfolding toward the more perfect has been a dominant metanarrative. Tehranian (1992, 1994) examines the multitude of theorists and interdisciplinary backgrounds that try to understand how media influence cultural and national development. He describes normative theories that suggest desirable social change and the role of media in accomplishing such change. Liberals have argued that the media bring new information, modernization, and a consensus public. And Marxists have been critical of much modern media for creating corporate dependency and being pro-capitalist. The main theoretical issue is how a medium affects long-term change. Early theories were simply naive, assuming that modernization for the sake of modernization was desirable. Moreover, early diffusion theories misunderstood information as a commodity. But clearly, the two most important theoretical consequences of media are the diffusion of information and commodification of information. This commodification means that media are economic, rather than ideological apparatuses. This is consistent with information-society issues and continues to feed debates about either the liberating or subjugating effects of media.

The liberating perspective on media is born from the idea of natural progress. The assumption that change is inevitable, and along with it, increasing rationality, democracy, and economic development. In this tradition, ideology is a pathology; it is a disease, a barrier to social health. The Marxist theory of development is heavily ideological and inadequate as any sort of explanatory framework for media. It simply states that the media are ideological tools of elites or a ruling corporate class. This neglects the specific effects of individual media users and the power of entrepenreurship and social action to upset these processes. Any analyses of the role of new media and development must accept commodification as an economic reality to which other ideologies will follow. This makes the process more predictable, on the one hand, because the consequences of commodification are more clearly related to economic principles, but less predictable on the other hand, because human social and ideological responses are less predictable.

The introduction of a new technology does not dictate some historical inevitability. Human consciousness always frames institutions. But it does so within the parameters of a society that must tame the beasts of exchange, power, legitimization, and meaning. The media influence development through four interrelated processes (Tehranian, 1994). *Information* is the most important, and truly begins with the advent of print technology (Eisenstein, 1979). The ease of diffusing information can have complex consequences, from unsettling the stabilizing foundations of cultures to improving health care and the quality of life. Computers, tape recorders, and video contribute to social revolution as well as entertainment. *Control* is a second theoretical influence, and it is most pronounced with modern electronic media. Computerized information storage and systems of record keeping on purchasing habits, taxes, and credit cards are Orwellian in proportion. These, too, can either serve state autocracy or modern efficiency (Tehranian, 1992). The third process that media exacerbate is *development*. In other words, change is very rapid and increases as media increases. As early manufacturing technology gave rise to capitalism and its development, modern media technology has stretched this innovation to the farthest reaches of the globe. Internationalism and an interconnected world economy, including global marketing and advertising, are completely dependent on electronic in-formation-processing highways. Finally, new media have strong empirical influ-ences on *democratic revolutions*, that is, they are very important for mobilizing people, communicating revolutionary ideas, and helping maintain control. This is a dialectical process, and one that can result in extremes from the social inclusiveness and equality of communitarians, to the hierarchy and exclusive-ness of Fascists. Clearly, modern electronic media make for a bias toward global-ization and all the attendant implications for culture, such as distancing people from their local cultures, and political stability. Historically, media institutions were wed to their own homeland. But satellites and computers and unparalleled speed make it more possible for media to distribute information and influence things worldwide including the development of a communication infrastruc-ture (Frederick, 1992).

The flow patterns of information are another important theoretical implica-tion of a medium, and these interact with all social effects including national de-velopment. Bordewijk and van Kaam (1986) outlined an interesting model that helps organize these issues, and I refer to it here. The interactivity effect of a me-dium can range from active to passive, slow to fast, and various levels of user control over time and material. There are passive forms of information flow (e.g., broadcast media, books) that provide information to a user but do not al-low for much user control. There is little interaction in such a flow pattern, and a resultant tendency for information to be commonly held and responsible for a more collective consciousness. Receivers of information have little control be-cause the media are mass media, that is, a single or few messages are available to the masses.

The preceding information flow pattern is termed *allocution* by Bordewijk and van Kaam (1986). It is the structure of mass media in which a center distrib-utes a message to outlying receivers. Radio and television broadcast messages, lectures, and church sermons are all examples of allocution in which informa-tion generally flows one way to many. The time and place are determined by the sender and there is little opportunity for receivers to influence messages. There is little interactivity. Control is paramount in this pattern and one reason why dictatorships and authoritarian political structures organize themselves this way. When information remains central, but the receivers and users of informa-tion have control and may access and use the information, then the pattern is *consultative*. Individuals at the periphery can shop at a central store of informa-tion. Libraries, data banks, newspaper archives, and the Internet are places where information is stored for use. This type of information flow is increasing in the era of electronic media. Information is commodified, but becomes more available and less expensive. These patterns allow for new publics to be created as groups organize themselves around common interests and have both information and communication opportunity easily available. Interactivity between individuals and information is high.

Two other typical flow patterns are conversation and what Bordewijk and van Kaam call registration. *Conversation* is an interpersonal or small group network and in complete control of the individuals. There is no center, and the participants control time, place, and subject matter. Electronic mail, letters, telephone conversations, and everyday, face-to-face communication are all examples. Individual psychologies are more at work and there is typically more equality (including political and economic equality) among individuals. The communication can be either symmetrical or asymmetrical, although modern media make asymmetry (e.g., faxes, E-mail, answering machines) increasingly important. Asymmetry increases the amount and efficiency of communication, but is more appropriate for routine exchanges rather than expanded discussion. *Registration* is another pattern that has increased considerably because of computerization. It is similar to allocution and consultation because there is a central store of information, but this central store requests information from users. It does not broadcast messages, and it is not available for search and use. Information is "registered" in a central place and then used to inform or bill individuals. A telephone company records phone use and then bills customers; the Internal Revenue Service keeps tax and financial information and requests periodic updates and payments; insurance companies keep accident and driving records and alter policies and bills accordingly. Registration is a matter of record keeping and is a principal means of surveillance in information-age cultures. Individuals have only slightly more control over content than in allocution.

All theoretical entities can be used for good or ill, and the question of whether or not media innovations are responsible for desired development or confining conservatism remains open. Nevertheless, many people (e.g., Beniger, 1986; Winston, 1986) suggest that the trend is more conservative than progressive, and that media innovations increase the opportunities for control and authority. Beniger argued that media and new forms of electronic contact have done more for governments, industry, and the military than anything else. Even if new technologies have liberating potential, they are very dependent on access to significant resources, and must develop without upsetting the established social order or threatening the status quo.

CONCLUSION: MEDIUM THEORY AND SOCIAL VALUES

The nature of the micro–macro link between media and society is tense and open to diverse forms of expression. One of the tensions is between science and normative theory, or between a rather detached and objective analysis of medium effects and one that deals with what the media *should* be like or how it *ought* to influence society (McQuail, 1994). Another tension is between the economic and the political conditions of media with respect to the value system inherent in each, and the social conditions they require (Garnham, 1986). These are essentially issues in normative theory or assumptions about how the media should perform and what society should expect from media. Much of the discussion about media thus far has taken place in a decontextualized manner; that is, we have assumed the evolution of a liberal democracy and noted the impact of various dominant media (oral, typographic, electronic) on the culture. Moreover, there is always the assumption in the West that freedom is essentially economic and the media are guided by the invisible hand of markets. This chapter concludes with some brief statements about what the organized political community should expect from the media, and about the perhaps irresolvable tension between commercial and political values.

Most citizens, and even media professionals, take the structure and daily working assumptions of the media as a given. Politics and ethics are left to others to speculate about. This is understandable because most social scientists want to avoid the messy subjective issues that surround political and ideological matters. As a consequence, prescriptive statements about how the media should serve a community have been marginalized.

McQuail (1994), drawing on earlier theorists such as Hutchins (1947), Siebert, Paterson, and Schramm (1956), and Hardt (1979), explained how the origins of such normative theories lie in the role traditionally assigned to the press. Uncensored printed publications were considered essential for political liberation and development. Citizen democracies simply cannot be sustained without a repository of quality information and an outlet for open discussion. McQuail also offered up suggestions about how the media can benefit the public interest with respect to freedom, diversity, information, and cultural solidarity.

Two opposing perspectives on all modern forms of media (e.g., newspapers, television, the Internet) are the economic and the political. These, I believe, are the most important social theoretical issues, with respect to the media. An economic theory of the media defines an individual as a consumer exercising production and purchasing rights, and the media sustain and foster these rights. A political theory holds that individuals are citizens with rights of expression and information, with communally defined goals and social structures. Advocates of an economic model argue for private ownership—typically justified as a check on oppressive political power—and unconstrained media operations. The political model, on the other hand, seeks to intervene in media operations to suppress inequalities in the market, promote freedom, and improve public access to the media. The clash between these two theories has each arguing for the restriction of the other as the solution. Free-market economic theorists argue that an unconstrained hyper media environment is the strongest protection against state oppression, and political theorists see the current commercial condition of the media as the greatest obstacle to improved communication and equality.

A resolution to the inherent tension between these two social perspectives is not likely. In our current stage of advanced capitalism and technology, characterized essentially by an elaborate division of labor and the interpenetration of government and business, only the market can allocate resources and power across the many sectors of the culture. But on the other hand, there are many social decisions (e.g., health, control of violence, compassion) that you certainly do not want to leave to the market. So the goal is not for either the economic or political model of media to prevail at the expense of the other, but to identify the contact points and necessary interactions between the two fields. This is particularly important because media institutions are both commercial enterprises and political institutions. This unique organizational situation has spawned a host of laws, obligations, and protections, and has resulted in a media history where only those with money and power had access to the media, even though ordinary citizens are endowed with rights to debate, information, and public forums.

One contact point in the contemporary media environment is not the issue of access to the media, although that remains problematic, but the changing relationships and consciousness that a commercial media fosters. These changes are very deleterious to the democratic process. When the political discourse is reliant on a commercial medium of communication, then the political discourse takes on the values and discourse forms of the commercial medium. When a broadcast medium must compete in the market for consumers, then the political discourse must compete with other commercial products. Thus, we have politicians who treat citizens as consumers. Political language sounds like advertising that must appeal to consumer interests, needs, and appetites. The argument that political discourse has become degraded into little more than attractive salable packages for easy consumption is easy enough to make (e.g., Hart, 1994; Jamieson, 1988; Kellner, 1990). The rub is that the political realm of society has no naturalistic control system and is reliant on informed citizens active in a deliberative democracy.

Kellner's (1990) rather hysterical critical theory argues that this degradation of political discourse is intentional on the part of the capitalist elite. He cited a report entitled *The Crisis of Democracy* (Crozier, Huntington, & Watanuki, 1975), issued by the Trilateral Commission (an organization of capitalist world leaders seeking ways to stabilize democracies), that argued that the media created too much democracy and instability. The media were allegedly creating an adversary culture that was undermining authority. He maintains that the goals of global media authority were realized in the Reaganism and Thatcherism of the 1980s and continue to the present. He also maintains that the media have undermined democratic processes by promoting excessive corporate power.

Economic market considerations, and modern electronic media epistemological assumptions, are probably better explanations of the current condition of the political sphere and media power than are capitalist conspiracies. Media have commodified information and exacerbated economic forces, which has resulted in power concentration and commercialization of information. About a century ago, when our culture moved from the farm to the factory and became primarily a manufacturing country, the processes leading up to this point were slower and more graduate. Moreover, the move to a manufacturing economy created jobs. But the electronic communication revolution, consistent with its medium-theoretic implications, was much faster, with a more drastic impact, and eliminated more jobs than it created. We now have markets without geographical and spatial limits. Conventional economic explanations would predict that better communication would improve markets and expand competition. But the experiences of the 1980s and 1990s suggests that highly commodified information altered markets and created more complexity than we are able to understand.

The internationalization and globalization that resulted from new media have made many organizations less competitive (Melody, 1994). New media make internationalization possible, but it is primarily government and transnational corporations who are able to take advantage of these new markets. They are able to control these markets and operate them from a few corporate centers. The creation of these new markets by new media is what has caused a rush of mergers and takeovers, creating corporate monsters (e.g., Exxon & Mobile).

Moreover, the complexity of new media makes it difficult for anyone but the largest corporations to enter the market, thereby making corporate concentration more likely. There is an automatic assumption that consumers must adapt to the usage patterns of new media and information services. Large organizations develop these services for their own purposes, and then expect smaller users to adapt. Often, there are many benefits of data, speed, and information for large international corporations, but costs are prohibitive and access to smaller communities is limited. DuBoff (1983) made this same argument about the introduction of the telegraph in the past century. It improved market functioning, but made for increased monopolization.

Finally, there is now a research task to which major social institutions must attend. It is the bringing about of major restructuring among the institutions responsible for information and the public at large. Public information institutions, including proprietary corporations, must bring information to the marketplace to meet public information needs. This requirement is a strength of the public-sphere notion because it assumes that any political decision must be coextensive with the population it controls. Membership in a state (a public) implies certain universal rights and obligations. All citizens must live with the consequences of decisions, and that is why simply winning a political argument still requires the winners to act responsibly. It is the concept of the "public" that guarantees this. And it means that no suitable democratic participation can result in gross injustice or inequality.

This is related to what Arthur Schlesinger called the "vital center." New media and the information society should make the standard differences between the left and the right less distinct because new technologies should empower people at levels lower than government and corporate conglomerates. This is not an argument that we are at the dawn of full-participation democracy, or that representative democracy is dead. On the contrary, it is an argument for the continued importance of deliberative democracy, but one in which citizen participation is enhanced. This cannot be achieved if information is specialized, expensive, portioned, and fragmented such that one group of true believers is only talking to another. This is the developing cellular model of social structure alluded to earlier in this chapter. Enhanced national political debate is the rational core of the public sphere. One thing is for sure: it is vital that the dominant forms of communication be re-embedded into social life. This is an essential condition of democracy.

❧ 3 ❧

Meaning, Discourse, and Society

No matter how eloquently my dog barks, he cannot tell you that his parents were poor but honest.

—Bertrand Russell

In developing an account of media suggested earlier, I have focused on the particular characteristics of various communication media. Essentially, the task was to identify the qualities of these media and note their communicative and social differences and consequences. Now, I turn to a second elemental theoretic concept in communication and society, namely, discourse. Humans have a distinct capacity for symbolization of the unseen, and these symbols are organized and amplified through the internalization of social language. This means that the relationship between language and society is not direct, but is framed as a process of production. That is, societal relations and knowledge are represented in our minds and these representations are the link or interface between texts and society. These representations are fundamental to the micro–macro link, that is, they serve as key producers of microinteraction processes, which in turn develop and sustain macrosocial processes.

The term *discourse* is common enough, but also one of the most inadequately defined terms in scholarly literature (e.g., Schiffrin, 1994). The principal reason for this is because the term draws on so many intellectual traditions and perspectives. Although I make some brief introductory clarifications, my goal in this chapter is certainly not to review and evaluate these traditions and perspectives, or propose a specific definition. Schiffrin (1994) did a fine job of overviewing the study of discourse, and I would encourage the reader to seek out her work. Moreover, the study of discourse is, by its very nature, an

68

expansive and complex enterprise. It cannot be reduced or simplified without doing an injustice to the phenomenon under investigation. What I hope to do is explain how discourse is essentially a communicative activity—yet one that can be isolated for some noncommunicative analytical reasons—which can account for a range of social issues. More specifically, I argue in this chapter and others that discourse is the empirics of social organization and structure. I cannot discuss or analyze more general social categories, such as ethnicity or social class, without grounding them in the empirics of discourse analysis. This chapter first clarifies some issues in discourse and communication, and does this by showing how communication is interactive language use, within a medium, where meaning and social structures are interactional achievements. These comments are followed by consideration of how interaction and meaning are a form of social action. The final section explores conversation and how it is the key phenomenological reality for people and social organization. It is the various empirical relationships between conversation and society that are formalized.

DISCOURSE AS SOCIAL INTERACTION

At its most descriptive level, discourse is "language as social interaction." It is this phrase that Schiffrin (1994) suggested "best unites (at a very general level) the different approaches to discourse" (p. 414). There are numerous approaches and analytical orientations to the study of discourse, ranging from Foucault's broad discourses of knowledge and history, to the more microanalyses of conversation analysts, with pragmatists, speech act theorists, sociolinguists, and ethnographers floating somewhere in between. But they are all concerned with functional language use, which is responsive to speakers, listeners, contexts, and designed to serve human affairs in some way by producing meaning. They all have the following features in common (see also Brown & Yule, 1983; Leech, 1983; Schiffrin, 1990, 1994). The following list elaborates on the role of discourse in producing meaning and reality:

1. Discourse is in the first instance *empirical*. The data are language forms and specimens—either oral or written—that emerge from actual use by individuals in a language community. In discourse analysis, as opposed to linguistic analysis, methods and analytical techniques explain data. Discursive language and forms may be analyzed by frequency distributions, sequential structures, or distributional patterns, and are subject to all epistemological assumptions of data (e.g., falsifiability, reproducability, etc.) including powers of prediction and explanation.

2. Discourse is *radically contextual*. The empirical data just produced are done so in a context that includes a medium that is performing local work. A context is an in-tact assembly of people, objects, and psychological pre-

sumptions and expectations. Perhaps even more importantly, discourse is understood and interpreted on the basis of its placement in a sequence of messages. There are many types of contexts, (such as occasions and encounters (cf. Goffman, 1971), and these not only supply structure and meaning, but are themselves organized and interpreted by discourse. Contexts do not destabilize meaning. On the contrary, they make meaning possible.

3. This language data, which occurs in a context, is also inextricably linked to interpretive schemes and social meanings. The discourse uses resources from language combined with routine and idiosyncratic interpretive schemes to produce a coherent message understood by the participants. In other words, discourse is not simply a matter of denotational meanings or mechanized communication sequences. It relies on an attachment to group and cultural frameworks for its coherence and sense.

4. The meanings and actions of discourse are constructed and achieved in the social interaction. This does not mean they are constructed out of airy nothingness, but rather interactants use mental models and representations to collocate symbolic data and organize it into meanings and actions. Language users engage in micro-momentary interactions that are attended to and then externalized through interpretations. These externalizations are meaningful when they are connected to established or evolving semantic structures. This process is metaphorically akin to what Weick (1995) called "sense making" and Shotter (1993) called "authoring."

5. There are a number of *assumptions and resources* that are typically important for how something is meant and accomplished in discourse. When a language user is constructing messages, there are a variety of resources that typically guide the construction. These resources usually play a very strong role in establishing meaning and deciding what has been accomplished. The following are examples: genres, medium, conventional discourse modes such as narrative and exposition, speaker intentions, sequential patterns of phrases and utterances, individual personalities and relationships; rhetorical expectations, and standardized cultural beliefs and practices.

COMMUNICATIVE REALISM

Now I want to explain the nature of discourse as reliant on assumptions and methods I call communicative realism. *Communicative realism* provides some necessary assumptions for making discourse the key to understanding social structure. Communicative realism considers language to be the essential constructor of social reality, and considers practical relevance to be extractable from "lived" language use. This analysis is fundamentally communicative because it keeps data and interpretation grounded to language and discourse, and directs attention away from other analytical categories such as politics, ideology, or religion. Rather, these analytical categories are themselves implied in a recursive relationship with language such that they are produced, reproduced, and sustained in discourse.

Meanings and various social categories are real, but still achieved, reproduced, and constructed. What is the reality? The reality is meanings, codes, genres, routines, scripts, language games, and sequences. How are these constructed? They are constructed by the acts of communication, including thinking, using oral and written language in contexts, and interpreting. I am not making the argument that there is nothing outside of language, but that social reality is filtered through language in a fundamental way dependent on its nature, structure, and use. I certainly do not deny the fact of physical reality, but insist that it is known and understood within language and the communication processes that drive language. And society is particularly composed in language.

These are the processes that we want to examine and focus on. Because it follows that if social categories such as gender, class, or ethnicity are constructued in discourse, then there is no extralinguistic thing called "gender," "class," or "ethnicity." These are constructed realities achieved in the communicative practices of naming, classifying, referencing, and related acts in ordinary and particular discourse. It is very important to guard against slipping into the libertarian notion that we can "construct" anything we want, or that remaking language will easily remake society. No, language and discourse respond to social and communication conditions that are very binding on users. Rules of writing (Ricoeur, 1976), speech acts (Searle, 1969), deep structures (Chomsky, 1957), conversations (Sacks, Schegloff, & Jefferson, 1974), implicatures (Grice, 1975), and various intertextual contact points bridle discourse and interpretive processes. Communicative realism does not cavalierly suggest that society is subjectively constructed, but it locates social reality in the communicatively real structures of discourse, rather than in the metaphors of external reality where language is simply a map between cognition and the supposed external world. Social categories are constituted using the communicative mechanisms of language users, and one of the most important regulative presuppositions is semantic realism.

Semantic Realism

Discourse and communication are dependent on a form of semantic realism. This is because any form of interaction requires a common focus, and this makes it dependent on a form of semantic realism. This is the same principle of realism as scientific realism. Historically, realism was concerned with the real existence of things that were not physically apparent—with the reality of abstract entities beyond human perception. So there were recognizable things such as lizards and squares, and realists argued that the abstracta of *lizardom* and *squareness* also had a real independent existence. However, contemporary versions of the argument do not debate the real existence of abstract universals, but shift the focus to the reality of theoretical entities. Scientific realism holds that the theoretical entities of the world do exist. That the world's furniture can be described and organized and these descriptions and organizational patterns constitute real phenomena. Rescher (1987) defended a position within the orbit of realism by suggesting that even if these theoretical entities do not exist, at least we are "on track." Such conceptions might be imperfect, but there is some consonance based on the quality of our evidence and reasoning. In the natural sciences, electrons and genes are examples of such *real* theoretical entities.

Just as biology and electricity cannot proceed without the assumptions of genes and electrons, communication cannot proceed without the assumption of meaning. Information is always something that we lay *claim* to. We defend information (e.g., words, electrons, genes) and the nature of meaning with various kinds of evidence, reasoning, and data. Discourse is thus undergirded by an assumption that we communally inhabit a shared world of meanings, a world of *real* meanings amongst which we live and that we use, even if they are imperfect. The mere act of communication is only possible when we have common access to the semantic order of things. The epistemic status of this stable-meaning world is not that of an empirical discovery, but of a presupposition.

Our commitment to meaning that lies behind messages is indispensable any time we move into the domain of publicly accessible communal interaction about a shared world. In other words, any time we read, write, or utilize any medium of communication, we assume the real possibility of meaning. We could not even imagine any activity called communication without the assumption of a common world of meaning (semantic realism) to which we direct our individual conceptions. The objective status of this common world of meaning is an assumption, not an empirical finding. It is important to understand the distinction between this assumption of semantic realism and the *content* of what we say. Semantic realism is a matter of frame; what we say, content, is picture. The picture is related to the frame. We are able to accomplish actual communication because we submit to a type of contract agreeing on the shared world of meaning. Part of this contract stipulates that the language we use will be the deciding factor in our communication.

In a sense, when we communicate, we intend to objectify. We intend to use language and a host of pragmatic features to muddle around in this shared world of meaning and make some decisions about how a speaker and hearer (or writer and reader) can coordinate their conceptions. In many cases, this muddling around results in quite automatic efficiency. Langer's (1992) and Kellermann's (1992) arguments and evidence that much communication is primarily automatic is relevant here. They argue that the reservoir of meaning is simply there for community use and the extent to which so many meanings occur with mechanical regularity is evidence of the efficiency of the shared world of meaning. When I speak or write about something—even on the basis of my own idiosyncrasies—I speak or write about the "real" thing by virtue of the conventions governing reference. Even if I am speaking about a "ghost," I am speaking about a *real* ghost by virtue of our interpersonally shared world of meaning.

The factor of semantic realism reflects our basic commitment to a communally available world that is the property of all communicators. This is more than just a mere agreement on referential meaning. Such agreement would be merely an a posteriori agreement, although our commitment to semantic realism puts things on an a priori basis. What links my messages to the messages of another is our common subscription to the a priori presumption that we are talking about a shared thing. We can continue to talk about this shared thing and alter our conceptions of it, but it remains a real thing that we are discussing. To communicate, we do not need the same view of our subject, but only take the position that we share a world capable of being communicated about. This provides a fixed point around which communication revolves.

The commitment to semantic realism is basic to the communication process. It is the reason that we distance ourselves from meaning and recognize that there is a discrepancy between what we say and what we "mean." In other words, we are continually trying to achieve meaning in our communication because we consider it to be attainable. If meaning were only based on an individual's "conception of it," then the result would be a cognitive solipsism that would, by definition, preclude communication. That is, if I argued that my personal meaning for something was the only acceptable criteria for meaning, then the possibility of interpersonal communication and communal exchange would be nonexistent.

It is not controversial to argue that communication is fundamental to human nature and a practical consideration. And given its essential nature, we have no real choice but to accept its presuppositions. Therefore, we might pose the following argumentative structure:

1. Communication is fundamental to the human animal.
2. We cannot act or function effectively without an efficient and workable system of communication.
3. Commitment to semantic realism is essential to communication.

Therefore:

4. Semantic realism—that is, a commitment to a real world of meaning—is a necessary imperative or a *sine qua non* for the communication process.

Only in subscribing to a postulate of semantic realism can we take the view of communication that we have. Without it, the conceptual framework for communication would collapse. Its importance is such that even if there were no semantic reality, we would have to invent one.

So if we really abandoned the assumption of semantic realism, we could make no reliable claim about discourse and communication. We need the concept of semantic stability to operate communication. A straightforward statement such as "Mary and Bill are friends" is communicative and true only if there is a world in which Mary and Bill exist, the concept of friendship is understood, and there is the ability to interpersonally share this world. This does not mean that there cannot be an infinite number of conceptions about friendship and its expression, but that the statement is true in that it characterizes a communicable reality.

Meaning Versus Significance

This leads to another problem that must be resolved if the concept of stable meaning is to possess any reliability. This is the problem of endless semiosis and interpretability. We cannot lay claim to a workable communication process if any message is always at the mercy of incessant and equally plausible interpretations. An essay a few years ago by Bochner (1985) described, at the time, a growing approach to communication as "textualism." Briefly, textualism is the notion that all messages and vocabulary are language-relative. All messages contain gaps of indeterminacy that can never be completely filled, and therefore there is never a final resolution to the meaning of a message. This perspective emerges from the confluence of current streams in literary and critical theories (e.g., Derrida, 1976; Foucault, 1984; Rorty, 1982) that have sharply attacked representationalist views of language and opened the floodgates of interpretation. It is the position that there is no distance so great as that between two minds, and that all message recipients can do is "read" the words of the other (cf. Peters, 1994).

But if it is true that any "reader" of a message cannot simply declare meanings with humpty dumpty-like freedom, then it must be possible to bind the semiotic process. One of the most important distinctions for the study of discourse and communication is the distinction between *meaning* and *significance* (Hirsch, 1967). This is a compelling distinction that has received too little attention in the debates about meaning. Hirsch (1967) wrote:

> "*Meaning* is that which is represented by a text; it is what the author meant by his use of a particular sign sequence; it is what the signs represent according to conventional techniques for establishing meaning. *Significance*, on the other hand, names a relationship between that meaning and a person, or a conception, or a situation, or indeed *anything imaginable*" (p. 8, italics added)

Meaning utilizes linguistic conventions within a context to access the communally shared semantic world for a purpose; significance implies a vast array of possible relationships between a message and any number of social and intellectual categories. Significance is variable, creative, liberal, and continually enriches the way we appreciate or respond to a message. Meaning is conservative. It builds on individual and linguistic tradition and resists change.

I am arguing along with Hirsch for the importance of the distinction between meaning and significance. Although one is not more important than the other, the concept of meaning is more central to the study and practice of communication. The required assumption of semantic realism coupled with the distinction between meaning and significance helps discipline the semiotic processes. Railsback (1983) successfully made a similar argument in her efforts to avoid rhetorical relativism. She maintained that defining language as an interdefining code network with no final terms is inadequate because discourse takes place within a structure that provides limitations on what can be meant. Otherwise, meanings, like thought, would be inexhaustible and no communication would be possible. Even from finite vocabularies, humans can exfoliate an infinite number of ideas and meanings. If meaning, as Eco (1979) submitted, comes only from within an unbounded system of other terms, then the number of meanings of something will always exceed our capacity for understanding. There will always be more meanings than we can capture at the moment, and it will always be possible to make arguments for the acceptability of one or the other. We know from Goedel's work that even formal finite systems can never be fully stated, so imagine the difficulties of real life where messages are not part of a formal or finite system.

Meaning requires a correspondence between interpretation and the text. This correspondence can be strong or weak, but there is a correspondence nonetheless. On the strong side, we would argue that a word or phrase was completely constitutive of meaning. This would be analogous to a one-to-one correspondence between a word and its meaning, and this state is at least approached in highly technical (e.g., scientific) communication. Weaker correspondence between interpretation and text would be when a word does not uniquely constitute meaning, but limits it within a range of possibilities. Lyric poetry, disordered language, and some realms of everyday interaction fall into this category. But linguistic norms always impose limitations on meaning. At the very least, there are limitations to the *medium* of communication. The same words spoken, written, or sung all constitute different meanings in the minds of receivers. Art and music are certainly not easily translated into linguistic communication, and spoken and written language have fairly well-understood criteria that impose limitations (Tannen, 1982). The meaning of any message that is separated from its originating medium is altered. This alteration is evidence of the limiting conditions of the various media, which makes the possibility of meaning more likely.

But anyone confronting a particular message understands that the pragmatic norms of language are not uniform, but composed of different ground rules that vary with different utterances. Language does not a priori narrow the interpreter's task, but intersects with individuals, contexts, and other discourse resources to make meaning possible. Nevertheless, sharability is the single overriding principle of meaning. Meaning takes place when certain conditions of language and discourse are sharable; when attitudes, information, beliefs, emotions, and feelings are part of the fundamental conceptions that the language and communicative mechanisms of one person have in common with another.

Certainly the most common argument against the possibility of meaning is what Hirsch (1967) called the "psychologistic objection." This is the simple notion that the recipient of a message must come to different meanings because he or she is different from the originator of the message. Some argue that this is true even when the originator and recipient are the same person because we are always changing. This argument just does not stand up to experience, nor is it particularly useful, given the regular achievements of communication. First, and most importantly, it confuses meaning with mental processes rather than the manifestations and targets of those processes. It relies on the simple premise that because I am in any way different from others, I must understand language differently from others. But just because one changes, grows, and develops, or feels good, bad, tired, or sickly is insufficient grounds for assuming that he understands things differently and his meanings for shared language change. Surely no sensible person would deny that different people come to different meanings. But one of the thorny difficulties here is that such a statement cannot be tested empirically because the statement contains it own logical impossibility; that is, if it is impossible for one person to understand the meaning of another, then how could we devise a measurement for what someone means?

Hirsch (1967) recognized these difficulties, but shows how these supposed psychologistic barriers are inadequate as a theory of meaning because they do not account for the "facts" of communication. In other words, different mental processes often produce identical meanings. Because there are many hearers or readers from very diverse psychologies who, in fact, do converge on meaning, there must be something about the speaker–hearer (or writer–reader) relationship that effects this convergence. This does not disprove that people come to different meanings, it just asserts that a pure psychologistic perspective on meaning is inadequate.

Meaning is a matter of consciousness, and we are always conscious *of* something. This consciousness of something is not related to my momentary perceptions and mental state. If someone uses the word "computer," then I am understanding the object of my consciousness, not my perceptions or feelings. My meaning for the word "computer" does not change if I am happy or sad, tired or sick, rich or poor. When I enter into communication, I enter into this shared semantic world and I direct my attention toward meaning. Meaning is something that I attend to and avert my consciousness toward. For theorists such as Hirsch and those in the tradition of phenomenology, the concept most associated with object-directed consciousness is intentionality (Schutz & Luckmann, 1973; Searle, 1969, 1979a). Intentionality is the undergirding for a definition of meaning based on the sharable content of a speaker or writer's intentions. Because this meaning is interpersonal, it can be reproduced in the mind of another. This chapter addresses some of the criticisms of intentionality (cf. Chang, 1992; Wimsatt & Beardsley, 1976) and demonstrates its usefulness for making sound judgments about meaning.

The *significance*—as opposed to meaning—of a message is established when we connect that message to some other realm of thought. It demonstrates that a message is also "something else." These realms are most typically—but not limited to—psychological, sociological, and intellectual perspectives. If I interpret what someone says or writes from a feminist, Marxist, psychoanalytical, or some ideological perspective, then I am establishing the *significance* of the text, irrespective of its meaning. Examples from the realm of literature are quite common. Kristeva (1986), for example, interpreted the work of Mallarmé from a psychoanalytic feminist perspective. She stakes a claim on behalf of women to an unrepressed flow of liberating energy, and argues that women are associated with the "liquid" and "fluid" pre-Oedipal stages, and that men are linked with the "law of the father," which values structure and hierarchy. Her analyses of Mallarmé conclude that his poetry subverts the law of the father and identifies with the mother through maternal flux, and that is why his poetry was revolutionary. Needless to say, neither Mallarmé nor his readers probably ever imagined his poetry as politically revolutionary, and certainly knew nothing of pre-Oedipal development. But Kristeva added significance to Mallarmé's work. Her conclusions might be quite unrelated to the words in Mallarmé's poems, but she establishes some relationship between feminist psychoanalysis and Mallarmé's meanings. She can do this by employing the entire language code to the interpretation. She moves away from the interpersonally shared meaning of Mallarmé's language, and enters the unbounded network of terms to make connections between the language of Mallarmé's poetry and the language of feminist psychoanalysis.

Analyses such as Kristeva's are quite common in communication among media and cultural theorists. Typically, these scholars establish "significance" by first identifying a media presentation (e.g., news, a commercial, prime-time television) or a cultural activity (e.g., leisure, sports, shopping), and then interpreting these presentations or activities according to some extensional social and political discursive practice. The search for significance is behind, outside, and beyond the text itself. This type of analysis is a result of a suspicion that texts are open and unbounded with their "reality" deep beneath the surface. There is what might be called a hermeneutical angst that language conceals a profounder meaning (cf. Nehamas, 1987). By way of example, Shah and Thornton

(1994) studied magazine stories of African-American–Latino interactions in magazines such as *Time, Newsweek, Atlantic Monthly,* and so forth and concluded that these stories were symbolic of racial hierarchy and racial ideology in the United States. None of these stories were "about" racial hierarchy or ideology—it may never have occurred to readers, authors, and editors that these stories were about racial hierarchy and ideology—but the conclusions are possible by taking the magazine articles (texts) as finished products and probing them to understand their participation in broader social, political, and ideological processes. This is only possible by positioning the text in a broad semiotic network.

Intentionality. If I pose the problem of meaning as making useful, rational, or defensible guesses about someone else's meaning, then these guesses are enormously assisted by the concept of intentionality and other cultural conventions. Intentionality is a complex and controversial construct that provokes heated debate (see Cappella, 1979; Chang, 1992; Searle, 1983; Stamp & Knapp, 1990; Wimsatt & Beardsley, 1976). But my purpose here is not to settle the matter, but simply to pose intentionality as a useful device for recovering meaning. Intentionality is a referential property of communication that directs it toward objects, ideas, and events. Meaning is not, as Chang (1992) described in his straw argument, delivered by intentions like a thought parcel from one individual to another. Rather, the acquisition of meaning results from the departing from the text and looking elsewhere for assistance with meaning. Intention is one place to look. One of the objections to intentionality is that it is an inner state, and therefore not knowable or identifiable. But this is quite an inaccurate contemporary understanding of intentionality or any inner state. As Wittgenstein (1963) argued in *Philosophical Investigations,* there is no such thing as a completely private state because inner states take from outward circumstances. Indeed it is only outward circumstances that make it logically possible to name and distinguish inner states. Intentionality is an inner state that represents the speaker at the moment of expression and includes his or her goals, strategies, purposes, and affective states. Intentions are substantive in that they are infused with the ideas, content, and empirical knowledge that the speaker uses to navigate the world. Speakers and writers use these intentions to assemble language that has an instrumental–representational link between the intention and the actualized language.

When a hearer encounters a message, he or she must reason from behavior to intention because this is the essential procedure involved in capturing the meaning of an action. Such reasoning is highly complex and logically intractable, but speakers somehow manage it. Intentions function as a global interpretive resource. Granted, it is very difficult to provide a clear chain of reasoning from a message to an intention, and messages build out of many tiny, quick, and unanticipated processes, but rational attempts to develop such chains do exist and can be afforded the same realist status as any theoretical model.

The conversation analysts have tried to argue that some mundane conversational activities are not explained or illuminated by intentionalist analysis, and that the examples used by intentionalists such as Searle are context free (Heritage, 1990/1991). These arguments are consistent with the goals of conversation analysts who seek to avoid actional terminology that invokes mentalistic categories to explain behavior. But these theorists misunderstand the nature of intentionality and its role in establishing meaning. John Heritage equates intentionality with "strategy" and with conscious awareness of the strategy, which is even more troubling. Speakers and writers need not be highly conscious of their strategic decisions. Often they are conscious of strategy and intent, but much of communication is automated because the goal of intent is to stimulate meaning in the mind of a hearer or reader. Heritage (1990/1991, p. 316) relegated intent in interaction to those situations where the participants (or analyst) conclude that "A is up to something and B knows it" or "A is up to something and B doesn't seem to have noticed it or is disattending it." "Intent" is when a hearer or reader recognizes that someone else is trying to establish meaning. The hearer or reader then employs linguistic conventions, which have been socially established and validated, to disambiguate an utterance. I can take Heritage's own example and demonstrate how the attribution of intentionality is crucial to fixing the meaning of a word or utterance. Consider the following example from Heritage (1990/1991):

1. S: .hh When d'ju get *out.* Christmas week or the
2. week before Christmas
3. (0.3)
4. G: Uh::m two or three days before Ch ristmas,
5. S: [Oh:, .hh]

Here, Heritage claimed that the particle "oh" carries informative meaning that is not subject to an intentionalist account. This is the use of "oh" that conveys to the listener that the information was "news" to the producer of "oh" (Heritage, 1984). Heritage stated that an intentionalist analysis will not do for the "oh" particle because "there is no conscious vernacular knowledge that 'oh' is a resource for showing that one has been 'informed' and, correspondingly, there can be no conscious intention to utter 'oh' to show that one has been informed by what a previous speaker has just said" (Heritage, 1990/1991, p. 325).

This assertion by Heritage seems to be problematic. All linguistic signs (even a single particle) can represent meaning because the range of possible meanings have been limited by convention. In fact, the *only* way to understand the particle is by linking linguistic conventions with the intentions of the speaker. Uttering the particle "oh" in the previous example—enhanced probably with the attendant vocal indications of surprise and gestural accompaniments—can be demonstrated to have meaning if a hearer can make a correct pre-apprehension. Any language user would come to our correct and normative understanding of the particle because the meaning of the word has been established by usage. The communicative act in the example was successful because the hearer's preunderstanding of the particle was consonant with the pragmatic conventions that governed the speaker's use of the term. Surely there is no certainty that a hearer's guess about meaning is correct. But in the process of forming a hypothesis about what a particle such as "oh" means, the hearer reasons from the language to the plausible intention. It is also possible to confirm that a speaker's meaning has been reproduced by examining responses of the hearer.

During the process of communication, the meanings of a hearer are significantly influenced by his or her expectations. These expectations are established by the hearer's understanding of the conventional meanings being expressed. Even the meaning of a particle such as "oh" embraces elements not explicit in an utterance or context. There are pragmatic relationships between the speaker and hearer, nature of the content, linguistic features, and so on. The hearer is always in a state of readiness about a "certain type of meaning." He has expectations about the intentions of the speaker and makes sense of words based on the fit between intentions and expectations. What we commonly consider in the vernacular as "misunderstandings" or "failures to communicate" are essentially the recognition that a hearer's expectations have not been met. The fact that the particle "oh" communicated that the information was informative was the result of this interplay between the speaker's intentions and the hearer's pragmatically informed expectations.

Bridling Meaning in Discourse

I have been examining principles of language, meaning, and discourse that make communication possible. But many contemporary theorists argue that the meaning of a text is unstable and quite a precarious affair (e.g., Gadamer, 1989; Rorty, 1989). They suggest that extracting meaning from a discourse is not possible because of uncontrollable linguistic and historical forces. There are many issues in such arguments, and I do not elaborate on them except to disagree and say that the process of using language is designed to produce meaning, and that certain evidence, reasons, and assumptions can be brought to bear on discourses that privilege certain meanings. In addition to the assumptions of semantic realism and the use of pragmatic principles such as intentionality, there is an important distinction that is often ignored by those who trumpet the intractability of meaning.

This is the distinction between a code and a message. Discourse relies on a theory based on the distinction between a theory of language and a theory of communication. There is a noble intellectual history that examines the nature of meaning and language. But as Giddens (1979) argued, this Saussurian tradition holds language to be all form with no substance. This has caused many to concentrate on the relations between linguistic values and sign differences rather than the *performance* of communicative messages. Theorists such as Derrida (1981) and Rorty (1989) can destabilize meaning because they are concentrating on the language *code* rather than on *messages*. A theory of meaning and *discourse* cannot cavalierly subtract context, pragmatic constraints, and intentionality from language to destabilize meaning and conclude that there are no preferred meanings of messages.

Discussion about meaning typically centers on disputes about its determinacy or indeterminacy. But the distinctions alluded to earlier between a code and a message, and outlined in Table 3.1, can be used to mediate this dispute. Moreover, this distinction summarizes the differences between those theorists who emphasize the intractability of meaning, and those who stress its determination and plausibility.

A *code* perspective on meaning holds that all terms in the language are defined by their positional structure in the linguistic system. Thus, the meaning of "computer" is determined by all other terms it is related to (e.g., machine, calculate, technology, intelligence, brand names, science, speed, etc.), and no term is final because each one must be defined by continuously relating them to other terms in an endless process of semiosis. As Table 3.1 indicates, and as Eco (1979) explained, this perspective relies on a "theory of language" that forms a "structure" or "system of relationships." The code perspective has its basis in Saussurean structuralism, where Saussure's claim that the signifier–signified relationship was arbitrary. This arbitrariness formed the basis of *langue*, an ab-

TABLE 3.1
Distinctions Between Codes and Messages

Code	Message
Theory of language	Theory of communication
Systemic	Contingent
System of meaning possibilities	Selective actualization
Intertextual	Textual
Form	Content (substance)
Relational	Isolated (connected to reality)
Unbounded open network of signifiers	Bounded individually contingent network
Structural	Functional
Transcends context	Context occasions meaning

Note. From Ellis (1995).

stract conceptual system that transcended context and allowed for infinite meaning possibilities. So again, it is this code perspective that allows a communication or literary theorist to take a piece of language (oral, written, visual) and continually relate that language to other terms in an unbounded network of signifiers. This is how theorists "get from" seemingly mundane television or talk to ideology.

A *message* perspective, on the other hand, bounds this network by placing limitations on language from the material world. This is a theory of "communication" rather than language, where a text is purposeful, fashioned from publicly accepted referential rules, and the context of the communication occasions meaning rather than frustrates it. A code perspective cannot explain intentional acts initiated by speakers. But a message perspective centers on what Benveniste (1971, p. 44) called "reality," or that language has a relationship with the object world, and although a "signifier" à la Saussure is arbitrary, its relationship with the object world is not so capricious. The code perspective elides the problem of reference, but a theory of discourse and communication (message perspective) cannot do so.

Communicative meaning must be at least partially achievable by reference to public norms if language is in any sense sharable. A simple sentence such as "Please pass the salt" would not engender any confusion because of its frequency of use. But this apparent simplicity conceals a complex process of judgments about meaning. Reference to commonly understood public norms of meaning are important, but still leave a bewildering array of possibilities. These possibilities are restrained, however, when we introduce a speaker with an intention and a context that impinges on meaning possibilities to keep it from escaping into utter relativism.

This message distinction is meant to ground language users in the empirical world, and avoid the theoretical world of codes. The empirical world includes, rightly or wrongly, people, their practices, beliefs, information, and space–time limitations. It certainly does *not* imply that broader meanings and interpretations are separate from microinteraction. Rather, there is a "link" between micro real-time communicative events and more abstract cultural, sociological, and ideological structures. This linkage between microscene discourses and a corresponding macro reality is just the relationship between language and society, and how society is constructed (e.g., Alexander & Giesen, 1987). No meaning is bluntly given, but cast in a conventional representation (text) that must be construed. This construal process results in meanings that are understood on their own terms, and as Collins (1981) explained, are compiled and translated until the text is also a representation of macroreality "standing, above all the micro situations that produced it" (p. 988) I examine the micro–macro link in detail in the next chapter. But it is important to underscore my commitment to empirical discourse, where the production of meaning is possible, but not completely fixed by time and space.

Discourse and Cognition

I have spent some time establishing the necessity and possibility of meaning because it is elemental to the development of social structure. Language users attach meanings to messages and continue a cycle of social representations that
influence future discourse and are influenced by it. Before discourse can claim
to affect social structures it must be possible for individuals to "represent" the
world. Communication is the result when these representations are shared.
When individuals experience the meaning process described previously, they
produce social representations (e.g., beliefs, knowledge, and attitudes) that become the interface between them and others, or them and the external world.
This interface is more important to discourse and social construction than are
individual actions and mental processes. These interfaces develop into epi-
sodes, systems, and sequences. These are the building blocks of society. Social
cognition is a representational process, a process whereby individuals develop
mental images, structures, and strategies that are *shared* by other members of a
group or society. These shared representations are responsible for the production of social life such as situations, groups, and institutions, and provide the
frameworks for the production and interpretation of discourse.

Social cognition is more important to discourse than generic cognition because it is organized around "socially" shared representations (van Dijk,
1990) of experience. Social cognition is related to semantic memory rather than
structural memory and is organized by networks of categories such as contexts,
goals, cultures, and expectations. Social cognitive representations are acquired
and modified in social situations. They are generated by personal knowledge
and experience that takes place in real, subjectively organized situations. Following are brief explanations of some of the mental machinery of social cognition. They are necessary for the production and interpretation of language and
discourse. More importantly, social representations have a *constructive* quality.
They do not merely mediate people and the world. They are the generative
mechanisms for the construction of a sensible world. They are the psychological
categories that intertwine themselves with others and form a chain link that
"constructs" society. We will follow these cognitive-like categories with a more
sociolinguistic orientation.

Prototypes.   The social representations necessary for the production and
interpretation of discourse emerge from prototypes, or models, that are subjective and unique. These prototypes carry current knowledge, opinions, and
strategies, and are an action model for how to communicate when the prototype
is activated. I have, for example, prototypical representations of "teaching in a
university." If I encounter a new situation (e.g., a different institution or foreign
country), I apply my prototype and then refine it as necessary. Because these

prototypes are social in nature, they are the central interface between the individual and social structures.

Situation Prototypes.   A situation or context is an intact assembly of people, objects, rules, and expectations. Language users represent other social actors and have predictions about their lines of action, speech acts, goals, and other qualities of context. These prototypes regulate discourse by informing communicators about how to behave and interpret messages. They provide cues about what information is relevant, topical, and coherent.

Frame analysis discussed by Goffman (1974) and Tannen (1979) is related to situation prototypes. Goffman's description of a frame is a social representation through which people structure experience, and these frames are socially situated so they continue to develop. Frames are the organizational principles and strategies by which situations are defined. What is important here is that social representations, situation prototypes in particular, move the self out of individual psychology and into the interactional world. We have Goffman, Gumperz, and other interactional sociolinguists to thank for this. Individual psychological constructs are only marginally important to the constructive qualities of discourse and society because the study of interaction is one of studying "traffic rules," or how the representation of messages and action are fastened together to make a structure.

There are other standard social representations, such as strategies, ideologies, and attitudes (cf. van Dijk, 1994) that are components of a prototype. But despite the complexities of social cognition, and the practical difficulties of their role in research, there are two key points that provide a unity for discourse and cognition. These are the role of situated language use between two or more interactants, and the centrality of contexts. Language is the index to the social world; it signifies an array of conceptual content. Language use between communicators "points" to cultural backgrounds, assumptions, social categories, and all sorts of hidden knowledge that plays a role in communication and society. There is no insignificant communication. There is no nonprototypic discourse. Language is also more creative than the signifier–signified relationship might imply. It surely serves a primary sociolinguistic indexical function, but can also interact with context cues and alter or change meaning, creating new combinations displaying different insights and intentions.

Intersubjectivity and the Construction of Discourse Meaning

From social representations, it is possible to link properties of discourse to communicative goals. These can be any sort of goal, such as the clear and accurate transmission of information, relationship development, deception, credibility of the speaker, solidarity, ad infinitum. But the complexity of the relationship between discourse structures and communication goals must be emphasized.

The relationship is not deterministic. A speaker or writer's message does not necessarily achieve the desired sociocognitive effect. Moreover, the relationship is equifinal because the same message can lead to different sociocognitive effects, and different messages may have the same effect. But the relationship is not entirely variable either. Consistent and repetitive social representations and contexts facilitate predictability.

Discourse structures are those qualities of any text that carry messages and perform the "work" of discourse. They are the stable features of a text such as "topic," "syntax," "lexical style," "schemata," and "local meaning" as opposed to "significance." From the point of view of the originator of a message (speaker or writer), these discourse structures allow the speaker or writer to achieve his basic communicative goals; that is, the originator of a message must take an internally represented proposition and make it accessible to another person. The originator draws on knowledge of a message code (Ellis, 1992b) and transforms it into accessible language signals. Discourse structures are the tools used to represent and display these language signals. The transformation process of internal propositions into a format accessible to the other person is only possible by the existence of shared representations, a sort of message code with discourse structures linked with meanings. One reason this is important is because it views the originator of a message as associated with internal representations, but also deeply implicated in the medium of communication. In other words, the originator of a message maps thought onto language on the basis of a message code that includes the medium of communication, and this is interpretable by a receiver who also has shared representations that include the code.

Note that this perspective makes intentionality an important element of the communication process. It suggests a distinction between communication (intentional and goal-directed language use) and information processing (and significance), which is language that is informative and may be interpreted regardless of its intention. Intersubjectivity is very important. It means that communication is greatly dependent on the existence of shared representations and interpretive principles. Taylor and Cameron (1987) maintained that intersubjectivity is fundamental to the communication process. Knowledge of a code of meanings and the fact of intersubjectivity is what is being assumed in communication.

Intersubjectively shared social representations that form a type of semantic code for producing and interpreting messages are also what account for variation in communication. Variation analysis in discourse (cf. Labov, 1972; Schiffrin, 1994) is concerned with change and variation in language and discourse, and the fact that different messages can "mean" the same thing, but carry additional social implications. It relies on the assumption that systematic analysis reveals how messages are linguistically and socially patterned. So, for example, there are different ways of saying the same thing. In the case of simple lexical variation, the words *house*, *abode*, and *residence* all have the same referent, but justify some different conclusions about the speaker and the situation. These surface forms rely on structures that are not apparent in the discourse. From a pure code perspective, each of the three lexical items are built on the same abstract linguistic premises. Each has the same propositional referent. But each is also a different realization of that underlying form. The task is to identify the social, cultural, situational, and linguistic constraints on these realizations.

The intersubjectivity of discourse representations would allow two communicators to understand either of the following sentences as representing the same propositional question:

1. Who were you talkin' to?
2. With whom were you speaking?

Language users have these syntactic options. They are not options in the sense of free choice by anyone to use either construction, but rather both are available in the linguistic system, and the use of one rather than the other is informative with respect to the influence of other social constraints. The use of Construction 2 rather than 1 would justify inferences with respect to education levels, class differences, or various relationship and situational constraints. Analyses of this type show how lexical items, syntactical forms, and phonetic expressions suggest that what might seem like the same thing at the propositional level is really very different at the discourse level. But there are additional steps in the construction process.

It is certainly not the case that intentions have to refer to propositions or direct thoughts. At a very basic message code level, which is definitionally necessary to the communication process, meanings are not context dependent. They are based on intersubjectively shared knowledge of a conventional propositional representation system. This is the level at which no one would disagree about the meaning of words. And intentionality at this level is simply the intention to transmit thoughts or information from my head to yours. So the meaning of Construction 3 "Karen is a good cook," is just that: *some individual known to be Karen is skilled at food preparation.*

But one can intend an utterance to "mean" something that is not directly implicated in the language of the message. I may intend to mean feelings, or attitudes, or emotions. My utterance about Karen in Construction 3 might be intended as a "compliment." To come to the correct conclusion that Construction 3 was meant to be a compliment, we need some way to supplement our reliance on the shared understanding of conventional signs. We need some other intersubjective system that allows us to account for how people communicate more than they provide for in their conventional representation system. This supplemental system is a set of intersubjectively shared *communication* principles. These shared communication principles allow for inferences, or in Grice's (1975) terms, implicatures. Gricean maxims assist with the inferences necessary to determine the actional nature of a message. These are very powerful principles that help an interpreter by providing signals about how a message should be understood. This Gricean contribution to discourse makes it easier to account for the inferencing that goes on during communication. Understanding these inferences is important for understanding how meanings link from messages to collective understanding, or broader social organization.

We now have a model of discourse that joins the conventional representational code (explicit meanings) with communication principles that make implicit meanings possible through the use of Gricean implicatures. The complexity and indeterminacy of communication is accounted for by the addition of a shared communication system that is inherently more open ended. Language users share two kinds of knowledge: one is of the conventional correspondence between certain sounds and a referent (conventional message code), and the other is of a set of principles that apply to communication and behavior. These principles are socially shared inferencing maxims.

There is one additional ingredient of this model that must be stated briefly. Language is surely instrumental and does the work of so much everyday behavior. But language is also open ended and creative. I often believe that some meanings are deep beneath the surface of language, that language is only an exterior expression of a tangled pathway to interior and "hidden" meanings that are unknown, strange, and "someplace else." Earlier in this chapter, I referred to a distinction between meaning and significance. Significance is at the extreme end of the inferential possibilities for language. Inferences based on Gricean implicatures remain grounded in strong, intersubjectively held knowledge about how a message should be understood. Normally competent communicators have little trouble recognizing acts such as compliments. But significance is much more subjective than intersubjective. It is the place on an inferencing continuum where language is part of an open network of signifiers (open code model) and participates in broad social, political, and ideological processes. Interpretations of messages that seek "significance" are the most difficult to account for and rely on some different emphases with respect to intentionality, intersubjectivity, and the role of message recipients.

One of the problems with a perspective on discourse and communication that fails to maintain the centrality of intersubjectivity is that the meaning and work of a message becomes too receiver oriented. There is a shift in responsibility from the originator of a message who has designed language for a contextual purpose to the recipient of a message who is an information processor. The meaning of a message is bound or bridled when it is the goal of a speaker or writer to display his intentions and fashion language for a contextual and communicative purpose. But when anything is available for interpretation, when all behaviors have "communicative" value, then you "cannot not communicate" as Watzlawick, Beavin, and Jackson (1967, p. 49) observed.

This aspect of the communication process that relies on the libertine interpretive preferences of a receiver makes for difficulties that must be addressed. One question that must be answered is how various small, unintended meanings are created from verbal and nonverbal behavior that was not designed for specific meanings. The nature of intersubjectivity reenters the communication process because we must assume that interpretation is based on common intersubjectively held background knowledge about how to draw inferences from behavior, and about what behaviors mean in various contexts. This very specialized information, actualized by a specific person or situation rather than the conventional communication code, is important to the type of communication that is personal, intimate, and psychologically based. Consider the exchange in Constructions 4 and 5:

4. How's Allie?
5. She's alright.

We could say that the exchange is a conventional routine designed to make "polite conversation." Or, we could say that the speaker in Construction 4 genuinely intended to "inquire" about the health or status of Allie, that he wanted his intentions to be understood. But as soon as specialized personal or situational information is allowed, as soon as the recipient can interpret anything, then the utterance in Construction 5 is a response not only to the information in Construction 4 but to the meaning that Construction 5 created from the utterance in Construction 4. In any case, when the importance of intentionality and intersubjectivity are diminished, then the recipient is assigned a more important role in the communication, and what is finally communicated emerges more from what recipients interpret or construct from the language.

I am now at a point in the progression of this discussion where I can accept that speaker intention is the foundation of communication, but I must also account for a recipient's interpretations. Although the interpretive possibilities of a message are theoretically unbounded, they are pragmatically constrained. One way this constraint is useful to us is by complementing the matter of intentionality with the principle of discourse strategy. An intention will always be internal to an individual and subject to uncertainty, but a discourse strategy is inferable from an interaction. I can infer it from the response of the recipient of a message. By combining intentions with discourse strategies, and using other pragmatic resources (topicality, local meaning, prior relationships, environment cues, etc.) to make decisions about meaning, I can strike a balance between what is observable and what is not. Communication analysis must posit constructs that go beyond the immediate context and what is seen and heard. Moreover, by making inferences about a speaker's or writer's goals and intentions, and using the responses of recipients, I can build generalizations from repeated observations of behavior. These generalizations are very important because they become patterns of language use and interaction that are the elements of social structures. As interaction processes develop over time, intersubjectivity becomes, on the one hand, static because communicators have intersubjectively held discourse strategies that serve as the foundation of efficient communication, but on the other hand, intersubjectivity mutates as recipient interpretations change, vary, and creatively evolve. And both contexts and cultures are assigned a role as the most obligatory and consequential constructs in the communication process.

In the following section, I examine in more detail how language is a socially and culturally constructed system that is interdependent with the macro social world; that is, language is the material of messages that carry the intentions of speakers or writers and acts as matters for broader interpretation by recipients. These interpretations rely on and influence cognitive social representations that both reflect and create macro- and microlevel meanings. Communicators use language to continually indicate who they are, what they want to say, and their relationship with social structures.

The Sociology of Discourse

I begin by offering a few observations about the sociology of discourse to clarify its relevance. First, what is the sociology of discourse? And second, why study it, and what is its relation to social structure? One rather simple response is that social order and social action is the stuff of sociology, that if I am going to talk about social structures, such as class and ethnicity, in chapters 5 and 6 as something other than vaporous generalities, then I must engage a rigorous sociology. But a better way to think about sociology and connect it with discourse is to focus on sociology as it is concerned with the persistently reproduced patterns of activity in a social unit. Patterns of activity are reducible to symbolic interactions that are discursive in nature. Or, as many authors insist (e.g., Alexander & Giesen, 1987; Smelser, 1986; Turner & Collins, 1988) *interaction* is the important unit of sociological analysis, not the individual and his psychology. Such interaction is symbolic in nature and organized by the cognitive, communicative, and discourse qualities previously discussed.

Spoken or written discourse is related to social action that is logically part of social structure. For example, imagine that you encounter the following utterance during a conversation with an African American:

6. He don't belongs with them.

You recognize this statement as nonstandard usage. You just code it stereotypically as associated with the low-status discourse style of African Americans. We assume that you have no special knowledge of the history and structural explanation of Construction 6 (e.g., the mistake the speaker makes in thinking that -s marks a plural verb, as it does a noun). You just interpret this as "bad English." An interaction has occurred and your social representation (SR) for the utterance produces the interpretation. The particular interpretation is the result of some very complex attitudes fashioned by your experiences with African Americans as an ethnic group. If you draw a stereotyped conclusion about the interaction and report it to someone, or have it influence a future interaction, then social action has occurred. You have interpreted this act as an ethnic quality, and you prospectively interpret the actions and reactions of generalized others including friends, coworkers, and neighbors. Further social action occurs as others respond to you. More specifically, you search for interpretive frames for the utterance and your response to it. You might consider the existence of such speech an example of a *faulty educational system*, where speech like this is a consequence of the breakdown in the educational system, and this may be the result of a *racist society* that denies proper educational opportunities to African Americans. Or, even more vulgarly, you might frame the utterance as characteristic of a substandard group of people. All of these interpretations will influence all of your future interactions with respect to ethnicity.

It becomes clear that all of this social action that relates to ethnicity happens through discourse in action. Discourse takes place in numerous contexts and, as we made clear based on the work of Austin and Searle, language does not simply refer to some external world, it performs social action. People blame, lie, evaluate, question, advise, and establish attitudes, prejudices, and beliefs in conversations. The goal of the sociology of discourse is to demonstrate how the interlocking of communicative behaviors by language users forms a sort of infrastructure that constitutes society (Boden & Zimmerman, 1991). This is an interesting and important departure from the general orthodox theories of society, those theories that pit systems and institutions against one another. The sociology of discourse perspective tries to pose social order as a practical empirical question. This is not easy because the matter of researchable material is difficult.

Nevertheless, the sociology of discourse must approach the question of social order through the categorization and normalization of action system (Collins, 1988; Giddens, 1984). The *facticity* of social structure as an objectively compelling social fact is achieved in ordinary interactions that routinize, categorize, and normalize language use, social action, discourse routines and structures, as well as relationships. Important questions are posed about how stability is possible. What regularities exist and how are they maintained?

The enduring structures of the social world are the result of coordinated activities that produce talk that generates our categorized interpretations. These coordinated activities exist on various levels, including ethnomethods, discourse structures and routines, relationship rules, and cultural expectations. Ethnomethodological work (Garfinkel, 1967), for example, illustrates how language users engage a practical consciousness that is never really called into question to accomplish the work of communication. Garfinkel's term *ethnomethodology* refers to the commonsense knowledge of humans. But this is not content knowledge of something, it is knowledge of ordinary practices that make communication possible. The goal of ethnomethodology is to uncover these ordinary practices to explain how communicators have a stable organization for their activities. They are constantly engaging in "understandings." And these understandings provide a sense of intersubjectivity so that normal discourse can be sustained. Communicative action, then, produces and reproduces the knowledge that makes individual actions intelligible.

Conversation analysis is the essential analytical mechanism of ethnomethodology and it approaches discourse by showing solutions to organizational problems that all communicators must solve. Among these problems are opening conversations, closing them, exchanging turns, displaying information, and managing topics. Conversation analysis is concerned with the outerlinguistic behavior of naturalistic conversations to discover how local-situated language indexes the "rules" that make conversation possible in the first place. This method is a reaction against any reigning theory of social science that holds normative structure as the cause of social action.

Conversation analysis in the service of ethnomethodology can certainly display the local technology of discourse. It provides an analytic structural bedrock for conversation that is not susceptible to cultural variations. The turn-exchange system and adjacency pairs, for instance, are pervasive. This pervasiveness makes them less socially interesting, if only because they can be taken for granted and do not vary in any sociologically significant way. But my interests are in more than local technology of discourse. More generally, I must be interested in how discourse assists with the production and reproduction of social categories such as ethnicity and class through the public displays of language. I can grant that humans have "methods" of organizing and coordinating social interaction. And these form the carpentered foundation of social structure. But I need next a higher order semantic concept that helps interactants find their way through the maze of expressions on their way to interpretation. I need a useful hermeneutic.

This hermeneutic can be found in the work that *categorization* performs. Categorization refers to the sociocultural methods that language users use to classify behaviors, linguistic features, actors, and events, into pre-existing structured organizational forms (i.e., categories). These categories form a mundane order that constitutes facticity; in other words, they reveal an assumed objective social order. Vocabulary and syntax sort experience into concepts and categories. Consider phrases such as "my assistant," or "my office." Being either this person or this place involves a relationship and an activity. The possessive + noun structure in English codes a person as an object and a place as a possession. Both of these are treated syntactically and psychologically as objects owned and controlled by the referent for the possessive. It is easy to see that these relationships embody ownership and dominance, and such processes can be seen as ideological. From here I can argue that these linguistic relationships make for cognitive categorization of experience that encourages habits of mind that are prejudicial to the possessed item. Vocabulary and syntax are descriptive of the world, but this description is not a disinterested report of external reality. Instead, it categorizes the world and functions as a set of descriptions, judgments, and inferences.

From the categorization of experience through language I can move to locating *social order in systems of interrelated activities produced by members of a community in their mundane and routine interactions* (Giddens, 1976). I will explore, in detail, these systems of interrelated activity and how they work in the next chapter, but with respect to the sociology of talk, I can conclude that contiguous talk exchanges are linked to larger patterns of social activity and structure. So, ethnicity and social class—the two macrosocial categories I explore in analytical detail in chapters 5 and 6—are reifications of material communicative conditions.

Mundane and routine interactions embody the infrastructure of social organization and sense making. But an interactant's message is doubly contextual, that is, it is first shaped by a prior symbolic action and understood within the context that it participates, and second, simultaneously either renews or redefines the next action (Heritage, 1984). This context-shaped and context-renewing property incrementally establishes a sense of the whole, a gestaltlike process. Again, I can borrow the idea from ethnomethodology that symbolic messages engaged in context shaping and context renewing operate as a fundamental sense-making practice. Ervin-Tripp's (1969, p. 93) example of an African-American physician stopped by a policeman demonstrates double contextuality and how it is the site of a struggle for the definition of the relationship:

7. "What's your name, boy?" the policeman asked …
8. "Dr. Poussaint. I'm a physician … "
9. "What's your first name, boy? … "
10. "Alvin."

The police officer in line 7 clearly signals the racist nature of the context and the extent of his power. Dr. Poussaint in line 8 responds to line 7, but shifts the attitude of the relationship toward symmetry and equal status. The police officer in Construction 9 reasserts his authority and rejects Dr. Poussaint's attempt at equality. Dr. Poussaint in line 10 retreats from his effort to redefine the relationship. He responds to the request in line 9 and sets the context for the ensuing interaction. The exchange serves an interactional task, which is to support a particular definition of the context, and categorization on the part of the police officer designed to create a disjuncture between the two interactants. He wins this contest and is able to control the organization, interpretation, and legitimazation of the situation.

In examples such as the preceding one, the resultant relationship, status, and power of the individuals emerge from the talk exchange and is anchored in context-shaping and context-renewing structures. From these sequences, conventional action emerges and is categorized as such as a result of mapping the actions onto the sequences. If racism, ethnic identity, class, and power are critical social structures, then it is these talk sequences that are the primary vehicle of reification. These structures are inextricably interwoven and legitimized by *forms of talk*: who says what, and how it is negotiated within a context, is contingent on the social organization of the criminal justice system and the individual's participation in the larger structures of ethnicity. What I seek to discover in this sociology of talk instance is how the practices of communication embody the structural properties of racism, ethnicity, class, and power. I seek to discover how a system of ethnicity and power interpenetrates with conventional interactions to shape and categorize our thoughts and feelings—in short, to frame our meaning for the situation.

More specifically, social categories such as class or ethnicity are theoretical entities instantiated by types of interactions and contexts. The theoretical entities contain their own ideologies and assumptions—for example, representing power, status, judgments of good and bad—and the observable interactions differentially distribute speaking rights, language use, and various discourse strategies and responsibilities. Together these realms of reality intersect and, in the previous example, represent the relationship between ethnicity and everyday police interactions. I examine this "duality of structure" (Giddens, 1984) in more detail in the next chapter, and continue to explicate its underlying dynamics.

It should be noted here that social structures operate very covertly. They are an obscure and shadowy reality that carry efficient rules and constraints. For example, "ethnicity" has inequality structured into it as well as mechanisms of obedience. But these inequalities and mechanisms are not explicitly stated anywhere. Their rules and principles of operation are written nowhere. This, of course, makes these structures more insidious, intractable, and difficult to study. But it also means they must be continuously instantiated and reproduced. Bluntly enforcing inequality is difficult, expensive, and usually socially unacceptable, so it relies on more unstated mechanisms and subtler symbols that signal these differences.

In the previous section, I took it as my task to draw attention to the centrality of discourse and interaction for sociological and communication theory. A subsidiary goal was to identify the organization of talk-in-interaction as a focal point. I have now an empirical site from which I can pursue the goal of suturing micro–macro levels via structurational theories (see the next chapter). With this in mind, there is nothing exotic about the analysis of language and social interaction for sociology. Human communication is primary to the production and reproduction of social structure, and to the objectification of social structures and the problems they give rise to. Next, I move from this more theoretical foundation to a more substantial one.

CONVERSATIONAL FORMS AS AN EXPERIENTIAL BASE OF STRUCTURE

Everything that happens to individuals in a society happens to them in the flow of momentary experiences that are punctuated and organized into coherent categories of meaning. These meanings arise out of conversations and symbol experiences of many types. My approach here is to describe the conversation forms that people use to enact macro-social categories and structures. This approach enables us to deal with structures without imposing preconceived forms. It allows for plural realities and all of the disorderliness of interaction. This is important to a more mature and sophisticated theory of communication and society. My interest in the conversational forms that follow is not in the close analysis of the sociolinguist or the interactional researcher, but in establishing some foundation for everyday life and to further explore theory. I can only take a cognitive approach to the extent that the cognitions are social representations situated in the real world of human contact, the world of strong symbols that give us the regularities I call social structure.

Social structures are composed of networks of relationships and the fluffs of subjective reality that swell when people interact. A paraphrase of the rather common definition of communication that is "who says what to whom, through which channel (medium), in what context, with what effect" (Lasswell, 1948; Shannon & Weaver, 1949) is good enough to describe most social structure, especially if we include the fact that communicators incorporate their past in present conversations and construe future prospects. It is true that symbolic interactionists and subjective sociologists have leaned in this direction, but many of their abstract statements about the "definition of situations" are not very useful. I must move to a more manageable set of categories that describe situations and the type of talk they encompass.

Forms of Talk

Forms of talk can mostly be described as either coordinative talk, ritualistic talk, social talk, or professional talk. These are not meant to be mutually exclusive and exhaustive, but I have satisfied myself that they are sufficiently fruitful in that hypotheses and conclusions can be drawn with respect to the conditions under which they occur and the consequences for social structure. I certainly have no illusions about developing extraordinarily clear and comprehensive typological categories. Such things have their place, but are hardly the essence of explanatory theory.

Human interaction is a form of negotiation. It is not a formal negotiation with each strategic move planned out, but a sustained participation where each person tacitly agrees to contribute and establish subjective realities and social relationships. It is a relationship and a cognitive reality that is being negotiated. In an institutional setting, for instance, one member "negotiates," moment to moment, such relationships as power and agreeing to one person's right to exercise power, and each receives various material and symbolic benefits. Much of this interaction is tacit and "understood" and, interestingly, fairly routinized as the result of a form of developmental communication competence. On the other hand, some interactions that are formal and coordinative are quite explicit. In either case, there is always some emotional symmetry between conversational partners (Goffman, 1971).

Interaction takes place on many levels and does all sorts of psychological, sociological, and personal work. What the principles of ethnomethodologists fail to include is the fact that individuals bring different resources and influences to a conversation. Techniques, methods, skills, and approaches to interaction are not equally distributed in the population. Many of these resources can be traced to stratificational differences, such as the ones explored in the final two chapters of this book and alluded to earlier. But people have different abilities to construct discourse and carry out communication. These different abilities are part of a recursive cycle in that they are both the consequence and the source of social structures. There are all sorts of goals and objectives of communication, such as warm relationships, gratification, belonging, power, material goods, ego satisfaction, and so on. One needs resources to achieve any of these goals; resources that come from prior experiences.

Coordinative Talk. Communication is very instrumental. It is practical and gets things done. Coordinative talk is all that form of interaction that carries out tasks. It can occur at work, or at home, or in public. It can be something everyday such as "Let's empty the dishwasher" or more specialized to the work environment such as "Open up your database." Much of the talk in families in the morning as everyone gets ready for the day is coordinative talk (i.e., "What time will you be home?" "Pick up the laundry please." "Come on Allie, it's 8:30, time to go"). Interactions at work around getting things done are coordinative in nature (i.e., "You set up the data, I will run the analysis." "Copy and collate these please." "Which machine am I assigned to today?").

Not all coordinative talk is explicit. Manipulation, ulterior motives, and playing politics are attempts to coordinate things, but without apparent motive. Concealed coordinative talk involves alliances and special organizational knowledge that is covert. Language users must be particularly skilled in these cases. They must be able to "read between the lines" and understand things that are not clear cut. Advice giving, directions, and orders are all forms of coordination.

Authority is an important dimension of coordinative communication. Coordinative communication assumes various rights and responsibilities that shift from moment to moment. Intimate couples organizing their day exchange authority rights with respect to the distribution of responsibilities in the relationship. In work settings, authority is legitimized within the organizational structure and recognized when someone has knowledge that others need in order to complete their work. The power that accompanies authority is measured by how well and with what authority you coordinate others by controlling their resources and outcomes. One's demeanor and various paralinguistic features of timing, voice, and language use are also important to successful coordinative communication that is endowed with authority.

Stratification, social differences, and division are probably the most important causes and consequences of coordinative communication. Coordinative talk is basic to the structured inequalities that are stratification. Holding power, authority, and status means managing and participating in instrumental communication. In fact, performing various types of work means, more than anything else, being able to engage in coordinative communication of a certain type. The structure of organizational hierarchies is such that superiors initiate conversation, give orders, and provide information. The same type of coordinative action takes place during more horizontal relationships, but it is more voluntary and lacks the endowment of legitimate authority.

The sheer importance of talk increases as one moves up the status hierarchy of work. Manual labor requires little interaction. The quiet, taciturn farmer and the verbose and effusive entrepreneur are engaging in patterns of communication occasioned by their work and its requirements. Both use coordinative talk, but require vastly different amounts of it. Professionals define themselves by their specialized discourse, as all occupations are little worlds of language. But this is more than vocabulary, more than argot. Language in use that is highly defined by contexts relies on an implicit grammar and tacit conventions. And, seen in chapters 5 and 6, all of these forms of talk distinguish class and ethnic groups.

Ritualistic Talk.   This is a serious and impelling form of discourse in the culture where power is usually expressed explicitly. These are the rituals of personal relations, politics, and religion. Ritualistic interactions enact basic relationships that constitute the organizations of the state, work, and personal relationships. It is typically serious communication, where the structure of authority is firmly established. Group solidarity, power, and personal loyalty are the most typical byproducts of ritualized talk. The fact that a personal or societal function has evolved into a highly ritualistic form of communication is evidence of its importance and centrality. Marriage ceremonies ("I now pronounce you man and wife"), state actions (inaugurations, "Will the speaker yield the floor …"), organizational formalities ("This meeting is called to order"), and personal incantations (phatic communication, "I love you.") are all examples of ritualistic forms of talk.

Ritualistic forms of interaction are very common in the realms of family and personal communication (Bruess & Pearson, 1997; Goffman, 1967; Wolin & Bennett, 1984). They are the communicative enactments that honor the people and objects that are valued in relationships. They help maintain relational functioning and are sites of understanding. Interpersonal and family rituals communicate identities and beliefs, create personal and generational bonds, and perpetuate cultures and value systems. Ritualistic communication in the interpersonal world can organize itself around activities (work or play), habits, behaviors, events, and private communication codes such as jointly developed words, symbols, gestures, and communicative routines. And such ritualistic communication certainly takes on subtle but important differences for gender and relationship types (cf. Bruess & Pearson, 1997). Men have more conversations about politics and work matters and they invoke ritually anchored emotional loyalties. Women, as Bruess and Pearson (1997) explained, engage in more celebratory and symbolic sharing. Any of these forms of communication invoke a symbolic reality and generate emotional significance.

Official ritualistic communication in the work or political arena can be more or less formalized, but still gives legitimacy and particular characteristics to everyday life. There is probably less formal ritualistic communication in modern society—at least modern American society—than was historically the case, but the modern forms of rational–legal authority differ more in form and variability than in function. Certainly the mnemonic incantations of oral cultures, and even the traditional formality of print media, relied more on ritualistic forms than the modern electronic environment where change and variation are so easy, and where text has lost much of its authority. Traditional rituals were quite restrictive with respect to improvisation, although some of these are upheld in contemporary legal, religious, and family contexts. A decline in formalization is a mark of modern life.

Social classes and ethnic groups vary with respect to ritualistic communication. Occupational classes have different political values and patterns of interpersonal relations that encourage different ritualistic forms of communication. The higher social classes, who have greater communication resources and more diverse social lives, experience less ritualistic communication. Their relationships are more jointly organized, and each partner in a conversation has a more sympathetic concern for the other, at most in social relations, but somewhat in work relations. Most studies (e.g., LeMasters, 1975) of working-class work and personal relations report more ritualistic traditional role relationships between men and women, employers and employees. There are many complexities here when ethnicity, gender, and geography are factored in, but the conclusion that ritualistic communication increases in frequency as one moves down the class scale is sound.

Social Talk.   Social talk is for enjoyment that is based on rewards and pleasure. It brings forth conviviality and enjoyment and is satisfying as an end unto
itself. Social talk includes jokes, witticisms, bantering, gossip, verbal games, and
anything colloquially known as "shooting the bull" or "chit chat." This form of
talk is the opposite of instrumental in that it is a form of play that has important
consequences, but is not to be taken seriously at the moment. It is not designed
to achieve some immediate goal, other than momentary satisfaction. People
who participate in social talk are usually friends in both the individual and
broad sense of the term. In fact, friendship is typically defined as having a history
of valued conversational exchanges. Friendship conversation usually constitutes a desired shared reality in which the friends participate. They effectuate
this reality within the frame of their relationship.

Social talk mostly creates pleasurable emotions, but not exclusively so.
There can be topics of ideological and personal concerns that are more serious.
The topics of social talk are many and include sports, restaurants, scenery,
clothes, food, television, movies, music, as well as work and other people. This
sort of interaction depends on commonalities among interactants, and that is
why it is a key indicator of social groupings. People establish relationships
around what they like and find rewarding about others. Relationships and
groups are distinguished by their common interests and values. So jokes, gossip,
and stories are often at the expense of others. This is one way that even casual
social communication works to include and exclude people. Lots of backstage
behavior (Goffman, 1967) takes place during social forms of talk. It is a way of
holding others up to scrutiny or ridicule while cementing the bonds of your own
group. Gossip is a particularly powerful binder of groups. It is the casual sharing
of information and secrets about the character and qualities of others. Gossipers
reveal their own attitudes and values and bind themselves together.

Social classes are dependent on who is known and the value attached to social talk. Easy social talk is considerably more prevalent and valued by the upper
classes because they have the time and opportunity to develop tastes and attitudes about entertaining subjects. Being knowledgeable about and interested in
literature, music, movies, art, and food is just not possible for everyone. All sorts
of activities and types of social associations vary by class structure, so it follows
that the sociological functions of these activities would vary. The relative value
and beauty of certain activities is usually a point of contention among those
with different symbolic resources and class identification. For example,
Bourdieu's (1978/1993) essay on sport and class explains how the elites take
part in sport very differently than the working class. They value different physical activities—elites value leisure, health, and beauty rather than brute force
and competition—and physical "means" something very different to elites.
These differences lead to strains. Moreover, elites have more conversational resources to devote to purely social talk. This means that conversations among

different class groups is usually superficial and strained. The upper classes value performance for the sake of performance and have an idealized image of pleasure and enjoyment. Finally, social talk and gossip are subject to different rules about how they should take place. In the upper classes, social conversation is more idealized and restrained, with certain topics being taboo, and with expectations of manner and propriety.

Professional Talk.   This last form of interaction I call professional talk. It is somewhat more formal in nature and different from the others. It has its pleasurable and social aspects, but these are not its defining features. It focuses on the verbal art of communication, and is less concerned with the emotional dimensions of communication. Professional talk takes place during meetings, conferences, oral presentations (e.g., sales pitches), and all sorts of professional settings. It is often, but not exclusively, an intellectual form of talk about ideas or specialized information. It enacts relationships based on membership in professional communities and associations with others of like mind and interests. It maintains its boundaries to identify insiders and outsiders according to knowledge of a subject matter. Whether the topics be the intricacies of automobile repair, Victorian literature, engineering, or marketing, the ability to hold your own in the conversation marks you as a member of this subcommunity.

Certainly professional talk distinguishes among stratificational slices both within and between these slices. Those who are specialists in a subject matter can carry on conversations (either orally or in print) that is unattainable to the less sophisticated. Membership in an elite is based on these conversational abilities that include specialized language use and discourse structures. The ability to perform professional discourse also demarcates individuals with professional groups. All groups—whether they be academics, business people, or employees of various kinds—have a range of intermediaries with better or worse conversational abilities.

The working classes of various skill levels surely spend less time in professional talk, whereas the educated upper-middle classes spend more time in such talk. But even someone performing manual labor has a rudimentary professional discourse that relates to knowledge of equipment, the organization of time and activity, patterns of work accomplishment, history and future development, as well as other "insider" knowledge that makes one more expert or a "professional." Of course the more educated professionals (lawyers, doctors, academics) spend a great deal of time in professional discourse that permeates more of their personal and social lives. Their image of being prosaic and emotionally controlled is probably due in no small part to the pervasiveness of professional talk in their lives.

Professional talk takes on an authority that is increasingly significant. Mediated forms of communication, print in particular, carry authority. They record reality and create a sense of objective information (see chap. 2). Authority re-sides in various legitimate bases, such as occupying a particular role. But it is also highly correlated with professional talk. It is not a statistical accident that the authority that accompanies professional discourse is more common as one moves up the class structure. Authority is also more media determined. Knowl-edge derived from a book is considered more authoritative than individually de-rived knowledge. We thus enter into authoritative relationships with those who control a professional communication that we need or desire. We agree to a tacit bargain relationship where I benefit from the professional discourse of an-other in return for some reciprocity. Finally, these professional discourse rela-tionships are also the site of considerable conversational conflict and disagreement where personal ties can be either shattered or redefined.

Consequences of Talk Forms

When we are not in the light of interaction, we are in its shadow. We are inter-nalizing its conceptions and images of ourselves, others, and ideas. We are mak-ing silent conversation. What we think about and how we make connections between ideas comes mostly from conversations. These are the consequences of interaction. These internal social representations are pallid in comparison to the radiant experiences of actual communication. The acts of speaking expres-sively, reading deeply, and confronting the multiple sensory images of modern electronic media provide the content of what we think about and the reality that we share.

The political activities of other countries are real to those who communicate about it (mostly the upper classes). Everyone in their world of work, friends, and family engaging in all forms of talk create real images in people's minds, and these images disappear when they are no longer sustained in interaction. It is easy to see that societal values, moral commitments, and political convictions are really just points of agreement resulting from interactions of various types. The invariant rituals in a culture, such as religious activities and public ceremo-nies, are really just dramatic reenactments of other communicative exchanges that affirm a reality. When communication disappears, so does the reality it spawns. In this sense, interaction becomes the place at which one orients to-ward the world. This orientation can capture elements of complex social moti-vation because stratificational differences can be defined as existing in different conversational milieux. Interaction becomes a form of defining the present and moving into the future.

The institutions of a culture are networks of people carrying on regularized communication. One's work and life are a series of interactions with people. So-cial classes and status groups are formed along lines of age, ethnicity, work, and other specialized patterns of interaction. The effects of all these contacts and forms of talk is cumulative. With respect to individuals, the developed relationships can be rewarding or punishing and have the expected consequences on individual psyches. From a societal level, one can change positions in the communicative market, thereby improving or impairing social relations and practical successes. Improvement in social relations is usually linearlike in that success in one form of interaction, whether it be social, political, or some other, leads to increased confidence and the ability to draw rewards and resources from those lines of interaction. These successes lead to specialization and a loss of other possibilities, thereby keeping people within their circumscribed groups. These groups form the essential structures of a society.

I develop these processes in more theoretical detail in the next chapter and empirical detail in chapters 5 and 6. I turn next to a more elaborate outline of social structure and its relationship to social action. The basic dualism of micro-versus macroprocesses in society is best addressed by Giddens' structuration theory; however, I examine other theoretical perspectives, as well as structuration, in the next chapter. We must satisfy the requirements of recursivity in order to show a workable link between microinteractional levels and constraining social structural levels of analysis.

4

Principles of Interdependence and Structuration

... there is One man, —present to all particular men only partially, or through one faculty; and that you must take the whole society to find the whole man.

There is simultaneity, not coincidence.

The most elemental components of communication theory are media, discourse, and the nature of interdependence, which is the subject matter of this chapter. In essence, interdependence is how various elements come to coalesce and organize themselves into a whole of some sort that has structure. It is how parts are connected and form a collectivity that has organizational features. This collectivity may be large or small, simple or complex, formal or informal, but it adheres to principles of interdependence nonetheless. We simply cannot talk about a theory of interaction or any type of social bonding without considering theoretical principles of interdependence. What sociologists call the micro–macro link—the connections between the small world of individuals and immediate interactions, and the larger worlds of social structure—is one problem in theories of interdependence.

Communication researchers have generally ignored certain theories of interdependence, including the micro–macro issue, although this is less true of certain organizational theorists. Hawes (1974) in communication, and Weick (1979) in social psychology, are certainly notable exceptions. Both of these theorists have focused attention on interactional processes that produce larger organized relationships. They recognized that the concepts of collectivity and structure were the emergent forms of interdependence, which is created when language users participate in patterned interactions that meet individual and relationship goals, but have macrostructures as a byproduct. In the study of organizations, Hawes and Weick have tried to direct attention away from container metaphors of organizations—that is, the organization is a noun or an entity that holds something—and redefine organizations as verbs or processes, interactions that rely on principles of interdependence.

Their work is theoretically correct and innovative, and has caused many to think differently about organizations, but it remains at the margins of research and scholarship. Discussions of organizational structure are almost always based on bureaucratic hierarchy, and almost never concerned with examining the underlying nature of interdependence (Harrison, 1994). Structure in organizations is usually thought of a top–down hierarchy that is a means of distributing authority and decision making. There is nothing necessarily "wrong" with this, but it ignores the fundamental nature of interdependence. These principles of interdependence teach us more about communication practices and the ways in which interdependence is accomplished. These examples have been from organizational communication, which as I stated, has only prompted modest interest, but few have attempted deeper and more widespread analyses of how macrorealities are constructed from theories of interdependence. And even fewer have applied these fundamental communication principles to social structures such as class or ethnicity, Collins (1975, 1981) notwithstanding.

There cannot be a communication theory or a theory of sociology without confronting the principles of interdependence, to which the micro–macro link is related. We must face the connection between the small phenomenological world of real-time interaction and the large world of macrosociology. Surely the work of Giddens, Collins, and Alexander has generated interest in this issue, but much of it has been prepatory, showing how the problem is important but difficult if not intractable. In this chapter I turn my attention to some fundamentals of theories of interdependence. I briefly review some issues and theorists, and then attempt a model or analytic frame that may serve as an heuristic for the chapters that follow. Following, I quickly explore some history of the problem, followed by critical treatment of work by Giddens, Weick, and Collins, and finish with interaction ritual chains as promising conceptual tools that we can work from.

THE PROBLEM OF INTERDEPENDENCE
AND THE MICRO–MACRO WORLD

In one very real empirical sense, there is no such thing as sociology. There is no such thing as "structure," "order," or "macrosocietal forces" that influence individuals and cultures. You cannot observe or touch something called "the state" or "the middle class." These things are only reifications or generalities inferred from individuals behaving in relation to one another. As Alexander and Giesen (1987) explained, the debate over levels of reality and the existence of a micro- and macroworld have a long history in philosophical thinking. From Plato's *Theory of Forms* to medieval distinctions between the individual and the state, the issue of a micro- and macroworld has been a core opposition. Social scientific notions about systems, wholeness, and nonsummativity, and political issues about the individual versus the state are all part of the background of these controversies. This micro–macro problem is the first problem of interdependence we will address.

Interestingly, powerful and popular conceptual systems have been established for both micro- and macroepistemologies. The positivists' quest for a unified science based on atomistic principles of physics has been a very compelling and successful microposition. And Marx has produced the most influential macro perspective in the social sciences, concluding that objective circumstances rule people. Contemporary debates about the relationship between the individual and state are informed by this micro–macro distinction. Is the "system" responsible for the poor and jobless, or is it failed individual agency? The historical conflict between the populist Jefferson and the federalist Hamilton may be considered a micro–macro argument, one that pits what is called "big-D" democracy (principles of freedom, rights, and the state) against "little-D" democracy (smaller daily democratic acts such as participating in community actions and voting). Goldhagen (1996), in his book *Hitler's Willing Executioners: Ordinary Germans and the Holocaust,* challenged the rather facile explanation of the holocaust that inanimate social structures in Germany were responsible for the holocaust. Goldhagen cited Giddens, explaining how structural constraints (a macronotion) are never causal, and that the phenomenological reality (a micronotion) of ordinary citizens who perpetrated atrocities against the Jews had to be taken seriously. Much of the success and power of his study was attributable to his analysis of how ordinary citizens behaved consciously and intentionally.

One of the problems with this micro–macro debate is that the question is often posed as an antithesis, where one is expected to choose one side or the other as a deterministic entity. It was Durkheim (1895/1938) who melded social theory based on emergent properties from micro conditions. Durkheim conceptualized action as symbolic, and explained how collective order emerged from action, and later exercised constraints on voluntary actions. Nevertheless, Durkheim remained primarily concerned with macrostructures (Alexander, 1984). Marx and Durkheim remain as powerful statements about macro reality and formed an early intellectual foundation of modern sociology. But a reaction to structural realism was inevitable, and that reaction came in the form of pragmatists and theorizers such as Mead and Freud.

Mead and Freud represent a significant integration of pragmatism into social science. Mead's central claim that the response to an action by a language user is what determines its meaning, and the fact that patterns of actions and re-sponses determine social order, was a significant microsocial move. Mead then suggested that these patterns became so habituated that individuals carried around a portion of society with them. This "generalized other" was the reason that interactions were so smooth and often mechanical looking. But Mead car-ried this analysis no further. He had no link between the micro and the macro. In the same way that later Marx was completely dependent on macroforces, Mead ended up being dependent on the microexperiences of the individual. He was completely dependent on the position that individuals mediate all experi-ence and could not incorporate macrostructures into this theoretical position in any significant way. Most current constructivists (e.g., Gergen & Davis, 1985; Shotter, 1993) are left with the same problem.

This extreme privileging of personal microexperience remains a strong cur-rent in contemporary postmodern social science. For example, there is a group of scholars called critical race theorists who hold that people's perspective on events are completely determined by their own racial experience (e.g., Wil-liams, 1991). These scholars share the view that there is no objective reality, only competing racial versions of reality. And these versions are the result of patterns of communicative experiences. Critical race theorists do maintain that ethnicity is structured out of culture and history, but also have no link that joins human micro racial interactions with a societal structure of ethnicity or race. This link is important, because without it, we get either the subjective excesses of postmodernism, or the straightjacket constraints of Marxism.

Alexander and Giesen's (1987) history of this micro–macro debate explains how issues in philosophy (e.g., nominalism, realism) were translated into socio-logical theories about individuals and societies. These theories run the gamut from maintaining that rational interpretive individuals create society by engag-ing in individually subjective acts of free communication, to a position that ar-gues that completely socialized individuals simply translate structure into their microcommunicative reality. This dual paradigmatic debate went on for gener-ations, and is still influential in the social sciences, although less vital than be-fore. Moreover, the various syntheses of the micro–macro problem (e.g., Parsons, 1963; Weber, 1978) firmly established the interdependence of the two. Few would argue seriously these days for the deterministic priority of one over the other. Parsons discovered that "internalization" was the mechanism that linked micro individual action with macrocollective structures. Internalization is at the heart of how individuals carry order in their head, which works as a boundary between individual communicative action and social order. The cul-ture and society of a human actor influences the responses that he or she can make to momentary and unfolding conscious needs. Responses to the structural environment become part of the actors' perceptual or microworld. Those re-sponses are filtered and mediated by the preexisting cognitive makeup of the in-dividual. Thus, macrostructures have become part of the individual's microworld. This is a dialectic that continues and results in a socialized person who will subsequently influence macrostructures with his or her newly internalized microperceptions.

Alexander and Giesen (1987) chronicled the history of this debate and explain how "Mead and Freud outlined the 'other side' of Durkeim's macrotheory, portraying microsubjective processes that could be orderly without coercive constraint" (p. 9). This was accompanied by the work of the ethnomethodologists' emphasis on member practices in the microworld, and Marx and Homans' (1958) more objective micro theory, where mechanistic and rational choices were emphasized more than interpretation and emotion. Behaviorism is also a rationalistic version of microtheory. But the shift is now toward linkage of the micro and macro, and even though theorists might emphasize one over the other, no one fails to recognize the issue. Collins and Giddens developed similar theories that try to account for the "process" of developing structure by interweaving action and order. The following section focuses on their work and the concept of interaction ritual chains.

Communication and the Micro–Macro Dialectic

Among other things, the study of language and communication involves specific analysis of what people say and the stream of their moment-to-moment experience. Society (macrosociology) is concerned with broad and long-term social entities. Much of the history of the study of communication (speaking, rhetoric, interpersonal, and group relations) is micro in nature. And so is the ethnomethodology tradition in sociology. These concepts emphasize observational work that forms the empirical basis of broader social structures. Interestingly, we know that the study of experiential human behavior does not yield rational models of behavior. That is, actual human interaction is not strictly rationalist, but it does yield common features of social organization. Collins (1981) visualized this process in a useful table that has time metrics on one axis and a social and physical space on the other.

Table 4.1 illustrates the extent to which micro- and macroelements are continuous variables and relative to one another. Everything to the left of the table is more empirical than those to the right. And everything is more micro toward the top left of the table than those dimensions below and to the right. Interpersonal communication, much discourse analysis, pragmatics, phenomenology, symbolic interactionism, and ethnomethodology are concerned more with people and situations and are located more to the upper-left quadrant of the table. Organizational communication and media sociology are more toward the bottom-right sector. Lannamann (1991) made an interesting similar point when he explained how so much interpersonal communication research is skewed toward individual microexperiences at the expense of any emphases of social collectives such as class and education. He argued that this is a positivist bias that

TABLE 4.1
Time and Space as Levels of Sociological Analysis

Space Scale	Time Scale					
	Seconds (100-1sec)	Minutes/Hours (102-4sec)	Days (105sec)	Weeks/Months (106sec)	Years (107-8sec)	Centuries (109sec)
One person (1-3 sq ft)	Cognitive/emotional processes	Meaningful events Work Repetitive and intermittent behaviors	...	...	Careers, Life histories	Genealogies
Small group (3-102 sq ft)	Eye-contact studies Microconversational analyses	Rituals Group dynamics Exchanges Bargaining	...	...	...	...
Crowd/organization (103-106 sq ft)	...	Crowd behavior	...	Formal organizations	Organizational histories	...
Community (107-1010 sq ft)	...	...	...	Social movements	Communities Political, economic, demographic, and stratification patterns (mobility rates, etc.) "cultures"	Long-term social changes
Territorial society (1011-1014 sq ft)	...	...	...	...	...	

Note: From Collins, R. (1981). On the Microfoundations of Macrosociology. American Journal of Sociology, 86(5), 984–1014. Reprinted by permission of the University of Chicago Press.

emphasizes the unitary controlling individual rather than the individual as a socially and culturally influenced entity. Lannamann's own ideological biases notwithstanding, he is working with the micro–macro epistemological problem.

The most rigorous notions of empiricism and data tap into the upper left sector and characterize microsituations. Only these can be observed and measured with any degree of accuracy and precision. Therefore, as Collins concluded, "All macroevidence, then, is aggregated from such micro-experiences" (1981, p. 987). So, as you read these words or interact with someone in the next few minutes, you are forming social representations that construct a reality composed of all those macrocategories. For example, ethnicity, gender identities, and social class are the result of complex inferential processes from the microexperiences. They are a shorthand term for these multitude of experiences.

It must be clear that the micro–macro distinction is one of scale and ratio. The distinction should be considered a continuous variable that does not lend itself to rigid categorization. But our concern here is with communication and the problem of interdependence and the organization of people and messages. It is my contention that the important social categories and structures in a culture can and must be related to or translated into microcommunication experiences, and that communication is the only empirical reality for social structures. Social concepts must be rooted in microcommunication experiences. What are some of the advantages of rigorously requiring social concepts be translated into communicative actions?

The first advantage is epistemological. The state of our knowledge about social categories is stronger to the extent that these categories have empirical grounding in individuals behaving in microsituations. Any category summarizing a collection of individual behaviors is translating from a microreality to a macroreality and back again. This is how researchers and lay people generate social categories of all types and levels of generality. For example, Fitzpatrick (1988) spent a large portion of her research efforts studying family "types." One type of family is pluralistic (Fitzpatrick et al. 1996). "Pluralistic parents are committed to female equality and believe that personal preferences rather than role proscriptions should determine an individual's behavior" (p. 385). She then described a host of attitudes, behaviors, and communication practices that characterize pluralistic families.

These types (e.g., pluralistic) are macrocategories that serve as a shorthand for many microcommunication behaviors. The term *pluralistic* is a compilation of many microcommunication experiences that are coded and translated into this term *pluralistic* that represents some macroreality. A term such as this can be either the result of a researcher's efforts after observations and questionnaires, or a more amateur endeavor to describe experiences and behaviors. When a historian tags an era as the "Age of Jackson" or the "Ante-bellum South," he or she is glossing many complex microexperiences. The advantage, then, of requiring social concepts to be fixed in microevents is that they gain their most dependable empirical expression. Often this empirical grounding is complex, difficult, and perhaps only an approximation, but it is the best test of the macroconcept, and the best place to begin a reevaluation of the macroconcept.

And second, communication in microsituations is where real human action takes place. As Collins (1981) explained, macrosocial shorthands:

> do not *do* anything; if they seem to indicate a continuous reality it is because the individuals that make them up repeat their microbehaviors many times, and if the "structures" change it is because the individuals who enact them change their microbehaviors. (p. 989)

People are dispersed in time and place, and social structures are cumulative representations of microexperiences. Modern media makes distant and asynchronous communication possible, but such communicative acts remain microsocial actions. Individiual cognitive processing of messages is more central to microexperiences than is face-to-face interaction. Therefore, a computer interaction, E-mail, listening to the radio, or retrieving a message from an answering machine are microexperiences.

The Generative Mechanisms of Microinteractional Experiences

For all the normal cries about the complexity and intractability of communication and human behavior, it remains true that everyone communicates quite efficiently every day. How does this happen? One reason is the taken-for-granted stance (Garfinkel, 1967) of language users. There are simply many aspects of daily life that are taken for granted. They are assumed and unquestioned. We carry these social representations around in our head and call on them when necessary. This allows for efficient storage, such that every communicable experience is available for use, but stored in a sort of shorthand. This shorthand has an efficiency that does not require all representations to be present in consciousness but makes them available on request. The terms *frames, scripts,* or *schema* are related to this "shorthand" and are commonly understood in linguistics, artificial intelligence, and psychology. These frames help language users gain what Goffman (1981) called "footing," or the ways in which we position ourselves in interaction to manage messages. What is important analytically about using frames to gain footing is that communicators use linguistic markers to help them find their way, or to access a frame. These linguistic cues and markers provide a structural basis for analyzing interactions.

Conflicting or mismatched frames can be considered the reason for the common experience of "misunderstanding," "confusion," or "poor communication," as well as other interpersonal difficulties. Tannen and Wallat (1993) explained how a doctor and the mother of a child in a medical visit can invoke different frames and end up with either confusion or ill will. The mother can be in a "consultation" frame, requiring both lay language and sympathy. If the doctor mismatches with this frame and stays in an examination or medical professional frame, then he will fail to meet the mother's needs. This also accounts for certain types of racism, ethnic tensions, and problems because language users build cognitive models to represent other groups. When we encounter members of a ethnic group for which we have well-developed cognitive models, we activate special frames that are often in conflict with the other person (see chap. 6).

Indexicality is another mechanism that helps structure understanding; it is part of a set of principles that organize interaction. Indexicality is a simple concept. It means that an utterance always indexes or "points to" people, contexts, and background information for its interpretation. If I were walking out of a restaurant after an expensive meal and said "Well, that was enjoyable," the sentence could be used as a straightforward description of my experience, or a sarcastic comment. Indexicality means that any expression can be altered by its context. But all expressions are indexical; that is, their sense and reference are only settled by looking at contexts or occasions of use. All utterances require listeners to fill in meaning by referencing power, status, speakers, past information, and anything else that makes the message coherent (Ellis, 1995).

There are various structures that language users employ to produce a coherent sense of real-time interaction, and there is little need to restate them here. Scripts, indexicality, microlinguistic features, speech acts, implicatures, story structures, and rhetorical strategies are all part of the ethnomethods communicators use to stitch together a microcommunicative reality. What is particularly important for the theory of interdependence is that the microworld of everyday communication is the site of meaning that both produces social structure and is produced by it. This is a key theoretical principle of Giddens (1984)—to be elaborated on later in this chapter—that represents the most important contribution to sociological theory in some time. As is developed throughout this chapter and those that follow, creating meaning and understanding requires access to vast domains of culture and social structure.

We can visualize this microworld of communication and interaction with others as an enfolded order. Social structure and history enfold into the reality of individuals and act like seeds that produce an organized flowering of messages and meanings. The flowering is the world of appearances; the enfolded seed is the world that underlies appearances. The analysis of discourse is part of this observable flowering world. This enfolded seed world contains classical social structure in the form of history, culture, and language, and is accessible through the duality of structure, and the duality of analysis.

The duality of analysis is the fact that recurring patterns in the macrostructural world require methods for detecting regularities such as mathematical and statistical models. These are necessary to detect long-term and slow-moving patterns of regularities. But the microworld requires techniques for unearthing the quick and small movements of real-time interaction. The language of these techniques is different from traditional sociology and social psychology. It is the language of linguistics and communication.

Goffman was perhaps the best speaker of this microworld language. His study of impression management and embarrassment (Goffman, 1959, 1967) established the concept of "face" and the extent to which interactants were sensitive to momentary affirmation and negation of status and image. He showed how avoiding embarrassment and presenting the self in a strategically desired manner occupied most of a communicator's time. His analysis was important in sociology, and the social sciences in general, because he understood how to tap into the nuances and the modulating compass points of social encounters.

But to Goffman's credit, he did not completely turn his attention away from issues in the larger social order. He was mindful of the relationship between the micro- and macroworld. His work with mental hospitals and patients (Goffman, 1967), among others, always showed a concern with what the microworld told us about macrostructures. He described quite convincingly, for instance, how the variety of disputes and contests in a culture such as wars, arguments, feuds, revenge, and sport reflect the social order of cultural character and honor.

But he did neglect the cognitive aspects of interaction in favor of the interdependent structure of acts of people in interaction. This neglect of social representations limits his analysis and leaves him unable to offer much explanatory power. Much of my analysis tries to improve on this by including references to motivated social representations used by individuals. This improves the power of discourse and language analysis to describe lived experiences, and injects some life into these descriptions. The theoretical and methodological work of the next two chapters involves shuttling back and forth between observation of language and social structures. This will be an effort at describing the relationship between action and structure. The microlinguistic turn of Goffman and the theoretical directions of Giddens loom large in these chapters.

I should add here that a micro–macro interdependence is not captured particularly well by rational models such as exchange theory (e.g., Homans, 1958). A communication perspective does not assume that actors calculate rational choices and then behave accordingly. Actually, people operate on the basis of normalcy and regularity. As the ethnomethodologists have amply demonstrated, a taken-for-granted and assumption of routine are common for most interactions, not calculated decision making. Coherent interactions can only take place in the context of mutually understood and tacit understandings that are not even high in consciousness. Moreover, there are some powerful arguments (Williamson, 1975) demonstrating how human rationality is limited and that the natural tendency of long-term interactions is to evolve into repeated exchanges that end up having structural consequences. It would be, to switch languages here, biologically nonadaptive to incessantly work out and negotiate all interactions. So communication over time gives way to an understood basis for reality. This understood basis of reality is sociologically structural and logically related to microinteractions.

Interaction Ritual Chains

Collins' (1981, 1987) theory of interaction ritual chains is a useful conceptual tool. He is proposing a microsociology that explains macrostructure, and his concept of "interaction ritual chains" is central to a theory of interdependence. Briefly, Collins has been instrumental, along with the ethnomethodologists, in turning traditional sociological concerns into microevents, typically microcommunication events. It is possible to translate macrophenomenon such as class or the state into observable microbehaviors. Given that a macroevent is never seen by anyone, but exists only through the activities of observers labeling and classifying action, then it must be possible to compile summaries by translating a text or communicative exchange into an example of a macroreality.

The term *interaction ritual* comes from Goffman (1967) and refers to little more than the fact that a communicative exchange depends on the motivations, resources, and the language of the users. And these are produced out of cultural and biographical histories, stored memories, and linguistic socialization. An individual has certain cultural resources, and these are derived from previous interactions, invested in present interactions, and implicated in future interactions. Moreover, there is a tremendous variety and complexity of interactions that one may engage in. Some of them are everyday and routine, others are new, creative, and distinctive. Some involve asymmetries of various types, but all of them actualize one's membership is social networks and establish power, roles, and identity. This is also true for parasocial relationships (Horton & Wohl, 1956) where individuals cognitively interact with nonimmediate others. So some "emergence" is the result of all interactive situations. There is some emanation that results from this interlocking of actions and sentiments. It cannot be predicted, but some sound theoretical judgments are possible.

It us useful to invoke an economic metaphor for some of these processes. Collins (1987) and Bourdieu (1991) used the term *cultural capital* to describe the consequences of conversation chains. As individual's exclude and include different identities and relational positions, and as they engage in numerous symbolic exchanges with various forms of media, they store cultural capital; that is, they have a bank of things to talk about, language features, attitudes, and the like. People who successfully engage in power relationships, for example, will move into the future with the energy and confidence to enact new power relationships. And, conversely, those who experience capitulation and acquiescence will initiate similar subsequent conversations and have something else "emerge." Cultural capital consolidates numerous resources that circulate, including energy, motivations, image, identity, and verbal skills.

These interaction ritual chains that circulate cultural capital can direct one's attention to either micro- or macroperspectives (Collins, 1987), and I suggest that both professional and lay observers seesaw between the two regularly. A microperspective on interaction ritual chains focuses on the individual and his or her personality and psychobiography. We might notice or document his enduring nature or particular communicative skills and patterns. But it is the interaction unit—the encounter, and the ongoing interaction ritual chains—that is fundamental, and the individual's nature or personality are abstracted from these units. When we draw conclusions and label an individual's "personality" or "nature," we are simply using a verbal shorthand to encapsulate and describe patterns of thinking, speaking, and behaving. Intervening at this level is what therapists, friends, and family members do in the world of interpersonal relations and their daily requirements.

But as Collins (1988), Alexander and Giesen (1987), and others such as the ethnomethodologists explained, one can also aggregate these interaction chains into macropatterns. The stratified nature of cultures separates people by groups. But within these groups are associational patterns based on similarity of encounters. Just as a label describing someone's personality (e.g., "friendly," "aggressive," or "authoritarian") is an encapsulation of interactional encounters, so too are stratificational terms (e.g. "lower middle class" or "African-American ethnic identity") labels for status groups that regularly converse and employ language and communication patterns that produce and reproduce group membership. The term *middle class* is broad and crude, but conceals a narrower and more refined reality that lives in a network of communicative relationships. A group has a sense of reality and identity because of the communicative behaviors that mark membership. As Collins (1987) wrote, "if one wishes to describe accurately the condition of class consciousness, ideology, or culture across a society, the proper way to do so would be to sample the typical conversations across the landscape" (p. 201). I broaden what Collins meant by "conversation" but make an effort at just such descriptions.

Issues related to this micro–macro distinction (e.g., Giddens' structuration) are further addressed in the following section, but I should raise a warning here about too much emphasis on conversation. Life is not only a series of chats. Certainly some theorists (e.g., Marx) argue that human behavior, including communication, is responsive to structure in the first place. Employees, minorities, and members of social classes have internalized discursively created identities and positions in networks, and these are structurally responsible for whatever symbolic capital one possesses. But the concept of an interaction ritual chain already heeds this warning. The experience of an interactional encounter already includes previous symbolic accumulations, which means that macrostructures and patterns are influential in these interactional encounters. Yet, we cannot simply leave it at this and assume that structure determines behavior. The reality of communicating in a role or as a member of a culturally identified group is neither simply given from structure nor fashioned arbitrarily. It is truly crafted with some struggle out of the interplay of microcultural capital and structural constraints.

I would push this dialectical tension to almost radical levels by suggesting that microempirical phenomena and macrostructural phenomena are close to the same thing, but not exactly. They require theorizing. This is a somewhat more extreme position, but one that is satisfying because it makes for a very close articulation between specific human behavior and culture. Social practices and culture enfold on one another such that each informs the other. But what is even more important theoretically is that the concept of *objective structure* is advanced in an empirical way because the social facts of communication and language are available to the social sciences. The phenomenological and emic experiences of individuals in relationships would be a variant of the etic or "outside" structural variables generated by analysts. This helps solve the problem of how a rich diversity of interactive practices emerge as a macropattern, or how a stable structural characteristic of all cultures is represented by a great variety of linguistic and interactive practices.

This unity of microsocial experiences and macrostructures is an argument with more than its share of problems, but one that raises some intriguing points. One very interesting and theoretically important issue is the extent to which structure is part of anyone's reality-Gestalt. The ethnomethodologists try to claim that individuals conform to structure, and then that same structure is displayed in member social practices. But they do little more than claim the identity of the two. And they do little to make socio-logical and technical connections between interaction and structure. The ethnomethodologists seem to be increasingly pressured to make the connections between language user practices and various asymmetries of power, status, or other structural issues (cf. Schegloff, 1997). Recall that a language user's reality is enfolded into his consciousness and may be foregrounded without verbalization. So, for example, the role of power or status in a relationship may be operating, even though the individuals are not talking about power or status. This makes the indexing problem very difficult, and it becomes impossible to argue that real-time action is the same as structure. This is certainly true for many aspects of reality, and is one reason that sociolinguists such as Ochs (1992) are in a better position theoretically to connect social practices of language to aggregate social structure.

Also, except for Maynard and Wilson (1980), there is little work on the reification of conversational subject matter or topics. Global and background knowledge always plays a role in communication such that the horizons of knowledge impinge on the local time and place. But the content of talk also constitutes what a conversation is about and its macroreality. So, microcommunication events are accomplished by the same people who accomplish macroevents. Therefore, the important theoretical act for microevents is their classification into reality, and their subsequent use as documentation of the macroreality. The macrostructures are reifications and idealizations that are logically and empirically related to the microevents (communicative encounters). The macroreality owes its existence to microevents that in turn owe their existence, in part, to macrorealities. Thus, there is the coalition, through interaction rituals chains, of the micro- and macroobjects. This is essentially the spirit of Collins' vision.

The nature and content of conversation is truly important to the "ritual" part of interaction ritual chains. Every time individuals engage in symbolic acts such as reading, conversation, or media use, they are constituting themselves as members of a group. They form a conversational cult.

It is possible to criticize interaction ritual chains as nonobservable because they invoke an image of long, chaotic sequences of interactional events. Moreover, such chains have no apparent pattern, and it would be impossible to see them in such a way as to identify a totality. This is true, but mostly a methodological technicality. Interaction ritual chains are observable in principle, and more importantly, they are positioned in real time and space. They are not the same as classical social structures because they exist on a microlevel, and, unlike classical social structures, do not have patterns coded into them. Social structures are, by definition, summarized glosses that organize and pattern microphenonomenon. They exist in no other way. Interaction rituals are the empirically available behaviors that constitute structure. They are available on the basis of their concrete relations to people and situations. Their sequential structures, patterns, and simultaneities may be posited as a matter of investigation, but they are not given.

So, interaction ritual chains are events and activities in which micro-experiences occur. They are the sites of macrostructures. Interaction rituals are distributed around the social world and provide contexts for microstructure and macrostructure production. I turn now to the crucial problem of linking microevents with macroevents. In this vein, we must also examine further the relation between action and structure, which is a relation between microinteractional order—action that includes social representations, motives, reasons, and so forth—and the external orders that presumably operate outside of action—structure. In the next section I say a few words about the conditions of micro–macro linkage, followed by brief clarifying statements about structure and action. This leads to a brief discussion of Giddens' theory of structuration, followed by comments of my own.

LINKING ACTION AND STRUCTURE

As central as the micro–macro linkage problem is to the social sciences, it has not been very systematically analyzed in communication. The key concern is to identify and examine theoretical concepts that "link" individual- and encounter-level variables with larger social structure phenomenon. This is a theoretical problem, but also a practical one. Actual social systems must find ways to integrate individuals into collectivities. Gerstein (1987) suggested one framework that may be usefully adapted and altered.

When attempting to link the phenomenological experiences of individuals in interactions with macrostructures, certain principles must be respected. First, there is a very real sense of both quantitative reality and qualitative reality. Quantitatively, some elements of both micro- and macrolevels can be measured, counted, and aggregated. It is theoretically possible to measure various aspects of communication (i.e., events, topics, contexts, linguistic units, and role types) and link these with macrosociological levels regarding groups and summary data. All social actions produce cultural products through media and other forms of contact, and these may be counted, organized, and classified. It is also the case that simply recognizing part–whole relations between social action at all levels will provide necessary links. But links must also be qualitatively satisfying and meaningful. It must be possible to interpret them in a manner appropriate for the engaged language users.

These part–whole relationships are central to micro–macro links, but difficulties arise because the classification of a micro–macro distinction is not fixed and stable, but analytic (Gerstein, 1987). In other words, just as parts and wholes can change places, so can micro- and macrophenomenon. One's membership in an ethnic heritage may be macro with respect to its explanatory power for certain communicative behaviors, but micro-relative to the state. Communicating conservative family values is micro within the family system, but macro-relative to politics and the economy. None of these are clear empirical relations, but practical strategies for analysis.

We do not want to assume a microreductionist or macroreductionist reality. In other words, we do not want to assume that everything is microempirical communication and all else is just epiphenomenal or a classificatory gloss. And we want to avoid the reverse: that macrostructures are deterministic. Something interactive that balances the two will be most productive. Communication and social theory will be strengthened to the extent that we can shift causal directions from time to time. This requires researchers and analysts to make arguments about the location and direction of causal relations. Sometimes microanalysis will justify reifications and grant causality. Other times reifications may cause microcommunicative behaviors and relationships. This middle approach makes for a variety of theoretical approaches at the expense of certain empirical advantages.

Linking Things

We have been examining throughout this chapter the issues that help explain the movement from the moment-to-moment realities of interaction to general collectivities. The key theoretical argument being that society, and components of this macrolevel, has its empirics in microlinguistic and communicative interaction. But it remains difficult to explain and detail this vacillation between micro- and macrolevels. Just how does it work? We turn now to some principles that are typically associated with linking small to large, micro to macro, as well as action to structure.

The most conventional linking principles mentioned by Gerstein (1987) are aggregation and disaggregation. These are well understood and simple, but no less important and powerful. Aggregation is the formation of generalities and summaries by accumulating, ordering, and adding individual entities. Statistical statements and generalities are the most common. Disaggregation is the reduction of these generalities into component parts. For example, membership in the African-American ethnic group might be based on an aggregation of an individual's country or family origin, physical features, certain linguistic structures (e.g., zero copula), and so forth. These things would "aggregate" and form the macro category of "African-American ethnicity." The problem with these is that they do not tell us much about individuals. Moreover, a richer notion of ethnicity would have to include the aggregation of attitudes, group loyalties, behavioral tendencies, and additional language and communication styles. Disaggregation would take a group-defined individual and make finely grained assumptions about individual family origins, physical features, linguistic structure, attitudes, loyalties, behavioral tendencies, and communication styles. Statistics remain the primary tool for this sort of linkage, and they figure very prominently in modern communication and society. Census data, laws, hiring practices, and other structural-level activities rely heavily on aggregated glosses of ethnic groups. Crime statistics for minorities, for example, influence individual attitudes and behavior as much, and often more than, personal experiences with members of the same minority group. This is consistent with cultivation theory (Signorielli & Morgan, 1990), which predicts transformations in individuals because of exposure to institutionally created symbolic environments (e.g., crime on television). This socializes people beyond the limits of interpersonal interaction.

Taking an individual and his conscious agency, as well as ecological factors of life (e.g., significant dates and places), and making these "socially" relevant because they are part of the social order, and then generalizing from individuals to groups, is probably the best way to turn micro worlds into macrostructures. More simply, it is the relationship of individuals to the groups they identify with (Gerstein, 1987). Simply locating or calling yourself a member of group is not good enough. Individuals must identify with a collection of people who share and recognize information, language, and patterns of communication. But even the slightest commonalty and identity can result in a macro category. An individual can move along a sort of continuum of strength of group identity. From statistical groups with no psychological identity formed on the basis of pure arithmetic aggregation (e.g., "everyone born in 1947," "all males," "everyone who earns over $22,000," etc.), to strongly identified groups where people merge their individuality into the group (e.g., racial, religious, or organizational groups). The standardization that comes from these groups makes certain predictions and explanations more tenable. The movement from wholes to parts is also possible and makes for greater individualistic understanding. Racial groups, for example, can be segmented into different geographies, religions, or social classes.

This entire process of linking the actions and meanings of daily life to group and structural realities suggests the importance of communication systems in a society. In fact, any notion of linkage and interdependent relationships is definitionally a part of communication. It is communication that makes group boundaries real and concrete. The development of networks, ritualistic exchanges, sources of information, and "cells" as discussed in chapter 2 are the communication mechanisms that enculturate people and turn their communication practices into meanings that become material, and are then reified.

In chapter 2, I made the argument for the role of the media in crafting a culture. We can make the micro–macro link here. I use the example of television, but the principles apply equally to any medium of communication. What appears to be a simple television show, and is experienced as such by viewers, is composed of many small, varied, and complex activities. There are various texts (e.g., scripts, contracts, financial arrangements), meetings (business, rehearsals, distribution), groups (actors, executives, unions), and technological components (cameras, computers, lights), all of which assemble into a "whole" that is what the viewer sees. Moreover, people watch television with others (friends, family) and subsequently enter it into their conversations in other contexts.

This exposure to television constructs a social reality in the same way that earlier dominant media did. Television as a modern medium expresses communication patterns, dominant symbols, and discourse forms. This type of communication becomes somewhat normative and sets the expectations for human relationships. A medium such as television creates a series of interaction linkages that symbolically unite individuals and fashion them into collectivities. This linking process, which assembles many small processes into larger ones, works the same way for other electronic media such as radio, movies, computers, and newspapers.

THEORIZING ACTION AND STRUCTURE

I have been reconstructing some principles and issues in interdependence and the space between the micro and the macro. In the remainder of this chapter, I present a more comprehensive theoretical framework; one that suggests some more illuminating and important innovations in this perennial discussion of the individual and the collectivity: one that moves closer to the "communicative" reality of the micro–macro link. In the following sections, I try to theorize "action" and "structure" in such a way as to make them more empirically accessible, and to at least make some progress in closing the gap between a microexperiential and linguistic reality, and that of macroidealizations about social science or individuals. The important nature of interdependence that links communicative behavior with social structures, or "types" with "tokens," is the relation between "action" and "structure." Action is internal to the individual and interpretive, structure is an objective external constraint. But things are not quite so distinct, because structure is internalized and reenters the individual's interpretive frames, and action finds its way into structures. We must try to go beyond this simple dualism.

Action

The idea of action is based in the conscious and purposeful behavior of individuals. Burke (1966) drew the distinction between action and motion, where action is based on symbolicity. This is the symbol acquiring and using nature of humans. We may eat, heal ourselves, and reproduce out of our pure biological nature, but we communicate, plan, theorize, discuss, and coordinate out of our higher-order purposeful nature that requires us to use symbols. Human action, such as a speech act where we assert or promise, requires three things. The first is some choice. There would be no action if there were no choices or contingencies because we would then be behaving out of mechanical conformity. The second is purpose, or intentionality. We act for a reason; to accomplish something or achieve some end. Third, some material conditions are necessary for an act. Language, which is fundamental to action, is rooted in social life, which includes the nonsymbolic. Concrete nouns, of course, refer to the nonsymbolic physical world, but even abstract nouns are based in the actual experiences and conditions of life.

In general, I warn against the customary idea of action as one-sided commitment. And even though action involves intentionality, such intentionality might be at low levels of consciousness. Garfinkel (1967), Giddens (1976), and existential philosophers correctly argue that reflexivity and self-consciousness are central to action. Humans have the ability to remove or separate themselves from a situation and reflect on it. They can treat themselves and others as objects of observation and then "act" in a strategic manner based on various contingencies.

The two most important features of action are meaning and strategy. These are always present in action and do not represent only moments in time or different types of action. Action is understanding. It takes the basic act of meaning as one of observing in a reflexive manner some aspect of the world and then inventing a meaning for it. This invention is less subject to free creativity than it is to social contingencies. This invention results from typification, or the cognitive process of encountering something (e.g., a word, or behavior) and subjecting it to understanding. This understanding is a matter of taking what you do not know and "typifying" it by placing it in the context of what you do know. The word or act is considered to be an "example" of a social representation that the language user already possesses.

This is how individuals become members of a community or "socialized." They learn the standard frameworks of meaning in one's particular world. All members of the culture must learn names, processes, and patterns in order to be socially competent. You are considered "educated," or "knowledgeable," or "an expert" when you can take your understanding of something for granted; that is, when you can typify the objects and processes of a domain of experience. You are a dentist when you can typify dentistry, and a literary critic when you can typify artistic texts. These typifications imply easy and standard access to semantic reality, and are why Langer (1992) and Kellermann (1992) can argue that communication is often so automatic and routinized. Action, by its very definitional nature, requires meaning, and meaning involves the typification processes of interpretation. This is quite a unique human experience.

But action is not only interpreting things, but "doing" something and having some effect. Individuals use meaning through strategy and *praxis*. We achieve necessary goals by acting practically, by using our knowledge derived from meanings and then employing a strategy. The logic of human action, its dependence on meaning and strategy, is consistent here because strategy requires understanding, which in turn necessitates meaning. A strategy to do something with language (e.g., assert, blame, argue) never takes place in a vacuum, but only in terms of understood events. To act, to strategize, requires time, knowledge, resources, and energy. Human action is therefore constrained by these things and each must be allocated according to strategic calculations involving relevant knowledge and considerations.

There are always contingencies. One can expend considerable energy and resources calculating and strategizing and still know nothing for sure. Knowledge can be sketchy and the future always clouded. Strategic human action, then, always has an element of uncertainty and slippage. There are always errors introduced into strategic calculations about communicative behavior—albeit sometimes very little—so there is the appearance of automated communication. This error and uncertainty creates an intersection between rational decision making and irrational and idiosyncratic understanding. Consequently, strategy returns to meaning and establishes an interdependent loop. This loop-like principle of interdependence reminds us that meaning is itself dependent on strategy. When individuals are typifying and attaching meaning to something, they draw conclusions about meaning on the basis of practical resources such as time, personal goals, and the nature and extent of their knowledge in the first place. Our meanings are altered and managed in one way or another, and are unequally valued.

This means that human action, with its essences of meaning and strategy, is subjective. It always will be as long as humans can never be perfect calculaters.

By subjectivity, I certainly do not mean random or chimerical but refer to the mental interior of a person that is both psychological and sociological. Subjectivity is an individual's unique psychological dispositions that derive from his psychobiography and the circumstances of his particular social groups. It at least presupposes Habermas' "lifeworld," which is an intersubjectively shared world, and Bourdieu's (1977) "habitus," which is what connects social action with objective social structures. The idea of duality of structure is inherent in this notion of action. But for now, we are emphasizing the egocentric nature of humans. Individuals live in groups and have a sense of public, but are also always somewhat private and separate, while coexisting with the public. Thus, it is important to include in a social communication approach, some understanding of the individual as a separate subjective entity in the relationship between the individual and social realms.

I point out here that I disagree with the importance that Foucault and poststructuralists attach to discursivity and individual subjectivity. Certainly, the discourse environment influences subjectivity, but there is also much meaning generated by unique individuals and emergent properties of situations. The tendency to conflate discursivity with individual subjectivity is most pronounced by feminists (e.g., Weedon, 1987), who use subjectivity to explain the privileging of males. An individual's subjective nature, according to Foucault and poststructuralists, is simply the result of his or her identification with discourses. These discourses then regulate individuals. Hence, an individual holds an opinion or set of attitudes that are "subjective," only because of his or her exposure and participation in certain language patterns that position the individual in such a way.

Real human action, with its inherent subjectivity, cannot be understood solely in terms of discursivity, although it is unquestionably true that a recognition of how discourses constrain human behavior is warranted. The argument that subjectivity results from the identification of individuals with discourses seriously misses the point about the role of intrapsychic forces and their part in communicative encounters. Emotional motivations and the nature of individual identity are continually worked at, adjusted, negotiated, and altered. They are, at the very least, somewhat changing and fluid, and are not just assigned by the traces of one's memory for discourse positions.

If subjectivity were little more than a subject's position in relation to a discourse, then an individual's simple "role," or membership in a social category, would be sufficient to explain behavior. The behavior of an employee in an organization could be explained by the fact that he or she was "management" or "labor." We would look no further than "class" to explain one's choices in clothes, language, and comportment. But these things are only one vantage point for the investigation of how communication is divided, reorganized, and spliced through interaction events that evolve over time and are mediated through people and technology. All human agency is based on the concept of action, and the "act" of communication is the most fundamental. These communication acts are typically quite stable and recoverable, but still dependent, to varying degrees, on the divisions of identity and personality that must be marshaled for communication.

Structure

Despite some ambiguity around the term *social structure* (Porpora, 1989), the idea of social structure possesses some basic meaning that encompasses important concepts. Durkheim's early clarification of structure still has currency: Structure is objective, preexisting, and an external constraint on action. For example, the language system that I am a part of exists independently of my use of the language. I may employ certain words or phrases that suit my circumstantial needs, but these words or phrases are separate from my use of them. They are part of an external system of words and phrases that do not determine my communication, but certainly influence it. The basic arguments for structure are that it is objective because it is relatively stable and organized, and works separately from my understanding of it; that it is preexistent because it is bequeathed to us, we did not create it, and that it is external because it works in a suprareality that is autonomous and maintains a persistent stability and continuity. It is not a psychological disposition or a personal attribute. In the sense of philosophical realism (Rescher, 1987), social structure is real; it exerts influence on people and constrains, forms, and fashions their behaviors. Structures exert pressures on individuals that carry normative, political, and moral weight.

As I argued in chapter 3, language and meaning possess many of these characteristics that compel language users to conform. This conformity makes meaning and understanding possible. Even though there is room for individual subjectivity as previously discussed, most of what people confront in their daily communications are external institutionalized structures that are massively constraining. Social theorists of any stripe (e.g., sociologists, critical theorists, cultural theorists, etc.)—with varying degrees of circumscription—have these principles of structure in mind when they talk about race and ethnicity (Wilson, 1987), class (Hout, Brooks, & Manza, 1993), patriarchy (Weedon, 1987), labor markets, and other standard sociological structures. There are three other important qualities of structure.

The first is that structure is highly theorized. It establishes and predicts a range of options with principles that are predictable, but less so than the empirical choices. Merton's (1957) structurally induced deviance is a good example. A culture has a structural level of labor opportunities and mechanisms for choosing these opportunities. Some of these mechanisms are considered normative and conforming. Others are considered deviant. An individual who engages in deviant behavior (e.g., criminal behavior) has done so because the normative mechanisms of success in the labor market have been blocked or are unavailable. Thus, structure sets boundaries. It is a macroconcept that constrains microbehaviors. Structural membership and identification influence various participation and communication rights. Pressures on members of the upper classes to behave and communicate in predetermined ways, and participate in the culture according to normative mechanisms—or clever deviations from such norms—are considerable.

A second very important quality of structure, and one that is even more apparent in the next two chapters, is the usefulness of aggregation as a linking device to understand structures. Structures are formed and informed by statistical correlations among various empirical entities. For example, Sum, Harrington, and Goedicke (1987) explained chronic unemployment among African-American males according to structural change in the economy. The change from a manufacturing to a high-technology industrial base, and the movement of these jobs from the central cities to the suburbs, accounts for most of the unemployment. And statistics indicating that African-American youth employment rates decreased as the employment rates of other non-White youth increased reflect discriminatory hiring practices. These aggregate variables are the stuff of traditional structuralism, and new theorizing has softened this approach. But even when action and structure are merged and become more of a dialectical process, as in Giddens' structuration theory, the principles of statistical aggregation are fundamental to the relation between action and structure.

A third point about structure is its realist philosophy-of-science stance. The concern is with identifying real elements of structure that produce observable linguistic and communicative outcomes (cf. Ellis, 1995). These real structures give rise (not cause) to surface regularities that we work with daily. Hence, the observable attitudes, communication behaviors, and class consciousness of unskilled workers is the outcome of systems of education and production. But that subjective actional nature of humans cannot be ignored, and it is particularly significant when structures occasion opposing tendencies, which they always do. These opposing tendencies create crises, conflict, and synergies—which mediate subjectivity—and collectively transform social structures.

This conception of social structure is more in line with the notion of action and structure as braided entities. Structure constrains action, but is in turn changed by action. Structural racial discrimination as described by Bell (1987) in *And We Are Not Saved* illustrates how the legal structure negatively influenced educational experiences of African-American children, but the interaction of a discriminatory legal system with subjective senses of injustice promoted an activism that was responsible for changing the legal structure and subsequent progress in racial justice. So although structure is powerful and constraining, it is far from deterministic. It is a theoretical entity that conditions a range of actional options that may or may not be realized, and fosters an atmosphere of new arrangements and outcomes.

A major point here is that social structures are systemic. By that, I mean that they are whole entities, but composed of parts that form subsystems. These subsystems have their own characteristics, but are interwoven with one another and related to other hierarchical wholes. Structure is not a single dominating force with one generative nature. Accordingly, one social structure is implicated in another and cannot be fully separated from it. The class structure, for example, is part of an orbit of interacting systems—ethnicity, gender, economic conditions—each with its own complex set of principles and practices. The argument about which of these subsystems is the best explanatory candidate for some behavior is often confused, or at least more complex than expected.

For example, explaining a pattern of verbal violence (threats, intense lexicalizations, personal attacks) in a White household would require showing how subsystems interact to produce the surface action. A patriarchal ideology (MacKinnon, 1989) might interact with difficult economic conditions to produce a justification of the violence. Other structures are also involved. For instance, Hurlbert (1989) found that approval of violence was one of the five distinctive features of White southern culture. This approval would enter the verbal violence as an autonomous ideology. Each of these—patriarchy, economic conditions, cultural approval of violence—drive a set of discourse organizational properties that are also structuring. To reduce the pattern of violence to one dominant explanation, such as patriarchal ideology, would be possible but simplistic, even becoming dogma. A more considered analysis requires in-depth scrutiny of how action and structure are simultaneous and conjoint.

Finally, it is important to understand that structure exists as I have been describing because individuals make it exist. Structure, for all its effects, is still the result of individuals who process information, interpret, reify, and stubbornly define certain social phenomenon as real. Structure involves how the social facts of class or ethnicity are produced and reproduced, through the interdependent relationship of the micro and macro. Structural concepts emerge from a homodynamic environment where language users have converged on common meanings, expressions, and understandings. Structures are produced by people, so it is necessary to decipher this process more carefully.

I turn, then, briefly to Giddens and his ideas about structuration. Structuration captures the simultaneity of action and structure. It is an important move in the evolution of these issues for how society is organized because it is closer to a fusion of action and structure. One where neither side is privileged, but the process of how each is implicated in the other is more perceptible. But the goal is not yet another description of structuration, but to show how Giddens' model slights the important mediating role of interactional encounters.

GIDDENS, STRUCTURATION, AND CRITIQUE

The distinctions between action and structure have organized differences among social theorists for a long time (Alexander et al., 1987). The action-structure dualism has fixed many debates. Some suggest that external structural issues should be the foremost turf of social thinking. Others (e.g., ethnomethodologists) counter aggressively by claiming that you can never escape human beliefs, reasons, and motives, and structure is little more than a gloss of these things. Giddens (1984) denied the primacy of either structure or action, and shows how both are embedded in each other. What Giddens called *structuration* is a term deliberately designed to call attention to the ongoing and processual nature of structure, to the fact that structure is embedded in interaction and how these interactions thereby reproduce structure. Giddens altered one orthodoxy of structure by denying that it is external. Structure is not elsewhere. It is in individuals. It is instantiated in social life through languages, meanings, and communication patterns. Memory is what makes structures appear to be external, and these structures are foregrounded when they are actualized by language. This positions Giddens more toward the constructivist agency side of the argument, and is one weakness in his arguments.

Giddens (1981) used linguistics as an example when he illustrated structure by explaining that when someone speaks an utterance that utterance, is "understood by the listener in terms of an 'absent totality': that 'absent totality' is the rest of language which has to be known for the sentence to be either spoken or understood" (p. 170). This is an important point about structure because it preserves its nature as preexisting and constraining, but forces it more into the empirical world of communication (writing, speech acts, etc.).

Even a simple declarative sentence is part of a larger structure of grammar. The larger structure may or may not justify the realization of a certain surface structure. Giddens drew these ideas from Chomsky. Knowledge of structures is necessary for all pragmatic competence, also. Just as sentences draw on the "absent totality" of grammar, communicators draw on the taken-for-granted structures of their culture and society. The absent totality of "class" and "ethnicity" are a knowledge structure to draw on for various actional expressions. For instance, the structure of ethnicity always includes subsystems that organize offensive stereotypical discourse. If a speaker referred to a female as a "JAP," the speaker has engaged in what Giddens called a structurational performance. The speaker has drawn on and manipulated the structure of ethnic stereotypes to perform a communication action, namely, an insensitive generalization to describe someone's nature. This generalization is composed of numerous content-based subsystems in the culture, in this case pertaining to clothes, materialism, greed, and ostentation (Beck, 1992). The structure makes the action possible, but the action, in turn, influences the structure. This process is linguistic in nature because of the continuous interplay of presence and absence. The structure is absent until the utterance makes it present.

For Giddens, structure is more of a constructive process utilizing principles of recursivity and self-organization than it is an exterior fixed constraint. There is an additional important point from Giddens' concept of structure. The problem of creativity and social change concerns Giddens. It must be possible for cul-

tures and their structures to change; it must be possible for social action ema-
nating from one set of structures to create new structures. Structuration theory
retains the linguistic concept of recursivity. This is the notion that a few simple
rules can generate an infinite number of sentences. Structuration maintains the
centrality of the recursive interplay between structure and interaction. But
there remains an important addition to recursivity for Giddens with respect to
unintended consequences. Recursivity not only faithfully generates intended
consequences, but also unintended and unexpected consequences and conditions. This means that there is always the possibility for change. Social systems
and the various interconnections are so complex that sometimes the system
gets out of control, producing unintended effects. Thus, all communication is
constrained by structure, but also contributes something novel, something potentially transforming.Although structuration is a very complex process, and
there are few empirical studies that demonstrate how structuration works,
Poole and DeSanctis (1992) introduced a method for studying structuration.

Giddens' emphasis on the duality of structure and the process of
structuration captures structure as active and dynamic. There is no such thing
as structure apart from individual action. The strength of this duality of structure is that it preserves some inherited principals of structure—namely, its preexisting constraining forces in interaction—but always draws attention to the
rich details of interaction. But it is necessary to be even more explicit and formal
by forcing the question about how structures are drawn on and implicated in interaction. Enduring patterns of interaction are produced and reproduce structures by using rules and resources (Giddens, 1984) recursively drawn on to
generate social systems. Rules are procedures and "ways of doing things" that
are operable across situations. They are the mutual knowledge that interactants
have in situations. They are the shared intersections of that absent totality that
allows individuals to perform social action and make valid interpretations.

Mutual knowledge involves two primary rules. They are first signification
rules and second regulative rules. All interactants share signification rules,
which means that they have experience in common contexts and workable
methods for determining meanings and framing interpretations. Interesting
"communication problems" arise when there is little overlap in signification
rules. Regulative rules refer to how actions are to be performed and their moral
and normative force. Many rules are simple formulae that make the day-to-day
work of communication possible. Rules of language and coordinative pragmatic
procedures (e.g., turn taking, topicality, coherence) are of this nature.

Such signification and regulative rules manage the distributions of communicative options in an interaction. They oversee language choices and pragmatic strategies and thereby construct the rhythmic and coordinative patterns
of social interaction. But not everyone has equal access to this management system. The opportunity to manage communicative options and regulate the flow
of social interaction depends on the availability and use of resources. Resources

are the skills, and most importantly, power that one brings to a situation. Resources may be symbolic (language facility, education, relationships, image) or material (money, property, objects). Bourdieu's (1991) ideas about cultural capital (e.g., knowledge, technical skill, education) and symbolic capital (prestige, honor, position) are the best examples of resources that manage communication. And the single most important resource that emerges from having capital of various types and that is the predominant influence on social interactional systems is power. The constitution of meaning and social reality, the crafting of culture and society, is organized by power relations.

All formal institutions of society deploy dominational resources to control interactional contexts and constitute society. The court system (judges, lawyers, clients), enforcement system (police, victims), educational system (teachers, students, administrators) municipal systems (clerks, civil servants), as well as others of various size and complexity engage in a dynamic interplay of mutual knowledge and resources. When a police officer detains an individual, the officer has the authority to ask questions and compel answers by virtue of his position in a social organization, and the rights conferred on the police officer to symbolically (and physically if necessary) impose on the individual. Both the officer and the person have mutual knowledge about the types of questions and the expectations of the encounter. And each possesses resources in the form of overt legal sanctions and verbal skill.

More importantly, each must manipulate the unfolding discourse and finesse the process to their respective advantages. The police officer must begin by reproducing his social and power advantage over the detained individual, and he must do this against the resources of the individual, which are most typically legal and moral. He can accomplish this by physical restraint, including weapons, or by symbolic restraint. His linguistic capital includes various interrogatory devices, challenges, and required patterns of address (e.g., TITLE + LAST NAME such as "Officer Smith"; or, "What's your first name boy?" If the detained individual is female or African American, then the police officer can employ practical reasoning and racial or gender ideologies that become the dominant interpretive frame for the suspected offense and the individuals involved. These interpretive frames are not gender or racially neutral. Consequently, sexist or racist social structures are reproduced, and the power of these ideologies is enhanced, because they operate within the confines of a socially sanctioned interaction.

Signification and interpretive rules interpenetrate with resources and are constantly used to renegotiate power advantages. The ongoing dialogue between the officer and the individual is a constant battle over contested claims about meaning and outcomes. The rights and moral structures of a culture are primarily established through a legal system that is designed, ideally anyway, to offset unwarranted power relations and ensure some notion of "fairness." But because the ideal state of rights are never achieved, and there are ample opportunities to manipulate these structures, it is communication that becomes the foremost battleground where strategies are mobilized for various advantages. Because subordinates in relationships can direct the power dialectic to their advantage through mechanisms such as legal redress and symbolic capital, and can wrest control, superordinates are always trying to reproduce themselves. Hence the claim that laws are made consistent with controlling ideologies, taxes favor the wealthy, and aesthetic judgments correspond to upper class tastes.

This speaks to another point made by Giddens, which is the distinction between structures and systems. A system for Giddens is the set of relations and organized social practices in a collectivity. Systems are empirical. They are patterned, interdependent relationships that have instantiated social practices attached to them. Thus, there is a "legal system," or an "organizational system," and each has patterned articulations, including communication norms. Systems are not the same as structures; systems have surface features and exist in time and space. Structures are an absent totality and more theoretical in nature than empirical. Structures are used to make sense of systems, they are the stock of knowledge that individuals draw on to shape how they behave and understand things. Structures have cultural, political, and ideological content that provides a flesh for the skeletal framework of systems.

It is important to underscore that the process of structuring involves empirical and concrete instantiations of structures in interaction. This is an important theoretical contribution of Giddens, as well as Collins, that connects communication with structure. The tie between the moment of observable interaction embedded in a social system and the separate structural totality is maintained. The more traditional distinctions between action and structure have reorganized themselves.

Even though Giddens placed considerable emphasis on action over structure, he still fails to fully appreciate the role of the subjective individual and of various psychobiographical influences. Human interaction produces and reproduces structure, but it is also the site for the establishment of identities and personalities. Individuals are the emotional foundation of social life, and these emotions and subjective factors are registered in social encounters and thereby in structures. They become a resource used in the production of society. Goffman's discussions of embarrassment and deference notwithstanding, he too gave scant attention to these issues in his work on face-to-face encounters. Some of Turner's (1988) thoughts are concerned with these issues. He described the importance of individual security and stress in determining the success and maintenance of social encounters. And Scheff (1990) outlined an emotion–deference system in interactions where one participant's power is associated with emotional energy and the deferent person has his energies depleted. Interactants are very sensitive to gestures of respect and status in interaction, and these gestures are worked out in social encounters. Human interaction is a continuous dialogue of affirmation and denial of these gestures, which makes them socially produced and reproduced rather than simple intrapsychic properties.

The point here is that individuals deploy psychological skills such as dominance, deference, anxiety, and egocentricism to infect an interaction order to achieve a goal (such as identity maintenance). Giddens paid little attention to this, and Goffman did not emphasize enough the individual skill involved of the person who uses these. For example, a person who wants to create a sense of power and status can do so by role distancing (Goffman, 1967). As Goffman explained, role distancing is the ability to "stand apart" from an institutionalized role. It is the ability to recognize one's role and its obligations, and also separate yourself to either play another role or comment on your role. This means that roles were not rigid, but communicative, resources that could be managed. A teacher might distance him or herself from the role of "teacher" when dealing with a student's personal problems. An account of social skills is missing from the theoretical ideas of Giddens in that these things enter into the social encounters that produce and reproduce structure. Role distancing can be used skillfully or unskillfully, appropriately or inappropriately, with finesse or clumsily, depending on individuals and circumstances. These skills and individual subjective states can combine with social encounters to take precedence over system reproduction or the dominating constraints of structures. Surely the demands of systems and structures are insistent. But individual identity, uniqueness, ingenuity, and creativity sometimes take precedence.

In a sense, statements such as "we produce and reproduce society," or "action and agency are implicated in one another," or some other variant of these ideas are too indistinct. True, Giddens and others have written clearly about them, and they are well enough established social theory. But most interaction is routine system reproduction. This accounts for cultural stability and the possibility of meaning as discussed in chapter 3. But there are those activities that require more adjustment, talent, and facility with respect to identity and situational competence. In other words, the interaction order is more important than Giddens understood. Goffman's term *interaction order* is different from social orders, which are specific practices characteristic of an occasion. These occasions are composed of highly reproduced relations and practices. The interaction order is the set of concerns for the self and identity. It is the care that a communicator takes in presenting his or her social self and crafting an identity and meaning. An interaction order is present in all social settings.

Theoretical accounts like Giddens' that neglect the interaction order are underestimating its role in the structuration process. Foucault, Bourdieu, and Habermas are also quite deficient in this area because none of them paid particular attention to how individuals release their psychic qualities into social encounters. So what is this tie between individual agency and structure? What are the basic cognitive mechanisms that connect individuals to the structural totality? Habermas referred to a *lifeworld* and Bourdieu to a *habitus*. Each of these are generally related to the notion of an individual's unique motivations, perceptions, and dispositions. But other than inclusive terms like *lifeworld* and *habitus* are the social representations (SR) that predispose people to act in certain ways. Structures are not monoliths unfolding in an orderly manner. Social class, ethnic culture, and political ideologies influence habits and dispositions, but interactants also confront and creatively work through structural contradictions and tensions.

An example of one of these contradictions is the different conceptions of authority in democratic public institutions and private institutions. Harrison's (1994) study of democratic collective organizations and democratic employee-owned organizations illustrated how power, authority, and status were mediated by interaction patterns to serve the interests of the organization. Democratic collectives—characterized by ideologies of equality and participation—devolop richer face-to-face interactions that are more integrated into professional and social spheres. The structure of authority in these systems is relegated to the collective membership. Rights of expression produce an accepting atmosphere of discussion and conflict. These communication patterns, in turn, reproduce the structure of authority. To minimize status in democratic collectives jobs and the divisions of labor are not distinct, because status is most associated with expertise and knowledge. The employee-owned organizations capitalized on the ideologies of participation and equality, but mediate authority in a more hierarchical manner. The employees maintain status distinctions associated with work and organize themselves according to traditional bureaucracies. Information is shared only through formal reports and on a need-to-know basis. Thus, traditional authority is produced. Both types of organizations are produced by remaking what structures are already there. Employees take part in an interactional order embedded within organizations and use a "practical consciousness" to create individual, or even novel systems (Giddens, 1979).

Giddens made the distinction between "practical consciousness" and "discursive consciousness." Discursive consciousness is thought, intelligence, and information that can be put into words. It is reasonably well understood and talked about. Practical consciousness is knowledge and what people believe about circumstances but do not express discursively. They know what to do in certain situations, and know underlying rules, expectations, and requirements, but cannot necessarily put this knowledge into words. It is a tacit knowledge. Ethnomethodologists work to uncover and display this practical consciousness that language users have. The moods of communicators, their personality traits and psychobiographical predispositions, operate more at this tacit level of consciousness. These are not a practical consciousness in the strict sense of the term, because such practical consciousness is shared and routinized such that interactions are smooth and predictable. But emotions and subjective qualities do not produce smooth interactions. They introduce variability and unpredictable elements into an interaction. These play an important role in the extent to which interaction is purely routine and reproductive, or creative in resolving conflicts and altering structures and systems.

For example, the release of negative emotions into an interaction—for example, arguing, criticism, and personal attacks—could be the primary fuel of a communicative encounter where individual self-interest is more important than the accomplishment of routine social work that reproduces extant structures. One's ego, identity, or self-interest are at a premium and these psychic interiors are more important than routine social work. This flow of negative emotion can produce disharmony and dramatically alter the power relationship between people. And antagonistic, asymmetrical relationship can be significantly altered by the release of positive emotional energies. Family counseling, company picnics, and diversity training all facilitate smoothness and use positive emotions to alter interaction routines. By way of another example, Turner (1988) showed how people with low self-esteem alter situations according to their subjective states by working harder to maintain their sense of self. They place greater demands on others and destabilize situations. This psychic state operates at a more subterranean level closer to the unconsciousness than the conscious.

Duality of structure does not deal well with some of these more subtle intrapsychic strands in communication. It does not grapple directly with the fact that the consequences of social interactions are more multilayered and responsive to subjective qualities. Moreover, Giddens did not fully recognize the fragility and delicacy of these processes. They are always potentially productive or reproductive and can never be automatic or taken for granted. But when they are recognized and become more understood, they have tremendous transformational power. Change, creativity, and new social structures arise because meanings are achieved by the emergent outcomes of interaction contexts and routines, along with the subjective inputs of participants.

Finally, Giddens correctly criticized the distinction in social theory that insists on a separation between action and structure, but his "duality of structure" remains unsuitable. He, too, completely abandoned any form of objectivism and semantic reality and overemphasizes the micro side of the issue. He lost claims to characteristics of participants in social encounters and the extent to which they influence structures and systems. A better approach is to comingle features of contexts, interaction orders, and people to deal with questions about how they create social reality. The duality between the psychological and social world must not be drawn too sharply. The two are loosely coupled and traffic in a constant ebb and flow of separation and integration. Language is the key vehicle by which we move through this traffic, and language is not random, but materially related to people, contexts, and interaction orders. Language operates a micro–macro dialectic in a double generative capacity—to establish prototypes and macroforms and to be conditioned and altered by those forms. In order to work out these dynamics even further, I move to a description of genres as an analytic and ontological metaphor for the micro–macro dialectic. Communication necessarily entails penetration into generic forms (structures) and in turn, these generic forms construct speech (or writing) and the relationship between communicative agents.

GENRE AS A MICRO–MACRO METAPHOR

A genre is conceptually and empirically similar to a structure. A genre, like a structure, is an absent totality that refers to a distinctive category of things such as discourses (oral or written), behaviors, or experiences. Again, like a structure, genres are conventional but highly flexible. They are organizations of formal means that constitute frames of reference for communicative practice (Swales, 1990). Genres, too, have suffered from criticisms about being too global and fuzzy for detailed analysis. They are associated with literary theory, which suggests that they might not be too useful with respect to human interaction and sociological processes. Genres and social structures suffer the same fate of all classificatory interdependence schemes. There are always some empirical vestiges that just do not fit the structure or genre—or, which might be even more troublesome, these micro empirical phenomena fall into too many classifications.

But as we have seen, it is possible to treat this as a natural dialectic of integration and separation and use this duality to account for change, creativity, and revolution. Just as social structures are not mechanistic straight jackets, genres do not turn language into automated responses. Swales (1990) described four fields in which the concept of genre has been employed, and in each, the concept has been found useful and can serve as an analytic for the process of moving between the microworld of language and interaction and the macroworld of structures and genres. These four areas are folklore studies, literary studies, linguistics, and rhetoric. Analysis of how genres are conceived in each of these areas is beyond our concern here, except to say that they share certain commonalties. Whether the macrostructure (genre) is a myth or legend in folklore (Dundes, 1965), a literary genre such as a novel, essay, or roman à clef (Fowler, 1982), a speech event in linguistics such as a joke, lecture, or narrative (Hymes, 1974), or a rhetorical category such as a funeral oration, deliberative, or epideictic (Campbell & Jamieson, 1978), there are certain interesting issues with respect to genres as structuring devices.

Genres and social structures are both ideal types with texts and behaviors that deviate in various ways. But both have great classificatory power. They allow for interpretation and understanding as individual communicative acts are filed into explanatory systems. Macros also have forms that are established. In folklore fables, legends and proverbs have an independent integrity that withstands many social upheavals. These are always powerful indicators of deep cognitive realities that are preserved by discursive patterns. A phrase from Aesop's fable about the rabbit and hare ("The race is not always to the swiftest") maintains its cultural currency throughout the centuries. Lexical items designed to offend a member of a minority group emerge from the structure of prejudice against that group. Calling an African American "boy" as in utterances (7) to (10) in chapter 3 is deeply rooted in the unique structure of racism in America (see the next chapter).

Structures and genres also maintain functional relations in a culture. Certain groups survive and thrive, whereas others suffer. As I have been saying, structures are responsive to social values. They serve unique functions for a culture. The textual expressions of various forms are labeled according to what functions they serve for a community. Racist epithets maintain group asymmetries. So it is important to know more than a communicative routine. When an individual or government official engages in racism or some communicative behavior that reproduces racist structures in society, it is important to know more than just the communication. An understanding requires knowing why people engage in this sort of communication, why readers or listeners care about them, and why one type of interaction is routine over another. Functionally, the problem of a structure is not the text that it engenders, but why an individual or group finds the text meaningful and worthy of communication.

I have been consistently trying to find a place for change, conflict resolution, revolution, and creativity in the issues of the micro–macro dialectic of structure. The concept of genre from literary studies is a good place to look for similarities because literary critics are quite concerned with destabilizing genres in order to show how writers break conventional molds. In fact, changing generic structures is central to the creative arts. New literary genres are transformations in the same way that new communication forms (e.g., media) regenerate structures. Electronic media have altered the class structure from less vertical to more horizontal. Literary genres are a good analogy for the shifting, changing, and unstable nature of social structures. They show how actual works of literature do not often correspond well with genres, how stifling (structurally constraining) they can be, and their role in maintaining conservative values ("Shakespeare is the greatest"). Social structures in societies that allow for no change, growth, or development inevitably become restrictive and obsolete.

One of the interesting properties of both genres and social structures is that they have analytical and explanatory traction, even when they are modified or violated. In other words, there is creativity or change when a genre is violated, but the irony is that the original genre remains necessary for the creativity. I might creatively invoke a eulogy for humorous effect, but the eulogy genre, and the audience's knowledge of it, are necessary for the humor to work. But in linguistic science, as opposed to art, the goal is to maintain separation of genres in order to study and understand their special characteristics. I may deliver a eulogy for humorous effect, but it is not a "eulogy." The situational and social characteristics, including the goals of the discourse, are not the same. Offensive humor in the social realm works the same way. A "joke" about someone's racial characteristics relies on the structure of racism in the culture for its quality and effect. But the joke is taken seriously and considered inappropriate or offensive when the audience does not allow for the separation of genres from "racism" to "joke."

I do not intend any complete equation of genres to structures, except in a theoretical sense. Genres are classificatory communication systems that allow language users to interpret texts. But the text–genre dialectic is conceptually akin to the behavior–social structure dialectic. Both toggle back and forth to produce and reproduce texts and genres or behaviors and structures. Verbal and written texts realize genres, and in turn are constrained by them, in the same way that microhuman interactions realize and are constrained by structures.

Working Principles of Text and Genre (Structure)

Genres have been undertheorized in communication. They have been put to uses in ethnography and rhetoric, but scholars have generally assumed that they and their audiences know what genres are and how they work. We must be more precise in order to have a useful model to apply to the structures of ethnicity and class in the ensuing chapter. Moreover, we want to challenge the notion that structures are static and monolithic and place them within the sphere of human activity. But first I want to characterize the micro–macro dialectic I have been discussing. I proceed by making certain observations about the microworld (textual expression, interactions, language use) and the macroworld (structures and genres). I use the term *structure* because that is my primary interest as opposed to a literary or linguistic theory of genres. But as this section indicates, genres are an ontological metaphor for structures. They also provide useful clarifying examples. Following are four key principles, with commentary. This should be sufficiently adequate for others to use or modify, and to lead into more applied work in the remaining chapters.

Principle 1:   Communicative events are the fundamental microunits that form a generic class of events and constitute structures.

A communicative event is one in which language plays a significant role. This is not always easy to determine. Certainly a conversation, work meeting, lecture, or reading is very language dependent. But other activities (e.g., shopping, sporting events, driving) are less dependent on language, even though incidental talk is occurring. Moreover, the frequency of occurrence and importance attached to communicative events is also important. Communicative events can occur routinely every day (family talk, work talk, reading the paper) or very rarely (inaugural address, academic conference, medical exchange). And each can be considered anywhere from trivial to very important in a culture. All of these possibilities are marked for structure formation. Finally, a communicative event is more than just the observable text of speech or writing. It includes the individuals and their psychobiographies, and the environment along with historical and cultural issues. These are all necessary for a coherent (see chap. 3) conclusion about meaning.

Principle 2:   The purposes and effects of an aggregation of communicative events are the most important features that transform events into structure-producing behavior.

There are numerous qualities of communicative events that are important for the production of social structure, but their purposes are most central. Literary genres are more dependent on forms of communication for their classification, such as novels, poems, and essays. But social structures are more concerned with achieving something. People communicate for a reason, and these reasons inform the structural organization of a culture. It is true that purposes or the intentions of communications are not always easy to uncover. There are often cross purposes, multiple purposes, and mixed purposes. But these are accurate characterizations of the complexity of communication and the general difficulty of structure dialectic.

Some communicative purposes are very clear. A bold on- record racial epithet or a discriminatory legal system played out in the courts would be straightforwardly designed to produce or reproduce discriminatory structures. The structure of democracy constrains group meetings, parliamentary procedures, and voting rights. Other purposes are very indirect or opaque. There are subtle ethnic and class slurs whose immediate purpose is not apparent. There are unintended consequences of communication, such that communication is interpreted in some unanticipated way. Legal maneuvers and political discourse are often very indirect and designed for a purpose unknown to others. A newspaper, magazine, or television broadcast may have "informing the public" as one of its purposes, but they also "direct public opinion," "shape attitudes," "undermine credibility," and "serve corporate profit interests" among other things.

Privileging communicative purposes and effects recognizes the power of communication to shape the social world. But it also opens up the entire world of how communicative meanings are designed, framed, and interpreted. Linguistic and contextual cues that frame an utterance as "humor" or "irony" are all part of structure-producing communicative events because they very often determine purpose. It is well understood in genre theory that one must understand and be able to identify a genre in order to parody it. The nature and generic qualities of a romantic novel must be well understood by myself and my audience if I am going to successfully either parody the novel or alter it in some creative way. The same is true for social structures. Ethnic humor, for example, relies on the speaker and hearer's understanding of the identity structures of the particular group. Language users must competently disentangle the "real" from the "different."

Principle 3:   There is a varying specificity to the relation between particular microcommunicative events and the macrostructures they typify. Moreover, structural constraints will also be expressed with different levels of certainty.

In the micro–macro dialectic, there are occasionally highly specific properties of a communication that make it necessarily an instance of a macro structure in society. This is most clearly exemplified in the legal setting. A symbolic act can have the stipulated features that make it, for all intents and purposes, definitionally a part of a structure. Tate (1997), for example, described how educational research and legal structures contribute to existing belief systems and legitimate frameworks that result in educational inequities for people of color. In fact, Anderson (1994) explained quite explicitly how the structure of racism and the foundation of subordination of African Americans was formed in the constitution. The African-American–White binary opposition was the result of (a) counting African Americans as three fifths of a person, (b) delaying the outlaw of the slave trade, and (c) upholding fugitive slave laws. The Supreme Court ruling of 1896 in *Plessy v. Ferguson* that separate facilities for African Americans and Whites were constitutional encouraged all sorts of Jim Crow laws that made discrimination legal. So a communicative act between an African-American person and a White person in the wrong restaurant, workplace, rest room, or drinking fountain was specifically and identifiably related to the structure of racism. The simple act of human contact contained the defined properties of the structure.

But there remains great difficulty in identifying lists of defining characteristics of structures. Even scientific categories have little hope of identifying perfect defining features of categories. Jim Crow laws may have resulted in pretty explicit social definitions of discrimination and racism, but there is also the phenomenon that recognizes structural membership, even though defining characteristics are not explicit. The use of SAT scores to determine college admissions does not explicitly define a racist act and thereby reproduce the structure of racism, but there is a latent relationship. Even though the example of SAT scores is not directly communicative, it does serve an illustrative purpose because performance on the SAT exam is the result of a long and complex history of symbolic behavior. If these behavior and performance consequences are subject to inequalities, then so is the exam and its resultant, albeit unwitting, participation in racist structures.

It is the case, therefore, that what constitutes membership in a family of behaviors is based on something looser. It is based on relationships that share more abstract similarities and differences. Wittgenstein's (1963) well-known description of "games" as composed of family resemblances is pertinent here. Baseball, poker, track and field, tic-tac-toe, chess, crossword puzzles, a game of catch with a friend, jump rope, cat's cradle, ad infinitum, are all "games," even though there are considerable differences in nature and purpose among any of them. But they all have just enough features in common to be members of the same "family." Thus, "novels" are a complicated network of similarities and differences, where some have character types, structure, and language in common, but others do not. Wittgenstein's concept of family resemblances is not without weaknesses because its extended logic can lead to some pretty thin relationships (e.g., swimming pools and canteens are the same because they both hold water). But family resemblances remain workable because they are based on prototypes and how things cohere into structures.

These issues are quite pivotal to the action–structure and micro–macro dialectic. A microcommunication behavior, or an action, becomes representative of a structure or stimulates structuration because certain properties are privileged and cohere into a structural category according to psychological and cultural principles. Communicative goal, intent, and purpose are the most privileged property of social structures, but this certainly does not deny latent effects and unanticipated relationships, or relationships that are only later discovered. Moreover, all cultures vary their language use for the same social purpose. The patterns of interaction considered central to one kind of conversation, or narrative, or instructional form, differ from group to group (Heath, 1983) despite the fact that each considers its own microlanguage use to be the most sensible way to achieve a genre of communication and participate in a social structure.

Structures in society are never equal, and some are capable of exerting power and monopolizing access to avenues and activities of power. The upper classes, for example, have always taught their young the oral and written "genres of power" (Lemke, 1994; Martin, 1989), namely, scientific reports, theoretical reasoning, impassioned political oratory, journalistic quality, and academic argument. These are in contradistinction to personal reflections, diaries, and opinions for their own sake. These power genres provide entrance to the status occupations and the power positions that allow these structures and behaviors to be reproduced and maintained. Again, these forms of communication have tremendous differences in purpose and structure, but share a set of relationships based on how ideas and information are organized, sorted, and communicated.

Principle 4:   All structures exist only because there is some coherent justification for their existence, and this justification conditions the permitted interpretations of various communicative behaviors.

All cultures and communities have social structures that represent and realize their communities. These structures are recognized, even if at opaque levels of consciousness, by members of the community. Language users may be more or less skilled at this recognition, and more or less able to state these structurational relationships. And even with these structures changing and transforming, they still exert influence.

Some useful and interesting examples of this principle appear in the literature on turn-taking and the extent to which the speech exchange system exhibits different rights depending on location in a power structure. This has been demonstrated for numerous situations including, just to name a few, medical consultations (Heath, 1986), helpline calls (Watson, 1987), classrooms (Mehan, 1979), news interviews (Greatbatch, 1988), and police–citizen calls (Whalen & Zimmerman, 1987). Matoesian (1993),working with the societal structure of patriarchal power, showed how it is produced and reproduced in a courtroom in the dialogue between a victim and a district attorney. The following example is abbreviated from Matoesian (1993, p. 103). Some technical transcription has been eliminated for reading ease.

DA: how did'ju wind up in his automobile
V: I got in.
DA: Why?
V: Because he said we were goin to uh party at uh friend of is house
DA: But'chu didn't know his last name, where he worked, or where he was from, correct?
V: Yes
DA: You didn't know uh thing about him did'ju?
V: No

The theoretical issue here is that the macrostructure of patriarchy, and its power rationale, limits the possibilities and options of the microinteraction, in this case the exchange system. The structural distribution of options permits only questions by attorneys who also get to determine the trajectory of the questions. Moreover, the content and nature of the exchange is responsible for classifying the victim as a member of a certain class of people. The attorney's three-part list "But'chu didn't know his last name, where he worked, or where correct?" is a selectively designed device to invoke an inference about the victim. It directs the listeners to alter their interpretation about what happened by recategorizing the act as "consensual sex" and not a category called "rape." Moreover, the recategorizing the act into "consensual sex" makes it the normative standard of sexuality (the male normative standard) and thereby continues to reproduce the structure that informed the exchange in the first place.

Substantive structures filled with ideologies about power and dominance are implicated in the production of this interaction. They are interpretive resources for the communicative work of assigning blame and determining responsibility. Such exchanges as the preceding, including the three-part list utterance, occur in other contexts, but can be subject to other interpretive resources. Language users in a society or subculture can have a strong sense of the underlying logic of structures (District Attorneys, analysts) or weak one (victims, citizens), but understanding their nature is facilitative of communication.

In chapter 5, I focus on discussion, analysis, and illustration of ethnic structures. In chapter 6, I turn to the social class structure. These chapters are designed for more detailed and empirical demonstration of the micro–macro dialectic and the role of language and discourse processes in regulating that dialectic.

5

Ethnicity and Its Shadow

We hope that the world will not narrow into a neighborhood before it has broadened into a brotherhood.

—Lyndon Johnson

This chapter is about ethnicity and its structurational processes. It is not about any particular ethnic group—I draw from numerous examples and bits of data to illustrate points—but it does focus a little more on African Americans as an ethnic group, only because of the importance and interest in the issues and problems. I point out immediately that I understand the problem of labeling. The argument that the term *African American* fails to reflect differences in the community, and falsely implies similarity and consistency, is a reasonable one. Any single label will obscure class, religious, regional, and linguistic differences. But a continuous subdividing and classification of groups, attempting to account for any and all cutlural differences, is also impossible. It, too, can create rifts and false impressions of differences. Hecht, Collier, and Ribeau's (1993) empirical data suggest a reasonable amount of convergence on the term *African American,* and it is the term they use, so I adopt it also. I use the term only when borrowing it from previously reported research, or when it is appropriate for illustrative purposes.

I apply the principles discussed earlier of language used within some medium and social context to create meanings that structure society and individuals in the society, that are in turn constrained by those structures. This is one set of keys that might unlock some of the pathways to insight about ethnicity and culture. I make no pretenses about doing anything more than muddling my way to understanding, even if the results are incomplete understandings. Nevertheless, if we are to do anything more than gasp in exasperation at the problems of differences and diversity, we must make these efforts.

140

I profoundly disagree, and we must reject both intellectually and politically, positions such as those expressed by philosopher Richard Rorty. Rorty (1983) is representative of a position that we made reference to in chapter 1. It is a position based on extreme discursive construction, one that carries reality to extremes that cannot be sustained. It emerges from the Heideggarian notion of language where language strikes a difference; language makes distinctions that lead to incommensurate categorizations. If the world is discursively constructed (cf. Deetz, 1994; Shotter & Gergen, 1994), then the boundaries of discursive communities are impenetrable. Inquiry from this perspective has given up on the problems of meaning and the indeterminacies that people struggle with. It has given up on communication. So Rorty can argue that ethnic groups form their own discursive community, and their logic is only sensible inside their communication, that "conversation" between such communities (e.g., African American and White) is impossible. All we can do is stand apart from these communities and observe them at a distance, hopefully from a respectful distance.

One problem associated with Rorty's position is that he sees people locked inside a prison of language and society that creates a logic of action. And this logic of action is understood by and available only to those who are members of the community, those who have formed their subjective consciousness inside that community. It is sort of an extreme Whorfian view of language, one that has been roundly criticized (Rosch, 1975). Communication and meaning are not blocked by the boundaries of a cultural community, but are informed by them. Communication is an extensive system that carries its users into systems of meanings beyond the one currently in use. Navigating these new systems may be difficult and time consuming, but possible nonetheless. Language, by its very nature, has evolved such that it can map external worlds not of our own making.

SITUATING ETHNICITY

What is ethnicity? How do we frame it and situate it with respect to biological and social science issues? What are its unique communication aspects? The word has always referred to a group that lives together and shares language and social practices. The word has passed into everyday discourse and become important to the politics of group differentiation and power, as well as the personal identity matters that inform so much interaction. And there is certainly much confusion about the term *ethnicity* as it is so often confused with or related to nations, peoples, physical characteristics, and religion. The modern democracies of the United States and Europe are very culturally diverse and will become, perhaps, more so. Ethnicity is increasingly used as an analytic category for social and economic problems. Although we hear relatively little—at least little that is taken seriously—that uses race or genetics to explain group and political differences, it is not uncommon for "ethnicity" to be invoked as a legitimate reason, explanation, or cause of behavior. In its most extreme and distasteful form, ethnicity can become little more than the modern euphemism "racial hygiene."

This means that clarity about the concept of ethnicity is important. I do not devote too much time here to the nuances and complexities of defining ethnicity because I have other concerns, and such discussions are available elsewhere (cf. Jenkins, 1997; Anthias, 1992; Weber, 1978). But a few key issues with respect to defining ethnicity are important. First, people in an ethnic group must believe that their members share interests. These interests are typically political, but the pursuit of collective interests is most important. Ethnicity, like all social categories, is a dialectic that evolves in time. When individuals come together to pursue common goals they develop commonalties, and over time, increasingly see themselves as members of an ethnic group. The question of whether commonalties causes common interests, or common interests cause commonalties, is not simple. Moreover, because there are so many possible combinations of common interests, collective action, and group similarities, the specific types of ethnic groups cannot be easily determined.

Second, the people in an ethnic group must recognize their membership in the group. Usually they will have learned the ways of the group early and deeply, such that they know who belongs and who does not. Intelligibility of practices and patterns of communication is important. Members of an ethnic group must share a sense of behavior and meaning about communication rights and responsibilities and what constitutes "right" and "wrong." Group membership is an important resource in generating the coherence of messages discussed in chapter 2 that is necessary for meaning and communication. It is not, and should not, be easy to leave an ethnic group. One cannot easily declare that they are no longer a member. An Italian, for example, cannot simply declare him or herself no longer "Italian." It is possible to abandon the practices of the group and work to assimilate into another group, such as the case of many American Jews, but this assimilation process is long, slow, difficult, and there are always traces of the past manifested in the present.

Third, ethnic groups are keenly aware of who is "in" and who is "out." This is the essence of social identity that is based on the recognition of similarity and difference. To say that one has ethnic relations or is a member of an ethnic group implies a recognition of others who are not in the group, and forms a dialectic with groups members to define one another. Intergroup ethnic relations are perhaps the most important for defining and establishing ethnic identity. To understand a minority, it is imperative to study the majority.

The fourth quality, and most pertinent for my purposes, of ethnic groups is that they are communicatively constructed. Some very early sociology had ethnic groups existing as social facts à la Durkheim. But a better way to examine ethnic groups is as the outcome of social interaction. The emphasis is not on the supposed unvarying content of ethnic groups, or some final list of objective qualities of a group. The emphasis is on how ethnic identity is formed, confirmed, and transformed in the course of interaction amongst individuals and media. Differences and similarities are produced and reproduced by interaction with "others" that creates images of similarity and differences. This makes ethnicity a social identity that is both individual and collective, and places its generative nature in the communication process. I explore the implications of this in the following section, but here I emphasize that this interactional perspective means that internalized personal self-identification is composed of all sorts of social representations, and ethnicity is externalized into the culture at large through various language and social practices.

Distinctions Between Ethnicity and Culture

It is probably useful to make some additional distinctions between ethnicity and culture, and ethnicity and race, even though they are as Wolf (1994) stated, "perilous ideas." There is much confusion, overlap, disagreement, and controversy surrounding these terms, so they must be confronted directly if ethnicity is to be situated in such a way that we can recognize it. I have no pretenses about clarifying these distinctions once and for all. Others will disagree about certain points, but I think the issues here represent some of the best and most agreed on thinking. This allows us to situate ethnicity in a way that the general reader would recognize, but one that retains analytic traction.

Ethnicity is usually more associated with national origin and geographic location than is culture. It is also more often, but not necessarily, associated with phenotypic similarities. Ethnicity usually encloses culture. Culture is more the "symbolic construction of community" (Cohen, 1985). It is language, traditions, rituals, religion, customs, laws, cuisine, clothing, dance, and so forth. Culture is the content of an ethnic group. African Americans are an ethnic group that have cultural content. A culture or subculture is when a group of people share symbolically constructed commonalties, including some of the issues in ethnicity, but individuals might also be members of different ethnic groups. So, we refer to "gay" or "lesbian" culture, but you would not hear anyone use the phrase "gay or lesbian ethnic group."

But culture remains very important because it is what ethnic groups use to differentiate themselves from one another. Seemingly minor cultural preferences can take on serious and consequential meanings. Often, cultural content is the category most central to the definition of the relationship and boundaries between groups. Religion is an example of how a cultural category is used to define the nature of relations across group boundaries. The opposition between Catholics and Protestants in northern Ireland is the foundational category that defines "ethnicity" in this area of the world (Jenkins, 1997). But the concept of ethnicity, when used to distinguish Catholics and Protestants, is pretty anemic. The standard categories of culture are structured bodies of knowledge that say how the world is or ought to be, and these structured bodies can end up defining ethnicity. Moreover, these categories can always be reduced to something else. Religion may be a distinguishing characteristic in Northern Ireland, but politics and economics have more to do with the actual conflict.

Sometimes cultural content, such as religion, can be completely confused with ethnicity. Judaism is a good example. Judaism is a religious cultural category and not an ethnic group, although, as in the case of northern Ireland, the two are often confused, and it is certainly true that Jews have similarities of geography and national origin. But as a religion, Judaism is concerned with doctrinal, ceremonial, and cosmological concerns that make up an ideological system. These ideological systems are fundamentally symbolic in nature and therefore cultural. Cultural content is easier to adopt as your own. Anyone can become a member of a religious group and adopt the group's ideology, dress, and cuisine, but declaring yourself no longer a member of an ethnic group is difficult indeed. We must underscore, however, that in the everyday world, many cultural activities are essentially ethnically enclosed. Religion and family organization are cultural categories, but almost completely circumscribed by ethnicity because of historical and regional patterns. So, for example, it is certainly possible to be African American and Jewish, but very rare.

Culture and social structure are in a state of constant structuration, for it is the structures of society that influence group interactions; and, conversely, microcultural practices are responsible for structural change and modification. To illustrate the first part of this point, we need only think of adult organizations in U.S. life (e.g., community theatre, book clubs, political meetings) in which men and women come together, and how unthinkable this would be in a traditional Moslem society. These activities are cultural characteristics that are related to the ideological structures of the society. Changing these affiliational practices is one way of changing the ideological structure. The second part is easily illustrated by reference to "education" as a cultural value. The United States has long had a ideological structure that posed African Americans and Whites in binary opposition (the inferiority paradigm) and then constructed Whites as brighter and more deserving and African Americans as simple and less deserving. This has justified oppressive social policies (Tate, 1997), including the specific nature of education available to these groups (Herrnstein & Murray, 1994; Jensen, 1969).

The concept of a *subculture* is equally important because it represents a nexus of influences that is more phenomenologically central to the individual. We hear phrases like "middle-class culture," "gay culture," "rural culture," "working-class culture," "educational culture," "the culture of the athlete," "immigrant culture," ad infinitum. These are usually convenient semantic stopping points, but the concept "subculture" is useful and requires more rigor. A subculture is a division of the larger culture that is composed of recognizable symbolic constructions (e.g., religion, education, class status, regional identification, rituals) that are *functionally* integrated and have a strong impact on the individual. Subcultures are more organized, their members have more daily contact with one another, and their impact is stronger. Subcultures are formed by interweaving cultural factors, but the cultural factors are transformed by this interweaving, making them different as they interact with different combinations of cultural factors. In other words, being a middle-class professor is not the same thing as being a middle-class insurance salesman; being an upper class Jew is not the same thing as being an upper class Protestant; being a gay professional is not the same thing as being a gay unskilled worker.

The concept of subcultures stops us from talking about broad categories like "Southerners" or "African Americans" and directs us to more cohesive systems of interaction. It also animates more interesting questions about subculture access to power, the psychobiographical consequences of various subcultures, how more common elements of a national culture are manifest in subcultures, and the communication patterns and correlates of the subculture. The focus is more on interaction and behavioral similarities, than of "peoplehood" and historical heritage.

Distinctions Between Race and Culture

A distinction between race and ethnicity or race and culture continues to be a difficult struggle. There is a commonsense reality about the significance of race, and there are many folk theories of race that remain important to understand. And even social scientists who strive for the most objectivity and rigor do not agree about the nature and significance of race. Some (e.g., van den Berghe, 1986) claim it is a legitimate genetic foundation for ethnicity and promotes the advantages of group identity. Others (e.g., Banton, 1987) argue that "race" is purely socially constructed; that is, race is an imposed social category based on confusion about phenotypical characteristics and has little scientific standing. My intention is not to rehearse these theories, but to suggest that the problems of race and ethnicity are almost ignored in communication, and claiming that race and ethnicity are "socially constructed" does not justify our neglect of the issues. Race may be a sloppy scientific concept, but it is certainly a fundamental classificatory concept with substantial historical importance.

When *race* is used in everyday communication, it refers to phenotypical differences. That is, physical differences in bone structure, skin color, hair, and even invisible differences such as cranial measures. But this begs the question of the differences between phenotype and *race*. Are they the same thing? In a word, they are not. No one would deny the rich array of phenotypical differences among individuals, but the concept of *race* is a social categorization, not biology. Race is a second-order abstraction created by cultures to organize and classify groups of individuals. And these organizational and classificatory schemes are subject to historical, territorial, and social forces. Race, as it is used in everyday conversation, is an ethnic marker. We do not want to deny either race or phenotype, but they are different orders of the same thing: one is material and the result of genetic endowment; the other uses these things for cultural organization.

Ethnicity is a more important concept than race because it is a first-order social identity that begins very young, and is maintained as a primary personal identity. One may invoke phenotypical differences to make ethnic differentiations, but these differences are primarily in the service of ethnic identity as described earlier in this chapter. The differences between race and ethnicity are a matter of emphasis. Ethnicity is about inclusion. It is about believing and recognizing your membership in a group with common national origins. True, race is sometimes used as a dimension of inclusion, but it is more of a way to organize the world. Race is more a simple categorization based on assumed phenotypic similarities. Whenever someone uses race to pose a structured body of knowledge about the social world and groups, they have then simply slipped into the social groupings and identity that come with ethnicity, and using phenotypic characteristics to determine inclusion and exclusion. This is when race becomes this true second-order category that is an abstraction from ethnicity. Ethnicity is a central and ubiquitous social phenomenon; race is not. There is no shortage of ethnic parades and festivals all encompassing prideful differences in names, foods, accents, and communication patterns. Phenotype contains no such things.

Finally, even phenotypic differences are dissolving as reliable indicators of anything but physical differences. The National Association for the Advancement of Colored People estimates that 70% of those who describe themselves as African American are of mixed racial heritage. Martin Luther King had an Irish grandmother and some Indian ancestry. Some racial categories have grouped native Hawaiians with Asians, others do not. American Indians in the western part of the United States can be categorized with native Alaskans, but often argue successfully for important differences. Race is not a fixed and clearly definable scientific category.

How, then, does one communicate ethnically? What are the peculiar cognitive and linguistic features of ethnic communication, and how do these form a microreality that is in dialectic relationship with the macrostructure? Taking up the discussion so far, ethnicity is a set of concepts and communication patterns acquired in mutual interaction with others. Ethnic groups are symbolized, and individuals identify as members of them, by engaging in specific expressive patterns that are acquired in communicative interaction. The following sections address the details of how this works. I explore how individual language users acquire ethnic knowledge by selecting and modifying messages that create a "shared perspective, one in which the gap between the individual and his or her interactional partners is narrowed."

THE ORGANIZATION OF ETHNIC REALITY

One of the first microcommunication problems to approach is how conceptual reality is organized for an ethnic group. How understanding what is said uses extralinguistic knowledge and personal experience to acquire and organize knowledge into a cognitive system. I begin by drawing on some epistemological issues and a distinction made by Kreckel (1981) between "knowledge" and "concept formation." Concept formation is private and highly specific to the material conditions of group life. It is more group subjective. Knowledge is experience that has become publicly communicable. Knowledge has been established by regular contact with others that leads to predictable assumptions and conclusions about the world. Individuals acquire concepts by the reciprocal interaction of symbolic representations and environmental events. Acquiring additional concepts adds to one's cognitive and social repertoire and increases understanding about the environment. Moreover, because these concepts are based on past experience and the assimilation of new knowledge, they can change. Because no two individuals will interact in the world in exactly the same way, no two individuals will be exactly the same. But this does not leave us in an impossible situation, which excludes communication, but only places certain limitations and constraints on communication (see coherentism in chap. 3).

So, the likelihood of a collection of people having a similar concept of "how to communicate," "the 'sense' of certain word meanings," or "appropriate attitudes" is high if they live near each other, communicate on a regular basis, share common goals, and so forth. It is only sensible to expect a White (European descent) upper middle-class suburbanite to have different concepts for these things than a poor urban African American. And we can conclude that the more mutual interaction people have had in the past, the more opportunities for acquiring similar concepts with respect to specific subject matter and communicative behaviors. An example is helpful here. Any number of scholars (e.g., Hecht Collier, & Ribeau, 1993; Kochman, 1990a) have made reference to African-American emotional intensity and more vigorous and expressive communication style. European-descent Whites tend to be more restrained and keep emotional intensity in check. Each of these groups have conceptual convergence within their group boundaries about communication. This convergence is dependent on socialization experiences emerging from mutual interactions, but later on, retrospectively appropriating that mutual interaction and incorporating the appropriation into contexts. African Americans "share" a perspective with one another, as do Whites. And this shared perspective also includes a desire to participate in future interactions. This is a "prospective" stance that is crucial to the active part that members of each group play in both converting individual experience into shared knowledge, and continuing to define ethnic group boundaries.

When people live near each other and are socialized under similar conditions of language, culture, subculture, and region, they have conceptual similarities even if they do not communicate. There is, therefore, less need for interaction for achieving interpersonal convergence and a sense of group identity. Turning personal knowledge and information into shared knowledge requires communication, and the greater disparity in shared knowledge (e.g., a Tibetan farmer and an English literature professor, or a poor inner-city African American and a suburban White), the more complex, time consuming, and difficult will be the mutual interaction necessary for convergence.

Interaction is so central to the formation of ethnic identity, and to the relationship between groups, for many reasons, but the overdetermined nature of communication is one of the most important reasons. Overdetermination means that communication is repetitive, and as a speaker or writer continues, he or she discharges their attitudes, beliefs, likes, and dislikes repeatedly. Communication rarely happens just once. The hearer of these messages can check and re-check his interpretations and understandings. Interactants usually make necessary adjustments toward convergence. Moreover, there is considerable support for the linguistic and psychological tendencies of convergence and accommodation that results from extended interaction (e.g., Giles, Mulac, Bradac, & Johnson, 1987). Over time, we ignore differences and work toward a better communicative fit.

In an earlier study (Ellis, 1992b), I discussed the codes that develop from this convergent interaction, and one of them is termed the *pragmatic code.* There is an important difference between knowledge that is fundamentally acquired in mutual interaction and knowledge that is acquired individually and separately. Knowledge acquired individually, such as "syntactic code" (Ellis 1992b) is not the result of sharing the perspective of another person and continually closing the gap between oneself and another. The pragmatic code makes for shared knowledge rather than knowledge that two people might have "in common." The shared knowledge of a collection of people is pragmatic in that it results in tacit understandings of objects, people, and their relationships. Knowledge of others is presupposed; there is a social stock of knowledge acquired in concrete relations. This communication principle forms the basis of how the ethnic structure in a society is organized. The dialectic between the individual and society and how this social stock enters the subjective world of knowledge and vice versa is the essence of the micro–macro dialectic that we have been discussing.

Verbal interaction is the most important reality-maintenance vehicle. And this reality is implicit, not explicit. It is made up of a background of taken-for-granted information that is constantly being modified by dropping and adding, and strengthening and weakening various concepts. Socially proxemic members of a group continually interact and make a place for themselves in the world of other people. They use the same language to objectify their world and the world of others. Members of an ethnic group engage in within- group and between-group interaction. They acquire their identity and contribute to the structural organization of ethnicity in the larger culture by learning concepts acquired in mutual within-group interaction that carry symbolic particularized group meanings. One more version and consequence of how this ethnic reality is organized is presented in the following section. It makes even more specific the relationship between a concept and a system of concepts. Organized and coherent systems of concepts are codes and subcodes.

Ethnic Codes and Subcodes

A language user's sense of knowledge and reality are composed of concepts. This knowledge is shared and thus communicable; it has been established in contact with others and can be used reliably. It is composed of "sense" meanings that are pragmatic and rooted in the empirical world. When one acquires a concept, they increase the cognitive structures available to them, and improve comprehension available to them regarding the concept. They also increase their affective attachment or detachment to certain concepts. Codes are essentially systems of concepts. More precisely (see Ellis, 1992a, 1992b), a code is a predisposition to produce and interpret language and communication in a particular way. It is a collection of concepts organized according to pragmatic principles including context, appropriateness, feasibility, genres, and other situational features. Codes are particularly sensitive to language and are essentially responsible for regulating the flow of meaning in an interaction. Subcodes occur when the interactional signs that mark social categories are extremely responsive to group experiences. So the highly specialized interaction among African Americans—commonly referred to as Black English or Ebonics—is a subcode where only language users with certain group experiences can mobilize these features of language and communication.

The line separating a code from a subcode cannot be drawn explicitly. But a code reflects a broader array of history with a language and its users, whereas subcodes are more group specific. A code is more like a system of systems that a speaker or writer develops as a member of the larger society. Its principles and properties are more widely available in the culture, such as when minority ethnic groups communicate with the larger majority culture. But the communication and "reality" of groups such as criminals, working-class boys, corporate cultures, or various ethnic groups is more subcode specific. These groups express and interpret a more "subjective" reality.

As I said previously, subcodes and subcultures are more important than codes or cultures. Subcodes are language and conceptual elements that acquire their strength and meaning by the history of a social group and the functions to which language is subject. Subcodes reflect value systems and group-specific attitudes, values, and communicative conventions. Ethnic subcodes are typically rich in linguistic and cognitive principles that are highly differentiated with respect to the group's primary subjective reality. This reality is not merely expressed, but is constructed and maintained. For example, Kochman (1981) and Edwards and Seinkewicz (1990), explained how "uniqueness" is valued in African-American culture, a value that generates symbols and various demonstrations of individuality that indicate commonalty in interactions with others. So, all communication relationships have methods of greeting, but developing one's own style of hand slapping or verbally recognizing another generates both individuality (uniqueness) and community.

Subcodes carry very strong senses of rights and responsibilities. One must be a genuine member of an ethnic group and earn the right to adopt group-specific communication patterns. African Americans are encouraged from youth to be "real" and to express that realness in a unique way (White & Parham, 1990). A sense of flair, expressiveness, and individuality signals uniqueness and group membership at the same time. These communication patterns that are forged in tight ethnic enclaves take on the status of being truly representative of an ethnic group. To the extent that these interactions are devalued or seen as low status by the larger culture (European White culture) is the extent to which they contribute to the structure of racism. As Henry Louis Gates (1992) explained, what was troubling about the *Cosby* show was the same thing that was troubling about *Amos 'n' Andy*: It was not the representation, but the role that it played in the culture and their contribution to the structure of racism. The positive—and for the time statistically unlikely—upper middle-class image of *Cosby* made the offensive images of *Amos 'n' Andy* more credible. The analogy holds for African-American communication conventions. They contribute to the structuring of a stereotype—unjust as it is.

There is an additional distinction in subcodes made by Kreckel (1981) that is useful for understanding the organization of ethnic reality. This is the distinction between homodynamic subcodes and heterodynamic subcodes. Homodynamic ethnic subcodes are developed in mutual interaction. They are based on heavily shared knowledge and regular direct experience with others of the same group. "Homo" underscores that the acquisition of cognitive schemes and communication patterns has occurred under similar conditions for all interactants. It typically implies much face-to-face interaction because that is the communicative condition where different individuals share the most context information. Heterodynamic subcodes occur when language users acquire features of the subcode under different conditions and less intense regular group interaction. "Hetero" implies that two or more people may have knowledge in "common," but it has not been acquired under the same conditions and it is not shared in exactly the same way.

The research example that best illustrates the consequences of codes acquired homodynamically versus heterodynamically is Garfinkel's (1967) famous case of Agnes. Agnes had undergone a sex change operation from male to female and was confronted with the task of "living as a female." Agnes began to construct a female identity by reading and utilizing public media sources with hints and observations about female language, behavior, and attitudes. But her attempts to "pass" as a female were unsuccessful. Her female subcode was being acquired heterodynamically; that is, through the use of common information, but not shared information. Only when Agnes immersed herself in communication with other females, only when she shared an interactional identity with other women and acquired her cognitive and linguistic representations and skills in mutual interaction (homodynamically), did she pass as a female.

Ethnic groups that are highly circumscribed by neighborhoods and share numerous spatial and communicative interactions develop their ethnic subcode homodynamically. These conditions promote a strong sense of group identity where many verbal, noverbal, and attitudinal characteristics are shared. Ethnic neighborhoods maintain loyalties and sentiments and socialize new generations. The neighborhood houses businesses and institutions that cater to ethnic interests. Under these conditions, African Americans retain their sense of cultural specialty and psycholinguistic distinctiveness. There are many areas of cultural convergence that make for optimal communication. But there are also marginal areas of homodynamic subcodes that make communication across the margins possible, but difficult. This is the location of interethnic and intercultural communication. As members of a group become more assimilated and have more in common with other groups or a larger culture, they lose some of their ethnic distinctiveness. This is the case with American Jews and increasingly with African Americans as they progress into the middle and upper classes.

But the ethnic neighborhood is changing and, more interestingly, the impact of the neighborhood is diminishing with respect to the formulation of ethnic identity (Alba, 1990). New structures of media and information technology are the primary reason for the diminishing impact of neighborhoods. I discussed in chapter 2 how modern media have altered and reorganized the boundries between the public and private. Ethnic and cultural communication, like political communication, is not so bound to a common locale. But this does not necessarily lessen the frequency and intensity of ethnic messages. Members of groups develop mediated quasirelationships with others and still share ethnic identity although more heterodynamically.

A MICRO–MACRO DIALECTIC FOR ETHNICITY

In order to provide a unified micro–macro framework for ethnicity, we must try to demonstrate how the structuration process works. This involves various orders of structure including microcommunication phenomenon and macroinstitutional and social phenomena. I broached much of the theory pertaining to structuration in the last chapter, but here I examine more closely how different phenomenological orders of reality structure one another, and I examine this with respect to "ethnicity" as a societal structure. This is a question of how society is constituted. And the key to understanding how ethnic society is constituted lay in the shifting relations between the production and reproduction (Giddens, 1984) of social life. All aspects of human social life are produced by human language users, but this social life becomes "ordered" and recognizable when language users repeatedly reproduce actions and sequences. So the question becomes, "How is ethnic identity produced and reproduced?" And, "What are the main conditions relevant to the production of ethnic structure?" The answers to these questions are of the following kind: The communication messages of social actors; the patterning and reality of these messages; and the institutional forms that permit such communication.

The following sections outline a useful set of analytic concepts by which structures such as ethnicity in a society can be considered. Ethnicity is a discursive categorization. That is, ethnicity is a category to which one is assigned on the basis of various phenotypical, group, and cultural tokens that have pragmatic meaning. Meanings for these tokens have achieved some intersubjectivity and become interpretive frames by which we make sense of things. Borrowing bits and pieces from Goffman and Giddens, we can talk about three conditions of social arrangement. These can appear clunky and are not always the best terminology, but they are a workable analytic for thinking about the various weaves in the fabric of society, and how these weaves are structured. These are based on ideas discussed in chapter 4, but linked more closely to ethnicity.

The Individual Agent. This is the world of the connected person, the one who lives in a system of messages that have consequences. It is the world of the individual psychobiography and sociocognitive representations. This level of social arrangement has a large amount of literature dedicated to how it is constituted, but we will leave that for another time. What is more important for the micro–macro dialectic is that language users rationalize their action. This means that they maintain a continuing understanding of what they are doing. If you stopped and asked any individual to explain his or her behavior, he or she would have no trouble doing so. These, of course, would not be the questions, or the answers, of social scientists or philosophers. The layperson's explanations are part of selfhood. They are part of Mead's "me," fashioned from the "generalized other," which is the voice of the community. This selfhood is formed significantly in certain ethnic communities and less so in others. This is also Bourdieu's (1991) *habitus,* or the set of dispositions that incline one to act in a certain way. These dispositions generate perceptions, attitudes, and orientations that are taken for granted and not under the conscious control of any rule or principle.

Giddens (1984) referred to this rationalization of social action as stimulated by "practical consciousness," and it is fundamental to the process of structuring individuals and societies. The individual's practical consciousness is a sense of what is actually done, what is almost automatic and taken for granted because of its strong claim on reality. Practical consciousness can be compared to Goffman's (1959) "backstage talk," such that it is comprised of interactions that are hidden. It is a place where information can be controlled and can limit the power of others. Thus, when an African American shares an insight, behavior, or attitude, and describes it as a "black thing," the person is taking an element of backstage practical consciousness and moving it forward. This both maintains and alters the group's identity.

The development of the individual and the habitus begins fundamentally with primary socialization. This is the basic relationship between self and others or the Meadian "looking glass." We see ourselves and the world through our interactions with others and this dialectic continues to establish a basic selfhood. It is especially potent during the early developmental stages of life. Ethnicity, or ethnic identity, is one of the most salient features of socialization and it is easy to imagine its impact. A child and young adult will develop a cognitive orientation to the world based on ethnic classifications and components. An individual learns that he or she is a member of a category (ethnic group), and this carries with it a sense of worth, esteem, power, and expectations of behavior. And what it means not to be a member of another group can be highly activated when racial categorization is a primary organizing principal of social situations and institutions.

Although most communication is intentional and rationalized, there are also unintentional consequences that feed back into the social structure. When a member of an ethnic group uses, for example, nonstandard and low-status grammar, he or she makes a contribution to the reproduction of a social structure that stigmatizes certain groups. The person using language may be simply trying to communicate, or even feel a sense of linguistic pride, but a negative attitude is an unintended consequence that reverberates throughout the social system and causes an aggregate effect.

Consequences of individual agency are important, especially so in interethnic communication. Consider the following structuring effect. An African-American man in a strange neighborhood is looking for a house address. A White homeowner hears a noise outside and believes someone is breaking into his house. He sees the African-American man outside and immediately gets a gun and calls the police. The police come and arrest the African-American man as a prowler. The man later files a suit claiming violation of civil rights. The African-American community is outraged and engages in protests that result in violence. Were these protests caused by a man looking for an address? No one intended protests, or police involvement, or violence, but these results are from what people "do," not from what they "intend." Even the White homeowner might have been "genuinely" concerned about a prowler, not motivated by racism, and certainly never intended legal action and protests. There are many complexities here, but it remains true that many small events and decisions trigger consequences far removed in time and space. True, consequences far away in time and space from their triggers are less intentional and pose a more tenuous relationship, but still figure into patterns of social conduct and structural configurations.

There is another structuring manifestation that differs somewhat from the one just mentioned. Rather than a structuring resulting from a long string of related events, it is possible to form a consequence that results from a multitude of unrelated events. Imagine a neighborhood made up of old businesses and aging families that used to work in these businesses. Over a period of a few years, the businesses begin to close and the families move away or slowly die off. The prices for housing and property decline and lower income minority groups move in. This results in a pattern of segregation not intended, but an economic outcome nonetheless. A whole series of small decisions and behaviors, each rational and sensible to the individuals, results in an unintended outcome that produces and reproduces a particular structure of ethnicity in a culture, namely segregated inner-city neighborhoods. And these unintended consequences feed back on individuals to further influence conditions of action.

The Interactional Realm. This is the communicative world where various individual and public selves meet and interact. Individual identities are "presented" and "performed" and become interlocked with others. These individual identities are not always wholistic, but parceled out in situations as strategically necessary. Weick (1979) explained how individuals partially include selected messages and behaviors from the repertoire at the individual level. The various behaviors that an individual is capable of are dispersed among individuals and situations, each one revealing shares of the self. An individual might be aggressive in one situation and submissive in another. Individuals can interact as friends, colleagues, sons, parents, members of an ethnic group, and so on. But any interaction is only a partial revealing of the self.

A sense of the "other" is a crucial part of the interactional realm. This directs our attention to the coordination, or lack thereof, between how we see ourselves and how others see us, and the match between our self-image and public image. These are very complex processes that can include much confusion and purposeful manipulation and prevarication. Moreover, there is always the epistemology problem of what we know about others and how we know it. But it remains impossible to completely escape who we are. There is always a connection between individuals and others that reveals selfhood, and in, turn forces an adjustment in the construction of identity.

Aside from the foundation of individual natures, the interactional realm is the arena where social structures such as ethnicity are constructed. This interactional arena includes qualities of discourse discussed in chapter 3 as well as a grammar of context. Participants in a culture interlock their communicative behaviors by knowing rules of interaction that include such things a select-ing vocabulary items designed for particular interpretations. And just as individuals use social representations and interpretive schemes to make mean-ing, they also employ rules for context construction. This grammar includes components such as scene, participants, setting, purpose, message form, se-quences, and the like (cf. Brown & Yule, 1983; Watson & Seiler, 1992).

Conversation analysis is a major microfocus on the structuring effects of the interactional realm. It is concerned with the machinery of the sequential orga-nization of talk exchanges that comprise the essence of interaction. Conversa-tion analysis is an analytical scheme for understanding and appreciating participants' use and understanding of what is being said and accomplished in the interaction. The problem is that so much conversation analysis ignores so-cial theory in its efforts to treat talk as autonomously organized.

Various interactional patterns that describe African-American–White in-teractions can serve as a clarifying example. Everything connected to the speak-ers in the interactional realm is a potential source of information. But not all information is of equal status or salience. Individuals monitor verbal and non-verbal behaviors, personal attributes (hair, clothes) of others, and the physical and social environment. What is distinguishing about this monitoring is the im-pact of various sources of information on the monitoring capacity of the individ-uals. The less people know about each other, the more they select and attend to various sources of information. People who know each other well (good friends, family members) attend mostly to verbal and nonverbal behavior and use these to index interpretive frames for meaning. The interesting and important ques-tion, of course, is how and why interactants take up some information and not others. What do they include and what do they omit?

African Americans and Whites of European descent in the United States both work to align their self-image with their public image. But they take up dif-ferent information and have different interaction goals that account for a sense of ethnic differences in communication, at best, and racism, at worst. Kochman (1990b) explained how verbal and nonverbal restraint are valued in White cul-ture. An index of tact, efficiency, and even a desirable class identification is as-sociated with a verbal style that is economic and minimalist. Moreover, in White culture, a sense of dramatic self-expression and exaggeration are more likely to emerge in private or in particularly selected contexts. But many authors (e.g., Abrahams, 1976; Hecht, Collier, & Ribeau, 1993; Kochman, 1990a, 1990b; White & Parham, 1990) documented the sense of liveliness, emotional vitality, and self-promotion that characterizes much African-American inter-action. This expressiveness has been explained as a legacy of the slave experi-ence and the adaptation of African culture to America (cf. Rose, 1982/1983).

But these verbal and nonverbal differences have their origins in very differ-ent experiences. In Kreckel's (1981) language described previously, they are a heterodynamic subcode acquired under quite different conditions of life and on the basis of little interaction between these groups. African Americans and Whites have this information in common, but they do not "share" knowledge of how to interact with others and the values of different styles. Each group attends to these verbal and nonverbal information channels in different ways, and this promotes negative evaluations of the other. African Americans and Whites have an element of choice in their identity, but within limits; the responses of others play an important role in the validation or invalidation of identity. There is greater distance and tension between the groups when they have little and infrequent contact. As the amount of contact between African Americans and Whites increases, then the decision to choose particular language and behaviors is based more on mutually acquired values and goals. Interaction is necessary in order to pursue daily personal, social, and economic goals. In the process, there is a gradual convergence of aspirations, behaviors, and self- and public images.

Cultural differences and heterodynamism of the sort described previously have serious cumulative effects if left unchallenged. The group-specific attitudes and values of these subcodes of communication styles construct a reality that becomes internalized. This reality carries labels, and we know quite well from both communication theory and the sociology of deviance that labels establish identities and categorize individuals and groups. As a consequence of this interactional realm, individuals and groups establish subcodes that are dialectically altered in the regular rhythm of internal and external definition that occurs within a communicative encounter. The reality created by terminology also carries a distribution of power and authority that will always work to the disadvantage of a minority group.

The cumulative outcome of labeling and stigmatizing the language and interaction of an ethnic group (e.g., African-American "style"), if unchallenged by any countervailing forces (e.g., education, affirmative action), is the development of emotional and cultural niches. The niches create ceilings that can have detrimental effects in numerous institutional orders such as occupation and economic mobility. We can see, then, how microprocesses interact with and produce the macrostructures. We began with a Goffmanesque interactional realm that, among other things, recognized the development of subcodes and the cognitive processes of information selection and interpretation in interaction. These interpretations lead to ethnic labels and a subsequent internal and external "reality" that becomes constitutive of discrimination and various social limitations. At this point, we have connected microinteractions to the next level of social arrangement, which is institutional order.

Institutional Order. This is the level of routine, patterned, and quasi-systematic interactions that compose the rules for accomplishing things. All cultures have patterns of social practices that "institutionalize" attitudes and values. And all groups in cultures are institutions; there are ways to identify a person as a member of group by his or her social practices.

What is interesting to us here is how ethnic identity becomes institutional-ized. This forces an emphasis on a collective definition of distinctiveness de-fined discursively by such things as communication patterns, groups organizations, forms of discourse, power, moral orders, ideology, and socializa-tion. The boundaries of ethnic distinctiveness—and one's location with respect to them—must be recognizable because ethnic identity is "validated" by others. And, of course, it would make little sense to talk about ethnic identity if this were not possible.

Any society is composed of numerous institutions made up of both contexts and processes, and ranging from the most formal (e.g., organized public admin-istration) to the least formal (e.g., everyday interactions). And none of these formality differences can be drawn too sharply because informal interaction can take place in formal contexts (hallway conversation at work), and typically in-formal communications can become formalized (some interracial encounters). The structure of ethnicity, and its relationship to microaction, is a matter of how one is categorized and interacts with social institutions, including group membership, communal relations, and the societal regulation of processes such as marriage and family.

These three analytical categories—individuals, interaction, institu-tions—are separated here for discussion purposes only. They are thoroughly in-tertwined and dependent on one another; they occupy the same space and even simultaneously influence and structure the individual and the context. As I have been arguing, each is produced and reproduced (structured) by the others. With this in mind, I focus on ethnicity and contrasts between one group and an-other as differences in discourse systems. In the section that follows, I focus on the communication that takes place across group boundaries that are defined by discourses.

ETHNIC DISCOURSE

The ethnic structure in a society is reflected in the language and communica-tion. When members of various groups (minority and majority groups) speak, they represent a taken-for-granted expression of knowledge and forms of inter-action. Each group has its own characteristic patterns of communication that they use with one another. This in-group discourse must be understood histori-cally and culturally. So, the language and discourse patterns of African Ameri-cans must be understood within the context of the larger White American society and the history of slavery. Groups also fashion a discourse between themselves that reflects some sort of adaptation that is sometimes successful, but often results in misunderstanding, conflict, and prejudices that mark the re-lations between groups.

My examples are taken mainly from African-American–White relations in the United States, yet I do not mean to imply that cultural communication problems, racism, and conflicts do not exist elsewhere. But although other ethnic discourse problems in places such as Bosnia, the Middle East, and Ireland have their unique features, I think the theoretical issues presented here are universal. They take on some different emphases and expressions, but are still useful for organizing knowledge about ethnic discourse. The issues in ethnic discourse are diverse and can draw from cultural studies, ethnography, linguistics, sociology, and psychology. My approach holds no illusions about a unified theoretical framework, but it does focus on how people talk and use symbols that are informed by ethnic issues. And it does draw heavily on sociolinguistics and communication theory to orient a systematic study of talk and interaction that "connects" itself to macrosocial structural issues. This connection is important, and of course dialectic, because it is impossible to adequately explain ethnic discourse by only focusing on texts with no broader socioeconomic explanatory base. In short, if there is an ethnic group reality, and they do have different ways of communicating, then these differences should be apparent in the theoretical properties of the communication processes. This can involve highly specified grammatical structures as well as broader discourse features such as topics, styles, and communicative goals. And these discourse processes take place within contexts where power and institutions continuously figure into interpretations.

Ethnolinguistic Identity

Language is the most elemental quality of the discourse of ethnic identity and group formation. All of the complexities of defining ethnicity notwithstanding, one's ethnic identity is bound up in the subjective symbols and emblems of culture that people use to differentiate themselves from others. This is quite consistent with current thinking in ethnicity that emphasizes individuals who carry their ethnicity with them in communicative contexts. Most people psychologically identify with an ethnic ancestry, even if they have qualities they consider atypical (Alba & Chaplin, 1983). So the display of ethnic identity is crucial, otherwise it is an ambiguous latent construct. Ethnic identity, like social identity, is constructed and maintained in discourse. And ethnic identity is the psychological condition that generates ethnic behavior, but it is the discursive world that represents the psychological condition called *ethnic identity*.

The term *ethnolinguistic identity* is associated with the work of Giles and Johnson (1987) and refers to the psychological and social representations that language performs with respect to ethnicity. Reviews of this work describe how it has moved from a more general theory of social psychology and ethnic identity, to a theory more focused on interpersonal encounters and how ethnic identity and language interact to account for intercultural communication and "communication breakdowns" (Gudykunst & Ting-Toomey, 1990). How individuals use discursive practices to maintain distinctiveness is a central theme in

ethnolinguistic identity theory. These include linguistic markers (lexical, grammatical, rhetorical) that establish individual and social distinctiveness. These
markers of ethnolinguistic identity are important to the structuration dialectic
because they both respond to and produce the ethnic structure in a culture.
   The more active and vigorous a group in the culture, the more it will demonstrate its linguistic distinctiveness. This distinctiveness declines to the extent
that a group is less important and consequential even if the group is not very assimilated. If there is structural racism in a culture—such as during the time of
Jim Crow laws that legally sanctioned group separation—and an ethnic group is
maximally distanced from the dominant group in terms of neighborhood geography, educational resources (separate schools), and places of employment,
then there will be much discursive divergence. At one extreme, groups will
speak different languages, but even if they speak the same language, there will
be very few points of contact and opportunities for communicative convergence. With very little out-group contact, within-group solidarity becomes
more important, and this is maintained by linguistic distinctiveness.
   Theorists such as Kress and Hodge (1979) give strength to the ideological
foundation of any system of discourse by extending Whorf and explaining how
no perception is pure and each involves some interpretation. These interpretations are symbolically loaded and stored in language. When something is given
a name, it is classified and remembered, and imbued with the beliefs, values, and
expectations of the interpreter and interpretation process.
   The discourse of ethnolinguistic identity is the most salient feature of ethnic
structure in a culture. Such discourse organizes group boundaries, determines
membership, expresses group vitality, distributes status, and sanctions language
use. There are any number of studies that make reference to African-American
identity, but conclusions are not very systematic and are fragmented among
topics such as Black English, the history of slavery, the civil rights movement,
and a variety of political and economic issues. The history of discourse and African-American ethnic identity is tied up in historical slavery and the various
manifestations of an economic ideology that has its roots in Utilitarianism.
Briefly, Utilitarianism is the idea that humans are essentially rational and economic entities, and that societies are the result of these economic interchanges.
Unfortunately, the practice of utilitarianism has led to some ideas similar to a
social Darwinism, where groups that succeeded most in the economic world
were considered superior to others.
   Historically, preindustrial European societies were like others in that economic activity was centered around the family and the local agricultural or mer-
cantile environment. But some new directions were apparent with
industrialization in Europe. Economic activity shifted from the family and was
redefined as those activities of technological work. And these people became
defined as *productive*. The individuals or cultures that did not evolve toward industrialization became less valued and associated with regressive or traditional

aspects of society. Industrial societies have developed educational systems, governments, and laws, all of which serve to promote economic interests.

All ideologies tell us how the world should be. In this sense, ideology is burdensome to those who are outside the ideological circle, and stigmatizes them. Such ideological systems encouraged and maintained the beliefs about African culture as inferior to White European culture. It stimulated a set of beliefs about African culture that justified a slavery that was rooted in beliefs about African inferiority. After these beliefs were in place, the dominant White culture set about the task of maintaining a sense of cultural inferiority with respect to Africans by engaging in practices and rituals—including the loss of cultural traditions, family life, religion, and even names—that continued to promote a structure of inferiority for Africans and superiority for Whites. American society came to embody the values of science, technology, and business and established a system of rewards and recognition commensurate with this ideology. This value system carried with it requirements for education and attitudes that promoted the utilitarian system of beliefs. Such opportunities for education and economic and social rewards were blocked from African Americans through the social systems of racism.

There is a discourse style that constitutes and is constituted by this ideology. This utilitarian ideology developed into an economic and professional, business-oriented discourse (e.g., Scollon & Scollon, 1995). Such discourse values focused communication that is clear and direct. It is a style of communication, and a philosophy of discourse, that values logic and argument, a clear organizational structure, and an understandable communicative goal. It is considered the most effective and "normal" form of communication. This way of speaking and writing has some codified principles listed in textbooks and taught in schools, and some uncodified expectations that circulate in daily interactions. This is the type of communication used by the professional and educated classes, and exemplified in books and official documents. It not only assumes that messages should be fashioned with clarity in mind, but that rules of grammar should be observed, language should used in particular ways, and words pronounced according to dictionary prescriptions. This type of discourse has been termed a *syntactic code* (Ellis, 1992a, 1992b), and emerges from the utilitarian traditions of business and professional behavior that accompany economic value systems and the literature of the written word.

As I develop these points, it becomes clear that the syntactic code system of discourse carries with it an ideology, methods of learning the discourse system, forms of communication, and types of relationships that are inconsistent with the general history and experience of African Americans in the United States. In other words, much misunderstanding, prejudice, and conflict can be attributed to the differing discursive experiences and habits of the two groups. There are certainly psychological, sociological, historical, and legal influences that contribute to these problems, but my focus is on the linguistic and communicative; it is on the focused communicative experiences that are the building blocks for macroissues, and on how these macroissues are again expressed in microdiscursive practices.

There are essentially four characteristics that describe a discursive system. A system of discourse arises out of these issues and they are in turn, influenced by discursive practices. This section briefly describes these characteristics and then compares the discursive practices of the dominant culture (White Western European syntactic code) with those of African-American ethnic culture. These four characteristics that give rise to systems of discourse are (a) ideas about how things should be, including concepts of right–wrong, good–bad, and common beliefs; that is, the *ideology* that undergirds a discourse system; (b) one's *identity*, or how an individual learns to use a discourse system; (c) the structures and *forms* of discourse that mark membership and establish identity; and (d) the nature of *relationships* among users of the system.

Ideology in Ethnic Discourse

The model middle- and upper middle-class discursive system—and the one associated with "power genres" (Lemke, 1994)—is what Scollon and Scollon (1995) called the C-B-S model, which stands for clarity, brevity, and sincerity. Or, what I (Ellis, 1992a, 1992b) referred to as the syntactic code. It is a mode of presenting ideas—through various means of communication—that are unified, analytic, and move forward with a purpose. This is a style of discourse that has its roots in literate traditions where semantic cohesion is constructed with internal textual relations, rather than relying on shared personal background and experiences, as in oral cultures described in chapter 2. This orientation toward the use and interpretation of language creates messages that are hypotactic, internally consistent, integrated, planned, and characterized by a sense of detachment, rather than personal involvement. Again, it is the style of language use taught in the schools and used in official capacities.

This discursive system draws its ideological impetus from the Enlightenment that arose out of the rethinking of authority away from the church and toward science and ideas about intellectual progress and the possibility of discovering truth. These new ideas about the pursuit of happiness and the free exchange of goods articulated by Montesquieu laid the foundation for ideas about systems of laws on which the Declaration of Independence and the Constitution were founded. There was a new interest in science and the specificity that accompanies it. People were considered rational and subject to "laws" of behavior and society. The individual was defined as logical and economic, and his language use reflected this. The evolution of the syntactic code was a system of discourse most appropriate for this means of communication. And, of course, this code and its attendant ideology is most associated with Western European cultures. Exaggerated class and group differences are justified within this ideology because rewards and benefits are thought to be a natural consequence of the most productive and deserving.

Much of what is African-American ethnic discourse in the United States emerges from a very different ideology. It is an ideology of orality (see chapter 2) where interactive storytelling, narrative, and personal identity are particularly important. Edwards and Sienkewicz (1990) explained how this results from the African-American tradition of preaching and the church where African-Americans sought solace from economic and social conditions. There are, of course, no true primary oral cultures in the modern era, but much African-American communication is representative of "secondary orality" (Ong, 1982), and Rosenberg (1987) cited the culture of preaching and religion—as opposed to science—as integral to African-American discourse.

Briefly, the traditional African worldview has the following salient characteristics. These are described by Daniel and Smitherman (1976) with communication examples for each. First, the spiritual world and the material world interact and implicate one another. This is a strongly religious ideology with lively gods and spirits and a belief in the supremacy of the spiritual ground. Religion is a daily affair and not something to be practiced on occasion. It becomes harmonious with daily life. Secondly, communities and one's identity in the community are very important. The individual must participate in the community and take part in its rhythms and patterns. There is no "I" individuality apart from the "we" of community. Third is the notion of time, which is more participatory than abstract. Performance and activity are more important than any linear notion of time. This includes the concepts of rhythms and patterns of activity. The phrase "what goes around comes around" reveals an ideology respectful of these rhythms.

The ideology inherent in this world view has implications for verbal performance, the tools of the performer, and the interactive relationship with the audience. There is a critical bond between performers and their audiences as they engage in linguistic exchanges such as praise, boasting, teasing, and the like. The aggregative and rhapsodic nature of the discourse is consistent with the ideology previously described. The call–response structure (Doob, 1961) reflects a world that is interdependent, interacting, and based more in community than individuality. Audience members in an African-American church participate with a preacher.

The secular world of banter and rap music also takes call-response and back-and-forth forms (Kochman, 1990a). Individuals or audience members will spur a performer on with expressions of approval and reinforcement like "you down, man" or "go girl" and with exaggerated nonverbal behaviors such as slapping hands and body movements. In the secular context, call and response is more associated with recognition as well as a "spiritual" connection to others. A lively and forceful call-response interaction facilitates spontaneity and personalized expression.

A traditional African-American sermon or street performance is certainly not composed of the "simple" structure of the C-B-S model, nor is it characterized by the tight cohesion of the syntactic code. An ideology that fosters emotional responses and deep involvement with both the material and spiritual world gives rise to discourse with more verbal elaboration and repetition. There is less need to maintain control and devise modes of expression that support controlled movement of ideas. As Mufwene (1991), Major (1994), Smitherman (1994), and others have shown, African-American language performances are considerably more endowed with narrative structures, formulaic repetitions, imperatives, vocatives, figurative language, and creative slang that constitute the deep structure of African-American discourse. This deep structure is a transformation of African ideology onto the experience of slavery and the social situations that obtain in America.

Learning Identity Through Discourse

African Americans learn their discourse system through a process of socialization that is generated by identity goals consistent with their history and ideology. The question is this: How does one develop this African-American ideological identity and the communication system that accompanies it? The most important distinction to be made here is between formal and informal socialization influences. The institutions of learning that are constituted, controlled, and sanctioned by the dominant culture are the repository for the formal principles of socialization. The informal ways of participating in a society are associated mostly with the family network, friends, and popular media.

If U.S. industrial society and the principles of free markets were going to be successful at generating wealth and opportunity, then it is imperative that citizens be subjected to an educational system controlled by cultural values. Historically, formal education was available only to a privileged few. Mass education of the citizenry is a uniquely U.S. phenomenon, and a pretty recent one at that. For about the past 150 years, public schools have been the standard context for teaching economic and political values consistent with mainstream U.S. utilitarian ideology. Compulsory public education is almost completely preoccupied with teaching science, rationality, technology, and forms of language use consistent with the syntactic code.

Although African Americans increasingly participate in mainstream U.S. culture, it was not until 1954 and the *Brown v. Board of Education* Supreme Court decision that African Americans were even allowed to join public schools in any significant numbers. They have been denied the fundamental socialization experience of the dominant discourse code. For generations, their schools were separate, unequal, and inferior. In many states, there were laws prohibiting the education of African Americans with harsh consequences for those who disobeyed (Marable, 1983). Certainly the perception of group inferiority is one consequence of a minority group's deviation from accepted ideology. Tate (1997) explained how the education of people of color was premised on their presumed inferiority. The predominant African-American ideology described previously became a legitimating ideology for an educational system based on an inferiority paradigm (Takaki, 1993; Tate, 1997). When a group is considered inferior, they are typically held in this inferior position by virtue of tools available to and controlled by the dominant culture. Padilla and Lindholm (1995), for example, show how IQ tests, White middle-class educational values—derived from experiences only available to the White middle class, measurement instruments, and attitudes that ignore differences are all apparent in the education of minorities.

We can see the macro–micro dialectic at work here. There is a history of macro structures (laws forbidding education, segregation) that deny micro socialization experiences (education) to African Americans. Mainstream White society evolves a system of discourse that emerges from the public school experience. This system of discourse is consistent with utilitarian ideology and has, according to Scollon and Scollon (1995), the following characteristics:

1. Oral and written language should not be too rhetorical; that is, facts should speak for themselves and style should be simple and unadorned.
2. There should be an emphasis on facts and proofs for what one says.
3. The relationship between an addresser and an addressee is less important than a text; it becomes a greater authority.
4. Individuality is valued, but for the sake of textual autonomy and integrity, not personal identity. Your speech or writing is "owned" by you.
5. Others who are part of the discourse system are treated as equals.
6. Your language has a "public" quality that means it is sanctioned by some formal institution.

I explore African-American forms of discourse more in the next section, but it is evident here that African-American discourse identity was forged in different circumstances. This identity is formed very early in life and is difficult to change. African Americans have not only been excluded from the crucial educational setting that prepares one for success with a dominant culture, but also from the larger sociopolitical world. Problems of crime, poverty, and unemployment are easy enough to document (Dennis, 1991). The socialization experiences that shape the African-American identity are slavery, oppression, and the experience of being a disdained "other" by the dominant culture (Jenkins, 1982).

Numerous scholars refer to the African-American identity experience as one framed by African-American culture, which is a blend of traditional African cultures with the realities of slavery (e.g., Covin, 1990; Franklin, 1988). Afrocentricity (Asante, 1987; Hecht, Collier, & Ribeau, 1993) provides a more contemporary ideology that serves as an infrastructure for the discourse system. This ideology, as described by Covin (1990) and discussed in Hecht, Collier, and Ribeau (1993), continues to emphasize (a) a wholistic rather than analytic experience; (b) a struggle between traditional values and the intrusion of Western European values; (c) a focus on harmony in nature, and rhythm; (d) an African-American culturally specific way of interpreting and managing the world; and (e) the power of the community. These theoretical ideas operate within a very complex social system that includes the influences of urbanization and the movement north by African Americans, civil rights, and the cycles of the U.S. economy.

The three primary institutions that foster African-American identity and occasion their ethnic discursive system are educational institutions discussed previously, the church, and the family. Unlike many other churches, membership in the African-American church has risen steadily. The church historically provided an organized experience for African Americans that was morally and community based. It became a retreat from the realities of a harsh existence as well as the social and intellectual core of the African-American community. The tradition of an African oral culture was transported to the church and spawned the rhythmic and call-response forms of worship, as well as the spirited interaction between the religious leaders and their congregates. This oral tradition created great church orators (e.g., Martin Luther King) and helped develop leaders who would be influential in the civil rights movement.

The impact of African-American church music on blues, rock and roll, soul, motown, jazz, and contemporary music cannot be underestimated. Spirituals and gospel music are the foundation of rock and roll (Davis, 1995). This music has tremendous impact on White performers and modern culture, and youth culture in particular. As Grossberg (1984) explained in his work on rock and roll, "you are not what you don't listen to" (p. 103). This is a statement of the powerful impact of music on identity and how music socializes one into an identity. Church music also expresses its negative. It signifies sin as well as salvation. It has to do with faith and the shattering of religious taboos. The falsetto wails and preening sexual semiotics of some performers (e.g., Al Green) demonstrate how the language of church music can be appropriated for secular expression. The various threads of sin and salvation are part of the fabric of African-American life, woven primarily by the church.

The African-American family is a complex institution with influences from both traditional African culture and those that emerge from slavery, poverty, and the pressures of social adaptation. It is the most material context for the conception of identity and socialization into language and communication. The traditional southern, African-American family was quite stable and maintained its group-specific traditions. But the African-American family since the 1940s has been destabilized by migration to factory employment in the north, divorce, and the rise in single-parent households (essentially female) with few economic and symbolic resources to deal with the difficulties of family life (Jaynes & Williams, 1989). Media stereotypes about African Americans and crime, drugs, and sex along with the criminalization of the African-American male are both a cause and a consequence of these conditions.

Forms of Discourse

Given an ethnic group's ideology, and a means of socializing an identity from that ideology, I turn now to the preferred forms of discourse and patterns of communication within that discourse system. I use the word *discourse* here to include broad functional uses of language in social contexts. The essential purpose of discourse is communication, or the process of using language and various rhetorical devices to direct the meaning of a listener or reader. Discourse for an ethnic group doubles as both the reflection of a group's values, structure, ideology, and as a defining aspect of the group. As an example, African-American Vernacular English (AAVE) in all its forms is a major defining characteristic of African-American culture. African Americans typically refer to language (e.g., slang) and "styles" of interaction as a defining factor of their culture. But European-descent Whites would not likely name language as a defining characteristic of their culture. Interestingly, various White subcultures in the United States based on geography, education, or class status would make the claim to distinctiveness, but not name language use differences very prominently. And U.S. Whites use language more to divide and separate than to unify. They use linguistic markers to recognize differences rather than similarities.

The idea here is not to describe and catalogue the unique linguistic features of AAVE. These features have been amply documented (e.g., Baugh, 1983; Dillard, 1972; Labov, 1970). It is the functions of a discourse system that are most important from a cultural point of view. Following are some interesting examples.

Representing and Respecting Ethnicity. It is culturally acceptable in contemporary society to represent the ethnicity of another group, but it takes skill to walk the line between accuracy and stereotype. Historically, social institutions (e.g., media) portrayed African Americans quite stereotypically and did so without recrimination. After protests and a period of time when consciences were raised about ethnic stereotypes, ethnicity is back. The melting pot is out; ethnic identity is in. Groups assert themselves, take pride in ethnic cultural expressions, and demand that their language and communication be recognized and respected. Consider an example from the corporate world of the Disney company.

Walt Disney, who was known to be ideologically and politically conservative, spent 50 years portraying African Americans and other ethnic groups as stereotyped "others." James Baskett in "The Uncle Remus Stories," the hipster Black-American crows in "Dumbo," and the Ape King who yearns for civilization (in the voice of Louie Prima) in "The Jungle Book" are all broadly sketched ethnic stereotypes. But in Disney's "Lion King," the character Rafiki is a baboon who is transformed into a Zulu-chanting priestess and African storyteller. The character grunts and hoots and guides the young king to his destiny. The hero of this movie is not a superman or an outsider, but someone who is trying to recapture his ethnicity, return to the "circle of life," which is the comforting embrace of your own group. Unlike other Disney ethnic portrayals, there have been no cries of protest as the young lion returns to his roots. These institutional media portrayals are important because a Disney film is often the only cultural experience many people share in a world where ethnicity and race are very charged words. This change in Disney's portrayal of ethnicity is no small matter and marks an evolution in consciousness about ethnicity and how it is communicated.

Formal Expression Versus Relationships. Given the various complexities and functions of language, there is easy agreement that all language in all cultures expresses both formal information and data about the subject matter of a message, but also serves a relational function (Watzlawick, Beavin, & Jackson, 1967). We communicate subject matter, but we also communicate how interactants see one another in the relationship, including expectations about power, intimacy, and control.

The syntactic code, which is a standard White, middle-class discursive system, is oriented more toward formal expression of ideas and information than relationships. African-American discourse is much more relationship oriented and concerned with relational solidarity and involvement. There is considerable research that supports this claim. All messages accomplish both information and relationship functions to some extent, but some are clearly more directed to one than the other. Rose (1982/1983) and Hecht, Collier, and Ribeau (1993) explained African-American culture, with its tradition of orality and the power of relationships in oral cultures (see chap. 2), value sharing, intimacy, solidarity, and reinforcement of ethnic identity. The call-response pattern discussed earlier symbolizes connectedness and interdependence.

African-American slang and jive stimulates immediate recognition of group membership and is a powerful communication form that is exclusively African American. Although it contributes to stereotypes for out-group members, it is a discourse form in the African-American community that is very rewarding (Abrahams, 1976; Cogdell & Wilson, 1980; Kochman, 1990b). Jive is composed of creative, informal, and metaphorically extended language. It serves to demonstrate humor, cleverness, and that elusive "cool." An expressive style is used to present oneself as an appealing member of a group. Many African Americans effortlessly switch from standard English to AAVE as situations and other participants change. This code switching is designed to signal the relationship between communicators and mark the value of subtle aspects of feeling and attitude.

The difference between a discourse style that focuses on relationships rather than the more routine goal of information transmission can account for problems in communication, including misunderstanding and personal offense. From a functional standpoint, a White syntactic code user might want to speak directly to make a point and then move on. The African American might try to make the same point with emotional intensity that calls for a response from the other person, and signals his or her identity, which acts as an interpretive frame for the relationship. This is contrary to White norms and may be the basis for discomfort, confusion, and even hostility.

Research by McLaurin (1995) is a powerful example of the real consequences of this mismatch in discursive systems. McLaurin studied the effectiveness of prosocial messages designed to change the attitude and behaviors of at-risk African-American youths. The study found that messages typically fail because they fail to account for the sense making and interpretive frames of the youth. The messages do not appropriate the central cultural images and issues of the youth. Moreover, McLaurin (1995) concluded the following:

> the design of these messages incorrectly assumes that the linear communication style used by mainstream culture, with its accompanying syllogistic reasoning, will be persuasive with an audience that communicates in a highly interactive, oral style utilizing a more horizontal mode of influence. (p. 301)

In other words, messages formulated according to the principles and ideology of the syntactic code were ineffective and prompted the young people in the study to state that "no one is talking to us" (p. 320).

Individuality Versus Collective Identity. The communicative expression of individuality, and the symbolic forms that promote this individuality, are also defining qualities of African-American ethnic discourse. Presenting oneself as a unique member of the community is important. Rose (1982/1983) explained how activities such as hand slapping and dance have a group vocabulary for African Americans that identify one as a knowledgeable and competent member of the group, but individual variation and style are also important. What Kochman (1990a) called flair and style is very developed in the African-American culture. Children learn very young to express themselves through verbal and nonverbal behavior that calls attention to their uniqueness. Attempts to be more conspicuous, colorful, and assertive through walk and talk are all examples. Bragging, boasting, verbal aggression, and stylized self-presentation are some of the means of signifying individuality. All of these are quite contrary to the syntactic code of White culture and certainly responsible for negative perceptions. The biases and misperceptions that undergird the structure of racism are assembled out of these intercultural mismatches in communication.

Boasting is certainly one way to direct attention to yourself. Middle-class White culture was shocked when Muhammad Ali in the 1960s bragged and boasted in rhymed couplets. Communicators merge themselves into performers when they boast to proclaim their own virtues. In oral cultures, words perform action, and boasting is the primary way to assert power and perform desired actions (Edwards & Sienkewicz, 1990). Dancing in the end zone and spiking the football after a touchdown are mechanisms for calling attention to oneself. Boasting gives rise to serious misunderstanding and negative perceptions of African Americans. In most North American and European contexts, there are expectations of humility and self-deprecation.

Boasting functions positively in that it can prevent a situation from degenerating into a fight, and it can serve as an effective psychological shield against harsh realities. But these micro communication behaviors (boasting) crystallize an attitude about African Americans and structure our interpretations to reproduce stereotypes about narcissism and inferiority. Boasting and a preoccupation with uniqueness creates categories through which we classify actors (Whites: African Americans) and their actions (humility: bragging). These classifications become preexisting in the culture and are therefore socially structuring (Jayyusi, 1984). Boasting becomes part of a dynamic web of words composed of interpersonal details and social structures that display these categories. If the world were objective and there was a one-to-one mapping between boasting and its interpretation, then our task would be to simply reveal objective reality. But given that our interpretations are not disinterested objective reports, they become motivated by things like ascribing blame and enhancing one's own psychological standing. Social structures are an intertwining of description and interpretation that makes them a judgmental process. This is how the forms of ethnic discourse produce and reproduce the structure of ethnicity in a culture.

Relationships and Discourse Systems

This issue is concerned with the way members of a culture organize relationships among members of the group and the discursive system that supports this organization. There are some aspects of relationships in a culture that are most important. Readers should keep in mind that many of these differences are a matter of degree, and no group is purely organized in one way and not the other. What is important is to understand the nature of these influences and the contexts in which they are most influential.

In some cultures, family membership and kinship ties are powerful and of primary importance. Scollon and Scollon (1995), for example, explained how in Asian cultures the family is a powerful force that holds people together. The sense of self and belonging emerges from the kinship system. U.S. culture, by contrast, often sees family as a barrier to individuality. Kinship is less important than individual expression. This aspect of Asian culture explains much of its respect for hierarchy and a resultant communication system rooted heavily in politeness and respect.

West African oral performances pay particular attention to genealogies (Edwards & Sienkewicz, 1990). I mentioned previously that the family was the prime context for identity formation, but the African-American family is historically rooted in a strong community that respects differences in rank. Although we would not want to overgeneralize the current influences of ancient African family structures, it remains true that contemporary African Americans maintain a system of kinship respect based on generational differences. This is different than the White Western attitude, which is one of individuality and egalitarianism. The change in the African-American family structure (e.g., Jaynes & Williams, 1989) has led to generational communication problems. Some of the increasing efforts to be individual and resist authority are motivated by individual interests rather than the altruistic ones that are encouraged by generational respect.

How you become a member of a group is also very important. Family and generational membership is organic and based on natural processes of learning and enculturation. This forms a solidarity based on the powerful influences of shared history, traditions, and goals. Other groups are formed simply by mutual interest and the fact that the group can be of use to one. The second process of group development is more professionally oriented than family. It teaches the modes of communication and forms of discourse consistent with schooling and the syntactic code. In the first process, meanings are directly ratified in interaction. One learns gender, individual identity, and a sense of place primarily through the oral forms of the community. Intercultural communication problems between African Americans and European White cultures can result from differing assumptions that emerge from these processes.

REPRODUCTION CIRCUITS AND ETHNIC DISCOURSE

I finish this chapter with a more direct confrontation between theory and data. I have been drawing on Giddens' heavy theoretical language and structuration to try and explain how different ethnic structures might become visible in society. This requires a move more toward models of interdependence to explain the development of society and its structures, in this case ethnicity. Typically, ethnicity has been seen as a natural characteristic of a group of people and the response of another culture. This "naturalization" has been so fundamental that it is difficult to imagine any other process, especially one that foregrounds interdependent relationships and the dialectic production of interaction and social structures. But such a question is central if we are to understand how members of a culture draw on structures to produce patterns of communication. Differences between African-American ethnic structures and the dominant White ethnic structure can be illuminated by how each produces and is instantiated by certain communication practices.

Typically, one focuses on either social actors and their communication practices or institutions and their social features. But Cohen (1989) and Harrison (1994) suggested that it is what is in between communication practices and social structures that is important. This is what Cohen (1989) termed *system analysis*, an extension of the principles of interdependence that we have been discussing here and in chapter 4. The first important term here is *reproduction* because we must focus on repeated communication patterns as these are the ones that become prominent and most influential, and are responsible for the creation of structures. As Giddens (1984) described, elaborated by Cohen (1989) and Harrison (1994), this reproduction produces processes that are considered *reproduction circuits*, or as Cohen (1989) wrote, "a cycle of routinised activities and consequences which are reproduced across time-space within and between institutional locales" (p. 124). These reproduction circuits help explain how systems of interaction—for example, ethnic group (e.g., Black: White) discourse described previously—are integrated, their position in relation to other systems, as well as how the groups signify meanings.

One set of issues that pertains to the two sets of discursive practices is system issues. These are what Giddens referred to as *integration* and *position*, and generally refer to the patterns of practices between the participants who compose social systems such as different ethnic groups. Questions of how closely they are tied together, where interactions take place, frequency of contact, and positional relations among members are of chief concern here. Another set of analytical issues are more symbolic in terms of how social actors produce meanings, their interpretive frames, and how the ideas and practices of one group are granted legitimacy and power.

For instance, African Americans are a group system aimed at maximizing their position in society and establishing a healthy ethnic identity. They do this through the communication forms discussed previously. The same is true for the White culture, even though the characteristics that produce their discursive system (ideology, identity, forms of discourse, and relationships) are different. As we know, communication in these groups is organized by geography, workplaces, and group history. More specifically, within-group interaction practices are regionalized around the home and neighborhood. Between-group interaction practices are marked more by workplace locale and public commercial enterprises. The type of communication that takes place in the home is fundamentally different than that which occurs in the workplace. These regionalized communication practices are how communication and social contact are "stretched" across time and space.

Individuals in these groups are parceled across these regionalized spaces and possess the appropriate discourse forms and rights and responsibilities. These individuals are distributed in social space, but maintain their differences with respect to class, income, education, and related demographic factors. Consequently, there are spheres of interaction among different social classes such as upper middle-class African Americans interacting with lower middle-class African Americans or Whites, poor Whites with poor African Americans, privileged Whites with underprivileged African Americans, and so on, including all the possibilities in a matrix of subcultures. Thus, certain forms and types of communication (e.g., African-American identity displays, mutual respect, racism, information giving, orders and directives, ad infinitum) take place between individuals in different regions. There are deviations from patterns, but these are idiosyncratic or, more interestingly, designed to alter social structures and disrupt accepted practices. These deviations play an important role in social change and conflict.

The conditions of copresence and regionalization are most important for system integration. When members of an ethnic group maintain contact and communication patterns over time and space—and the smaller the group the more likely it will be systematically integrated—then its level of integration is high. This is why African-American cultural identity is high. But when participants become increasingly geographically separated because of movement to new land or neighborhoods, migration for employment, or pursuant to skills or economic opportunities, then integration is threatened. It can then be held together only through technological mechanisms of contact and control. These would be mechanisms such as computers, letter writing, telephones, and other forms of media. Historically, the White culture was more reliant on these mediated mechanisms of integration and accordingly has always been less integrated and more dispersed into subcultures of class and geography. In more recent times, African Americans, too, are mobile and less tied to the inner city and countryside, which makes them more reliant on mediated forms of contact.

Use and skill with discursive systems such as the syntactic code or oral style of discourse also facilitates the level of system integration. When an individual is skilled and comfortable with one system to the exclusion of the other, he or she is more integrated into that system, but alienated from the other. These discursive systems are forms of literacy that have rules (sometimes highly codified) that act to coordinate and control individual actors. When one system is preferred by a dominant culture (e.g., syntactic code) it becomes hegemonic and associated with power and the accepted standard of communication.

The patterns of communication that constitute an ethnic structure are based on codes of signification, cultural principles of legitimation, and legal and psychological mechanisms of dominance. These are all devices that provide understandings and legitimations that reflect the tacit but mutual agreements about the rights and responsibilities of participants. Power is the essential factor that sustains differences among ethnic group positions in a culture. The possession and control of capital—both material and symbolic capital—makes for the asymmetry that is the essence of racism and cultural conflict.

The power of the dominant White culture over the African-American culture legitimizes certain interests and discursive systems. It legitimizes ways of speaking (syntactic code), behaving (understated behavior as opposed to emotionality), and other cultural characteristics related to food, clothing, and aesthetics. Each of these legitimized practices has "technologies" with their own vocabulary and frameworks for interpretation and understanding. Writing, computers, finance, management information, and so forth, are the technologies of the dominant group, and these require experience and training not easily available to the minority culture. As ways of speaking and behaving are de-legitimized, they go underground and establish different conditions for discourse by defining who can take part, what counts as valid communication, what issues are important, and what attitudes, values, and arguments are acceptable. This results in an ethnic discursive genre that involves standard and acceptable forms of signification, routines, and interpretive guidelines. This ethnic discursive genre is a way of existing. It constrains the culture and suppresses other, sometimes liberating, ways of thinking, and opportunities, but also performs powerful and attractive identity function.

Ethnic discursive system reproduction circuits perform an impressive transformative function. These discursive systems are transformed in communication by social actors. This is how change occurs. Communicators employ the practices and technologies of communication, and by doing so, they influence others. This transformative process continues as the others go through the same cycle. We have the situation described by Giddens and others as feedback that is reflexively monitored and continuously cycled. An example would be the talk and communication (microphenomena) that occurs in a meeting pertaining in some way to African Americans. This could be a consciousness-raising session, political meeting, legislative activity concerning affirmative action, crime, or any type of social policy. This communicative contact produces results of some kind. These results could be official policies and legal procedures, or minor changes in attitudes and beliefs. The results are then either implemented as policies, or incorporated into the consciousness of actors. Such policies and changed consciousnesses are then re-employed in future interactions. This is an accomplishment of skilled cultural members, but not one that is wholly understood or comprehended by them. This process of reflexive monitoring and reproducing has many conflicts and fits and starts. But "the seed of change is there in *every act* which contributes towards the reproduction of any 'ordered' form of social life" (Giddens, 1976, p. 102).

The process of reflexive monitoring that accounts for change is more ordered and causal in highly managed corporate systems, but much looser in less integrated social systems, such as ethnic groups. It is worth noting that systems such as corporations and government agencies have a long history of highly codified structures including intelligence and learning from specialists, educators, and experienced individuals. Many of their structures are clear and repetitive. It is no wonder that most people can understand and reproduce these bureaucratic practices and systems. There is less knowledge, experience, and predictability when it comes to looser social systems organized around an ethnic heritage.

In this chapter I have tried to encourage some appreciation for the relationship between communication and ethnic structure. I make little claim to dramatic innovation, but do believe that directing attention to the micro–macro dialectic can be an important rethinking of scholarship in this area. The micro–macro dialectic emphasizes the daily practices of communication, acknowledges changes as well as stability, and recognizes individual agency as well as collective identity and structure. There is no shortage of elasticity in the concept of ethnicity. It can be fixed and solid in the minds of some and responsible for rigid ideas; for others ethnicity is perpetually being fused and negotiated. In either case, it is a social construction that will not fade into the background of consciousness, but will continue to be an organizing category for individuals and cultures.

❖ 6 ❖

Class: The Presence That Dare Not Speak Its Name

An unlearned carpenter of my acquaintance once said in my hearing: "There is very little difference between one man and another; but what little there is, is very important." This distinction seems to me to go to the root of the matter.
—William James

Social class is America's dirty little secret. Even though Americans have a vague sense that they live in a culture permeated by status and taste differences, they do not like to talk about it. The subject is confused and obscure. But curiously, you can infuriate people and make them squirm in discomfort by even mentioning the topic of social classes. If you use class as an explanatory category (e.g., "Her makeup and big hair betray her lower class background") you will silence a group (unless they laugh) and present yourself as crude, elitist, or particularly nasty. Moreover, most people are quite uninformed about social classes and the system of stratification in the United States. They believe that the only class determiner is money, which is far from true, and most people self-identify as a member of the middle class, which they are often not.

Skeggs (1997), in her study of gender and class, explained how young working-class women do not speak of their class membership, but work hard "not to be recognized as working class" (p. 74). This is different than for males who often take pride in their working-class language and status. But females know that the label *working class* signifies that they are dangerous, without value, and sexualized. These women had subjective images of the standard to which they ascribed (middle-class respectability), and these images became generative devices that instantiated a set of behaviors and attitudes. Their class consciousness did not figure directly in their lives but was constantly present. It was a structuring absence.

Class may be a four-letter word, but marketers, writers, and political operatives are very skilled at exploiting it. In the 1996 presidential election, Pat Buchanan referred to the fiscal policies of wealthy Steve Forbes as cooked by "the boys down at the yacht club." Others called Forbes "Richie rich" or "junior" in an attempt emasculate him. When *The New York Times* columnist Jason DeParle (1996) described Buchanan's appeal to the "lunch bucket crowd" as bringing a "class sensibility" to the campaign, Buchanan cringed and said "I don't think I want to go anywhere near that one" (p. 41). Class is invisible and touchy, but political candiates know it has market value. Candidates explain how they grew up poor and imply that they understand the plight of the poor. Or, they admit to being rich (e.g., Forbes, Bush) and either cannot be bought, or defend themselves as proof of the American dream.

The reason that class identity does not have a powerful grip on the American conscience is easy enough to understand. We have a strong ideological tradition of equality that has achieved the status of a civil religion, even if the ideology and the reality are quite disparate. And mobility is an important factor of U.S. culture, so class categorization is somewhat more changing and complex as individuals move throughout the system. Moreover, we have other powerful sources of identity, such as ethnicity and religion. But class is very real, and the subject of considerable scholarship in sociology, but not much in communication. Data (e.g., Hout, Brooks, & Manza, 1993) show that class-based stratification remains very strong. There are new sources of inequality that now accompany the old ones. Class standing continues to affect politics, the economy, and the family. Following is an exploration of the stratification system in the United States and a theoretical rendering of its relationship to interaction.

The distinguished French philosopher Jean Rousseau became noted for his essay on the origin and bases of inequality among men. Rousseau celebrated "natural man" and argued that only equality among people was "natural" and that inequality was unnatural. He indicted property, money, and the state as the causes of inequality and inequality's natural cousin—oppression. Rousseau was correct that unequal distribution of resources of any type occasions inequality, but he was probably wrong to claim that inequality was unnatural.

Defending the position that differences among people are natural is not my concern. It is easy enough to identify the persistent differences among people and demonstrate how these differences are typical and important. Even when objective material conditions are the same, the "perception" of these may differ and produce inequality. Or, different material conditions can produce the same perceptions. It is repeatedly true that both historically and currently rich people are treated differently than poor people, men from women, educated from noneducated, Whites differently from non-Whites, upper class differently from underclass, and so on.

But more importantly, each of these groups acquires and expresses its identity in social interaction. Communication is a ubiquitous social activity that is the building block of all collectivities formal and informal alike. In the following pages, I examine the nature of social stratification—or how and why people are parceled into various groups—and the intersection between these macrostructures and the moment-by-moment processes of communication. The goal is to understand how the concepts that are used to describe certain commonalties among people (e.g., ethnicity, class, education, etc.) are grounded in the real communicative experiences of human beings. This intersection of the micro and macro serves as the essential theoretical focus as I discuss how social stratificational categories traverse linguistic and communicative practices. Throughout this entire volume, I have continually patrolled the boundaries between "external" social categories that are descriptive of groups, and the "internal" and "online" communication processes that constitute social categories.

I begin this analysis of communication and social categories with individual biographies. These biographies cannot reveal much about social or communicative processes, of which is of most interest here, but they do make apparent the influences that shape these lives and, in turn, how the communicative realities of these lives modify and maintain the macrostructures of the culture. Three life histories in the United States are presented here.

Willis

Willis was born in 1963 in a low-income, predominantly African-American area of Detroit. He lived with his mother, Cheryl, and three sisters until he was 2 years old. Cheryl knocked around from job to job the best she could. She cleaned buildings, was an aide for a government project, and even sold some drugs on occasion. When Willis was 2, his mother was caught stealing, which lead to a 1-year jail term. Willis lived with his aunt during that year and was a pretty happy child.

Willis was reunited with his mother when she was released from prison. Cheryl had trouble finding work and she and her children lived in about a dozen places over the next few years. The unemployment rate was high and jobs that paid enough to support a family were scarce. Cheryl settled on welfare for her family. Still, the welfare check was not enough, so Willis and his family moved into the spare bedroom at a relative's apartment.

When Willis was 10, his mother married a man who had a janitorial job. They moved into their own low-income apartment and provided as best they could for the children. Cheryl was a good mother during these years and Willis remembers how she always left him cute notes in his room. Christmas presents were few, but they always had some.

The pressures of money and life began to wear on Cheryl's husband and he would disappear for long periods of time. There were fights and he increasingly turned to alcohol. Cheryl and the children left and went back on welfare. Willis was in high school by now and remembers being embarrassed at his clothes and the things he could not afford.

One day Willis' older sister was beaten so severely by her boyfriend that she had to be hospitalized. When she was released, her speech was slurred and she could not walk properly. During this time, Willis was increasingly attracted to street gangs and saw a man killed during a minor holdup. His mother felt she was losing control of her children and cried every night. Willis was arrested for minor thievery, but was placed on probation. Later, he spent some time in jail.

In 1983, Willis' mother was found dead. He mourned the loss of his mother, but after a period of time tried to forget about it and find a job. The unemployment rate was higher than ever and Willis could find nothing but low-paying and low-skilled work. He went on a few job interviews, but always felt awkward and uncomfortable in the presence of White men in suits. Willis still works odd jobs in and around Detroit and collects welfare.

Nancy

Nancy was also born in 1963 in the San Fernando Valley region of southern California. Her father Russ was a salesman for a radio station in Encino. She lived with both her parents and a younger brother who was born in 1966. Nancy's father went to work in the morning and came home around 5 p.m. Sometimes he took calls at night from clients. Her mother, Dorothy, stayed at home with the children until the early 1970s, when she took a part-time job as a substitute teacher.

Nancy's father grew up in Pennsylvania and graduated from the University of Scranton with a degree in business administration. Dorothy also went to college, but dropped out after a couple of years to get married. Russ worked at an insurance company for a while before taking the job at the radio station. He has been in radio sales for 10 years and plans to stay there.

Nancy's family lives in a small stucco house in Van Nuys, California. She goes to the public school in the community and was active in Brownies and Girl Scouts. Dorothy was a den mother for 3 years and was respected for the gingerbread houses she helped the girls make at Christmastime. Dorothy also regularly collected cans for her church food drive.

Russ and Dorothy liked to go out to dinner and would get a babysitter for the kids every couple of months. They took car vacations most summers. They would drive to northern California and go camping, or, on a few occasions, they rented a small cabin by a lake.

When Nancy was in high school she was a slightly better than average student and active in drama club and girl's softball. Her younger brother played on the little league team that Russ coached. Russ had a pretty steady income and he received regular raises. When Nancy was a senior, Dorothy started to work more hours and the extra money went into a college fund, family trips, and the added expenses of a teenager. During her senior year in high school, Nancy worked part time in a Baskin-Robbins ice cream store.

When Nancy graduated, she went to a California state university to study nursing. Her mother now worked full time and she and Russ began to redo the house. One night in 1983, Russ had chest pains and was admitted to the hospital. Even though he did not have a serious heart attack, the doctor put him on a special diet and exercise program.

Charles

Charles was born the youngest of four children in Greenwich, Connecticut. His father was the primary stockholder and chief executive officer of a New York publishing company. Charles' father, William, was the son of the company founder. Like Willis, Charles grew up in a number of households, except that all of them were owned by his family and he went from one to the other during different seasons of the year or for particular occasions. The houses were clean, spacious, and had people attending to the various needs of the house or its occupants.

During most of the school year, Charles lived in Greenwich and went to Greenwich Country Day School. His French au pair dropped him off in the morning and picked him up in the evening. On weekends, Charles often went with his family to their Manhattan townhouse where they would spend time in museums and go to the theater.

Charles and his family would summer at their house on Martha's Vineyard. Many friends and family members would gather on weekends for big dinners and summer parties. Often, his parents would visit friends and Charles and his brothers and sisters would hike around the island.

Charles was a bright boy and curious about his surroundings and world events. Unlike Willis, he had a stimulating and safe environment to explore with many expensive objects and activities. And unlike Nancy, he had many opportunities for travel and his parents encouraged reading, artistic endeavors, and high academic performance.

Charles attended an expensive private school (the Choate School) for secondary education, and then went on to Yale. He was popular and successful at Yale (he played baseball and was an honors student), and went on to Harvard for an MBA.

William recognized that Charles was bright, ambitious, and responsible. He immediately began to prepare him for the company business in anticipation of Charles managing the family estate. In the meantime, Charles liked sailing and collecting wine. He traveled often to Europe for wine auctions and even bought property in the south of France. Charles married a girl from Wellesley and they live in Westport.

In the future Charles would sit on numerous corporate boards, hold university trusteeships, and be talked about for government appointments.

These three life histories describe the obvious fact that people in the United States are different. Some are rich, some are poor, and some are in the middle. There are certainly more people like Nancy than either Willis or Charles. But these biographies are rich in implications. Assuming they adequately describe the personal and social lives of large numbers of people, they suggest the following questions:

1. Why is Willis poor and Charles wealthy? Is it because one is smart and the other is not? Is it because Charles is simply naturally more talented than the others? Is there something inherently inferior and less moral about Willis? If all three of these people differ with respect to natural abilities, then what accounts for those differences? Is it genetic, or attributable to different backgrounds or experiences? If rich people are biologically superior to poor people, then how is it that many people are born rich but do not succeed. And, conversely, how about the poor person who is exceptionally talented? Purely individual explanations of behavior and life's circumstances are typically difficult to defend. So this prompts additional questions.

2. What role does social class background play in the assignment of someone in the class system? Is social class responsible for determining education and opportunities, or is it more responsible for shaping personal characteristics such as motivations and aspirations? If social class is the controlling factor in determining one's fate, then the parents of Willis, Nancy, and Charles are to be either blamed or praised for their outcomes. If this is the case, then how far back do we go in blaming parents, grandparents, great grandparents, ad infinitum.

3. What role does race and ethnic origin play in determining our place in the social landscape? Does it matter if one grows up African American, Hispanic, American Indian, or Asian? If it does matter, then what is the difference, for example, between being a Puerto Rican raised in Puerto Rico or one raised in New York City? More importantly, how do ethnic origin and social class interact?

4. Putting aside the causes of differences, how are differences between people maintained? Why is it the case that if you are born poor, you are

likely to stay poor? What patterns of behavior, in general, and communication, in particular, are responsible for keeping people in their social groups? I have a friend who makes a joke about people who get tattoos. My friend says, "sure get a tattoo, it will guarantee you minimum wage for life." Are tattoos low status such that they prevent you from succeeding in certain situations? Do employers discriminate against people with tattoos?

5. Finally, what are the language and communication patterns associated with various social groups? This is a very important question that takes up most of this chapter. I explore in some detail how members of various social classes, ethnic groups, and substrata of society communicate and thereby reflect and reproduce their own social conditions.

SOCIAL STRATIFICATION

Social stratification should not be confused with social differentiation. It is possible to be differentiated but not stratified. Social *differentiation* is characteristic of all cultures and is simply a separation of roles and activities, a division of labor. Somebody fishes and somebody hunts; somebody delivers the mail and somebody writes books. Social *stratification* is when these differing activities and behaviors are ranked relative to one another. There is no stratification if the fisherman and the hunter are considered of equal status and importance. But if the fisherman is considered "better" than the hunter, or the author better than the mail person, if these two positions are afforded more respect, money, honor, and status, then the society is stratified.

So what is stratification? *Social stratification is the institutionalized social arrangement that determines who gets what and why, and rank and status are associated with these arrangements.* It is as Heller (1987) wrote: "a system of structured inequality in the things that count in a given society, that is, both tangible and symbolic goods of the society" (p. 5). These arrangements are structured because they are not random, but follow patterns of consistency and stability. Moreover, there is a legal and ideological system that supports these differing social arrangements; society holds beliefs (e.g., religious, political, racial, economic) and creates a legal system that supports these beliefs and thereby produces and maintains the stratificational system. In the United States, for example, we have evolved an ideology that values capital and its acquisition. The legal and economic systems encourage this (tax and finance laws) and even support the rights of one generation to choose who will fill these same positions in the next generation (inheritance laws). Americanism is equated with support for the business community.

Differentiation is surely natural and inevitable, but the universality of stratification is at least debatable. Most theorists, however, are less concerned with a debate about the universality of stratification and more interested in the degree of stratification in a culture. Minimally stratified systems are different than highly stratified ones. Most sociologists agree on a few principal types of structure that can be distinguished on the basis of some defining characteristics. These principal types are communal, slave, caste, estate or feudal, and class systems. Any standard work on stratification or social inequality will describe these in detail (e.g., Heller, 1987; Hurst, 1992; Kerbo, 1991). There are other ways in which cultures are stratified, such as gender and ethnicity, but these are usually part of the differing reasons people are placed within the stratification system rather than constituting strata of their own.

In addition to the principal types of stratification, there are four essential characteristics of stratification systems. These characteristics are actually more interesting than the types because they determine the nature and composition of the stratification systems. They are also more related to the symbolic and communicative features that are associated with structured differences between groups of people. The following scheme is certainly not exhaustive, but it does represent a fair degree of consensus (see Heller, 1987; Hurst, 1992). Although the criteria are relevant in each stratification system, they are not of equal importance in all systems. The characteristics of stratification systems are summarized in Table 6.1.

Openness Continuum

Are the strata in a culture open or closed? This refers to the freedom and ability to move in or out of your particular position in society. Some cultures, such as the United States, pose norms and values that prescribe the freedom to leave your present rank or class and move up or down. In a rigid caste system, the ranks of your social group are closed. The differences between groups in a caste

TABLE 6.1
Characteristics of Stratification System
(Adapted from Kerbo, 1991)

Type of System	Boundaries	Placement	Legitimation	Primary Factor of Strata
Communal	Open	Achievement	Tradition	Honor
Slave	Mostly closed	Ascription	Legal ideology	Economic
Caste	Closed	Ascription	Religious, ideology or legal	Economic
Feudal	Mostly closed	Ascription	Legal ideology	Economic
Class	Mostly open	Ascription and achievement	Legal ideology	Economic, authority, bureaucratic

system are very well defined and you are legally as well as ideologically prevented from social mobility. One difference between a caste system and a class system is that a social class system has many more ambiguous areas, and movements among classes is much easier. In India, a poor and uneducated peasant could never become a member of the Brahman caste. But in the United States, Willis could certainly become a member of Nancy's middle class and his offspring might even become members of Charles' class, although it would be extremely difficult. True movement through class takes time.

Berreman (1987) explained how race relations in the south were historically a caste system with the same sorts of justifications and prescriptions about contact that exist in the more frequently cited caste system in India. A tendency to symbolically value their own caste or class is one ideological reason that movement beyond the boundaries is difficult. Those in low castes (e.g., slaves) develop symbolic ways to either elevate themselves or lessen the stigma of caste membership. So there is, for example, the caricature of the buffoon who is "happy." Or, many stigmatized group members exaggerate the importance of their own language, customs, and rituals. No low-class or caste member says, "I am of low status because of who I am and I deserve it." People are not content to live a life of deprivation and subjection, so they must rationalize it to maintain a tenable position. Blaming the economic system, history, or some other group are the most common rationalizations. Berreman also explained how all lower groups make claims to higher and more noble ancestry. Communication patterns solidify the boundaries between groups.

How You Are Placed in the System

Related to the first characteristic are the differing methods by which people are placed in the stratification system. The two terms that bound the continuum of placement methods are *ascription* and *achievement*. Ascription is when individuals are placed in classes or groups according to criteria over which they have no control. These are determined by your parents, sex, or race. If you are born African American and thereby considered a slave, your membership in the slave caste is ascriptive rather than achieved. Achievement is when your group membership is the result of your individual merit.

Almost all groups in contemporary American society are a mixture of ascription and achievement. This continuum is the source of controversy in discussions about race, gender, and power. Racist communication is prompted by negative attitudes toward a race and embedded in an ideology about why races have the qualities they do. Ideologies generate specific attitudes. So holding the belief that an individual *should* be assigned to a "station" in life for reasons out of his or her control (e.g., race, gender,) is what is called "racist" or "sexist." When one has an ideologically generated attitude about a group based on belief in ascription, then any new information is nullified. Even if a member of a stigmatized group does achieve, such an achievement will be attributed to circumstances or extraordinary assistance rather than individual merit. In this way, the racist or sexist attitude is maintained and the person is continually "placed" in the group by ascription. Table 6.1 indicates that the class system determines placement by both ascription and achievement. This is so because of the stereotypes that place group members in particular social strata, and the fact that we use the legal and economic system to increase the chances for genuine achievement.

Legitimation

After people are placed in the social hierarchy, there must be some way of justifying this placement. In other words, those at the bottom of the stratification system must have some explanation for their position, and those at the top need to convince themselves that they deserve what they have. Sometimes social structures are maintained through force, but this is usually unsuccessful. Moreover, ideology of some type (legal, religious, traditional) is more effective.

Current stratificational configurations may be justified for any number of reasons. Often customs prevent people from considering alternatives to the structure of society. Legal prescriptions, state rights, privileges, and duties ensure the assignment of certain rewards and ranks. In some cultures, religious beliefs invoke supernatural forces to will a system of differences. But ideology remains the most potent legitimization force, especially as it is communicated in the United States. I take up this issue in other places throughout this book, but introduce it here.

Individuality as Legitimation. For an ideological system to legitimate a particular stratification system, it must be perceived as fair. In the United States, people believe it is the *individual* more than anything else that determines his or her own social condition (Kluegel & Smith, 1986), even when there is evidence to the contrary (Krauze & Slomczynski, 1985). Individual skills, motivations, and circumstances act as a differentiation system that determines the distribution of societal rewards and punishments. There is a dominant U.S. ideology that if you invest in yourself, there will be a payoff. An important question becomes how do we accept a legitimation system based on individuality when we know that contradictory evidence and reasons exist? How do Americans internalize an ideology that justifies inequality? Communication and the interaction of significant symbols in a culture play a key role.

To begin with, individuals make evaluations and judgments about fairness and what members of groups deserve as a result of their own interactions (Fave, 1980). Individuals develop only in relationship to others. Over time, we observe certain patterns with respect to others and how others behave toward us. This interaction forms what Mead (1934) called the "generalized other." This generalized other is really a subjective experience of society, but what is important is that we internalize it within consciousness. The "out there" becomes the "in here." The details of this process need not concern us here, but it leads to a deceptively obvious conclusion: Every individual is a product of society, and society is *in* every individual. Moreover, the mental structures used by individuals to comprehend themselves become stable over time.

This constant communication with others and mediated information creates a sense of objective reality. So if large numbers of people believe that individuals deserve what they get if they work hard, then this becomes a justification for the fact that some people are wealthy. For example, Davis and Smith (1989) reported that people believe that hard work and ambition are more important for making money than being from a wealthy family or any number of other variables such as race, gender, or religion. Those who are successful believe that their own actions brought about that success. This is because of the positive reactions to their success by others.

In a complex societal network, individuals piece together images of others and make evaluations of others and themselves on this basis. For the most part, these conclusions are based on surface information only, namely, wealth, status objects, language, and patterns of communication. But from a communication standpoint, it is primarily language that is responsible for these images and their consequences. Those in control of linguistic and communicative resources use these to manage the impressions of others. Those not in control of linguistic resources have this used against them by way of negative attributions. This all becomes very circular. Those with more communicative resources elicit greater respect, which thereby justifies an unequal distribution of rewards. Because others respect those with symbolic powers, they feel that inequality in the hierarchy of rewards is justified and implicitly legitimated.

Bourdieu (1991) made this point quite clearly by arguing that individuals from lower class environments contribute to a system of evaluation that is not to their advantage. This is the essence of his term *symbolic power*. It is in contradistinction to overt physical power. Symbolic power, as suggested by Bourdieu, is the invisible power that accompanies routine social interaction. The exercise of this power depends on shared beliefs. In other words, a linguistically deprived individual must accept the fact that there are certain modes and styles of discourse that are superior to others for him or her to be subjected by them. If the person has come to believe that certain ways of talking are better, more educated, or more effective than others, then that person is capable of being manipulated, managed, or controlled by those "ways of talking." These symbolic powers are endowed with a legitimacy, and make it so an individual participates in his own subjection. So disadvantaged individuals are not really the passive sufferers of abuse. They believe in the legitimacy of the power modes of discourse, and the individuals who manage such discourse, and are therefore actively contributing to their own social, political, and economic disadvantage.

Anytime there is symbolic power, there is the possibility for a next level of intensity into symbolic violence. As Bourdieu described it, symbolic violence is "gentle, invisible violence, unrecognized as such, chosen as much as undergone, that of trust, obligation, personal loyalty, hospitality, gifts, debts, piety, in a word, of all the virtues honoured by the ethic of honour" (Bourdieu, 1990, p. 127). It is not the violence of the sword but of the word. An excessive gift that cannot be reciprocated and binds the recipient to the gift giver is symbolically violent. The paradoxical messages that contribute to a variety of pathologies and disorders as described by Watzlawick, Beavin, and Jackson (1967) do great symbolic violence. If a mother says to a child, "you don't show your love for me" and then is rejecting when the child hugs the mother, then this interaction does considerable symbolic violence to the child. All of these, at varying levels of intensity and significance, are forms of power legitimated through communication and are fundamental to the differences among groups of people.

Institutions as Legitimation.   Of course most people are experientially rooted in their daily lives and unaware of the institutions and wider social structures that affect their lives. Social structures of various types are typically assumed; even those most oppressed by society's institutions rarely organize for significant change. Although individual interactional and psychological processes surely legitimate inequality, institutions are also directly implicated. The question becomes how do institutions justify and maintain the social stratificational system? An additional interesting question is how institutions intersect with individuals to legitimate social differences?

The beliefs and values endorsed by individuals are determined, in large part, by the institutional framework in which they are embedded. Institutions (e.g., family, religious, educational, media, governmental) are composed of rules and processes that circumscribe the boundaries of behavior. They define what is permissible and what constitutes issues and problems. In a word, they set the social and cultural agenda. Although there are advantages to these definitional rights, they also confine our thinking and limit any potential redistribution of resources. Smith (1987), for example, insightfully described how her own research on parenting and childrearing were influenced by school boards and their control over the definition of problems. The school board in my own neighborhood recently decided to change the Kindergarten (K) through Grade 5 system to one where some schools would be designated K through Grade 2 and paired with another school that would be Grades 3 through 5. The reasons pertain to class sizes, diversity, and economics. But this decision caused a firestorm of protest in the neighborhood because it interfered with the definition of family life related to neighborhood schools, attitudes about busing, the impact on children of changing schools every 3 years, prevention of some siblings from attending school together, parental choice, and interference with children becoming part of a neighborhood community because of changing schools. It is a good example of the reciprocal influence of social institutions and the individual life space.

The previous example is one way that institutions legitimate social structures and influence the interactive relationships in families. The institutions can legitimate either equality or inequality by framing images with particular concepts and terms. How language is used to describe "social problems" influences the communicative and psychological reactions to these problems. Terms such as *diversity, neighborhood schools*, and *parental choice* become conceptual resources in the lived world of families. A comfortable, White, middle-class family who never thought about the "problem" of diversity now must consider it a legitimate problem. When the concept of a "neighborhood school" becomes a "right," then people have a legitimation mechanism influencing the education of others. Institutions of all types use language and symbols to legitimate existing social reality. The evocation of images to encourage acceptance of certain beliefs is true in the spheres of class, economics, gender, and ethnicity. These evocations prompt certain interpretations about society and the "other people" in society.

We cannot improve our understanding of the relationship between individuals and social institutions—and the communication patterns that characterize this relationship—without realizing the power that institutions have to act on reality by the way they represent reality. For example, the educational system (especially the elite educational system) sanctifies and perpetuates an established order. In fact, systems such as these create such orders. The people who move through these social institutions are transformed by them. Others begin to behave differently toward the individual and one's self-understanding changes to conform to how the institution has represented him or her. Bourdieu (1991) is especially insightful with respect to how institutions legitimate boundaries by encouraging recognition of differences between the graduate of the elite institution and others. Moreover, social structures such as institutions or class systems direct attention to one's group membership rather than the boundary lines that separate groups. One is either a member of a social group or not. But the boundary line is the more important question. What does it separate? Such lines separate people. Anytime one is a member of a group, or experiences a rite of passage or investiture, or holds credentials, titles, or qualifications, that person can exploit differences. These differences become more fixed to the extent that they appear more objective.

Any act of boundary making is a communicative act. Each side of the boundary signifies someone as to his or her identity. Even the simplest verbal utterance, such as a ridicule, places someone in a position and then signifies that position. The person then becomes enclosed in this identity. The controversy over admitting women to the Citadel, a traditionally all-male military academy, uses gender differences and tradition to support the rejection of women. These arguments have been so naturalized that they have become the center of the legal arguments around the case. The Citadel utilizes particularly aggressive and demeaning hazing rituals, which are sometimes sexual in nature, in order to establish class bonding. It is quite well known from social psychological experiments that severity of initiation is related to the strength of the attachments to a group. This bonding signifies one as a member of an elite group. Allowing women to "cross the line" into this group fundamentally changed the group's identity. Sexually oriented hazing rituals function specifically to distinguish males from females. This results in assigning social differences to the two sexes that seem like natural differences. These differences then consecrate the differences between the sexes. All of this is part of the legal ideology that sustains the class system (see Table 6.1). I return to issues in legitimation and ideology later.

Primary Factors of the Stratification System

The predominant factor of social inequality is the last criteria by which to classify social systems. This is the quality from which all other inequalities flow. The primary factors of inequality are usually either status differences, economic factors, or power. Most contemporary societies have some combination of the three. And inequality based on one factor typically leads to differences in other factors. In other words, a person favored with respect or prestige can easily translate this into power and economic advantages.

In the warm glow of America, all people are born free and equal. Everyone has an equal opportunity to reach the top. But we all know that such equality does not exist, that some people have status that sets them apart from others. Status is when someone is assigned esteem, respect, or prestige on the basis of individual behavior or accomplishments, or his membership in a group. Status is a particularly sensitive barometer of signification. Because no object or activity is intrinsically worthy and must be assigned value by human agents, it is the semiotic process that determines status. Status is a powerful engine in all cultures, but especially in highly commercial ones such as the United States, where value and self-worth are significantly tied to material success. Clothes, cars, houses, and personal belongings are abundant with status implications. Interestingly, communal cultures, which are not based on material success, have functional status as their primary strata. Because of some important function served by a community member, he or she is afforded higher status without gaining additional material rewards. In primitive communal societies, differences between individuals are minimal, so no legal or ideological system of status justification is necessary.

Economic factors are probably the most fundamental reason for social stratification. Economic issues are predominant in all types of social systems. Even communal systems, where differences are minimized, typically apportion small amounts of status on the basis of economic contributions to the community. As we progress in this book in a study of the interpenetration of micro and macro social processes, we will continually encounter economic issues. Sociologists can explain easily enough how economics establish and maintain differences. The system of acquiring goods and services in a culture is conditioned by access to rewards and opportunities such that some are simply denied opportunities on the basis of power, credentials, or group membership; and differing abilities, because this is another way that people are discouraged from competing for economic advantages. Some of these are psychological, meaning that some people or groups learn ways of thinking about themselves that reduce their self-esteem and control, and increase their alienation and distrust. The system of acquiring goods and services is also influenced by connectivity of people and groups to rewards and opportunities, because this is another way of taking advantage of economic conditions. Upper class people are connected by marriage, kinship, private schools, universities, and clubs, all of which allow them to reap and maintain the economic benefits of their class. The same is true of working-class neighborhoods, where work (e.g., unions), family, church, and physical layout of neighborhoods serve the same functions. And finally, the system is also conditioned by availability, which controls access to opportunities and rewards.

The social categories we explore in this book are subject to these conditions in various ways, although Collins (1975) suggested that social class is the consequence of economic conditions more than anything else. Even though each of the four mechanisms occurs everywhere, they do not occur equally. Social classes, ethnic groups, and genders differ in economic circumstance. But even more importantly for our purposes, these social consequences are the result of people meeting and communicating in certain ways. All people try to establish a line of advantage as they navigate the economic waters, and they do this by maximizing the resources available to them and others. The role of communication is central here. Communication, conceived broadly, includes language, thought, emotion, and interaction, and social structure can be grounded in these processes.

Finally, some groups use power to sustain inequality. *Power* is the ability to control the resources and behavior of others. There is often a negative nuance to the word "power" because it is easily associated with domination, control, manipulation, and other unfavorable interactions. But power can be based on achieved status where one has earned legitimate rights. Weber (1947) called this rational–legal authority, which is most characteristic of modern industrial cultures, and it is based on the belief in the legality and "rightness" of established laws and rules. An "office," rather than an individual, holds authority, and the legal rights of the office bring compliance. This type of power is a particularly important stratificational principle in mostly open-class societies that use legal ideology to legitimate the workings of the culture. The United States is such a society.

The establishment of power in a culture is a developmental process. It begins the same way that all inequality begins, with the recognition of differences. As soon as some are more skilled than others, more intelligent, more athletic, taller, shorter, or have different skin color, then the possibility of inequality has been established. After differences are recognized, those differences are infused with meaning. It is only natural that we look for reasons and explanations for differences and it is not long before such differences become "right" or "natural." Skin color is a good example. By itself, it is a "mere" difference, but when meanings are attached to it, inequality is the result. Next, difference must be legitimated; that is, the social system must develop reasons to justify the differences. Power is crude and typically based on force before differences are legitimated. One group dominates another, but force is the basis of the domination. Power is legitimated by authority when domination is tamed. Then Weber's rational–legal authority is most important because it becomes the cultural and philosophical justification for the differences. At this point, differences are accepted as sensible, justified, rational, moral, and necessary. Finally, power must be symbolized so that people can be reminded of the power relationship, and can recognize who is powerful and who is not.

The "constructive" nature of the power relationship is important to underscore. By this I mean that power is established by people in social interaction. It may be possible to argue for some "real" and "natural" differences that are not subject to cultural influences, but such arguments need not concern us here. Most differences have no basis in biology, and for this reason, different meanings can be attached to the same characteristics, and different characteristics can have the same meanings. So gender and ethnicity, are quite disabling in some cultures and less so in others. Social perceptions and consequences of being labeled as a member of a stratified group (e.g., "female," "African American," "working class," "educated") are in no small way linguistic constructions. Instead of assuming that people have fixed relationships with each other and nature, it is useful to think about how people and power relations are constituted by language features, including traditional linguistic categories (phonology, vocabulary, syntax) and ways of talking, message strategies, forms of accountability, and the like.

COMMUNICATION CODES AND CLASS

In this section I advance some theoretical statements positing the relationship between communication codes and the stratification system. This is one more link in the micro–macro dialectic. There are three basic assumptions:

1. Institutions and organizations reflect the workings of the class system.
2. Speakers are socialized into a communication code that is sensitive to their own class code as well as others. Speakers develop different levels of skill and sophistication within their own class code as well as others. This "other" code is associated with the dominant class in the culture that uses the linguistic standard and the discourse of dominance.

3. Speakers are able to interpret and invoke more than one code at a time, which is the reason for communicative conflict, ambiguity, and confusion that is theoretically class driven.

These assumptions receive some of their most articulate and well-known expression in Bernstein's (1971) theory of elaborated and restricted codes. I am less concerned about critique of Bernstein here (see Labov, 1972) than in promoting understanding of the relationship between communication codes and social class. In doing so, I draw on other work in codes and class (e.g., Ellis, 1992b; Huspek, 1986) with special emphasis on the structuring role of communication and class production and reproduction. From a communication standpoint, classes are produced and reproduced in a significant way through meanings and class-specific values. Members of a class have access to and employ certain codes of communication. Bernstein described the working-class code as restrictive, and the middle- and upper-class codes as elaborated. These differences were measured by surface-level linguistic features that were signs of deeper conceptual and semantic mechanisms that were sociologically related to society: elaborated codes of the middle class were explicit and universal—capable of more sophisticated and complex expression—and restricted codes were particular and highly positioned (Ellis, 1994) and "restricted" to particular contexts.

The assumption that the elaborated code is superior and more appropriate for higher-level cognitive work has been controversial. It has led to a deficit thesis that promotes the idea that restricted code users are deficient. It also encourages troublesome stereotypes about the classes. But this difference–deficit hypothesis is not my concern. The various differences among the classes in codes and discursive practices is the result of the complex production of disadvantage. Scholars such as Labov (1972) have demonstrated that these differences exist and have practical consequences, even if modes of speech, such as restricted codes, do not literally produce cognitive deficits. Class categories are simply too gross to result in anything but more general conclusions. We will see, as follows, that class categories have traction in the public consciousness, and may be useful for theoretical discussion, but their measurement is too difficult for refined distinctions. Moreover, the most common and accepted distinction between manual and nonmanual labor is losing its meaning in the postindustrial age.

It is best to think of class codes as a collection of strategies and interpretive procedures for both the class-based use of language and interpretation of language. Class is "marked" in the sociolinguistic sense. Codes reflect the language user as a member of society with various social experiences, class being a fundamental one. Individuals have subjectively organized their reality, and these concepts are central to the production and interpretation of language. When an individual in a social world that includes a class standing forms a subjective concept about some aspect of reality, there is a sign relationship between the concept and the semantic reality that the concept represents. These subjective concepts are organized semiotically and systems of these concepts are codes. These systems of concepts (codes) are capable of evolution and development, but they can also stay stable. Just as adaptation is natural in the biological scenario, so too do systems of concepts change to suit contexts, individuals, historical developments, and cultural variation. The elements of the code may have both etic and emic status; that is, some language features and communication patterns are etic or quite objective and individuals are completely unaware of their presence. Others are emic, or part of the conscious knowledge base of the individuals.

For example, the young working-class men in the Willis (1977) study developed a subjective meaning for the concept *school*. The concept *school* formed a sign relationship with other various meanings such that "school" pointed to semantic categories about "resentment," "waste of time," and "conflicting authority," and these young men entered into an oppositional relationship with the schools and their authority structures. This attitude is part of their class code that sees school as an obstruction that offers them little, rather than a code that contained more positive signs for education. These codes develop from various symbolic contexts including interpersonal, family, and economic environments. The students regularly encountered the educational authorities and developed discursive practices that expressed their resentment. They would misbehave, fidget, make jokes, slouch in their chairs, and perform mock insubordination. They also expressed many class-specific meanings in their interactions with the authorities. The important conclusion here is that these young men do not simply reflect a class consciousness and reproduce their own class processes. They do more than that by producing and interpreting meanings across classes. Their own code is devalued not because it is so deficient, but because of prevailing institutional attitudes.

In our mobile and communicatively connected culture, it is important to expand the significance of social contexts in determining code usage. Contexts are not equally distributed across the cultural landscape. The more restricted codes of the middle and lower middle classes gain more currency in contexts where it is more useful. But these codes run into problems when they are used in contexts that reflect the norms of the more powerful classes in society. These contexts (e.g., schools, government institutions) are structured in a way to secure their own privileges. But recent changes in society, including mobility and new forms of communicative contact, have rendered social classes more malleable and encouraged a "relational" model of classes (Wright, 1985). This is a model that is more concerned with the points of contact among classes and with how classes are related. A relational model is more concerned with the structuring proceses of classes, of what forces play significant roles in constructing and reproducing the class. The focus is less on categorization and definition, and more on the various classes related to one another, and structuring mechanisms in the culture.

Communication codes are useful because they move beyond static correlations between classes and other variables (e.g., linguistic ones). These correlations are useful, but perform a more etic function than an emic one. Codes have increased explanatory power to the extent that they do a better job of explaining contexts and the various conflicts and struggles within these contexts. For example, the working-class code is very evident in the workplace, where language and relationships are regulated in ways that maintain differences in power, and differences between the dominant and knowledgeable individuals and those with little power and symbolic resources. Individuals in the middle and lower middle classes work in environments where (a) knowledge is unequally distributed and reserved for the controlling few, (b) decision making is not available in any significant way to subordinates, (c) their work and behaviors are monitored, (d) reprisals are a common occurance, and (e) they have class-based attitudes about work and leisure that are at odds with those in control. These contexts shape class consciousness and modes of discourse because there are always relationships among members of different classes and struggles over resources. So class-based codes are structured by contexts, but also transformed by their relationships with other realms of meaning.

A line of research by Huspek (1986, 1989) and Huspek and Kendall (1991) has offered useful empirical demonstrations of how class codes are responsive to relationships between classes, and improved Bernstein's theorizing by making codes something more than linguistic straitjackets. Class-distinctive codes reflect an individual's life experiences, but also reflect meanings shaped by particular contexts and contacts with members of other classes. This means that members of classes are not bound only by code parameters, but can tap into other codes and communicate in a way that reflects an accommodation between their own code and others. We can still posit class codes that look something like Bernstein's elaborated and restricted—or, syntactic and pragmatic, as discussed in chapter 4—where one code is considered dominant and standard and the other subordinate. But these codes exist in relation to one another and not in isolation. The dominant code is more prestigious and promoted within formal institutions, but it is not always available to everyone. It is essentially sealed off from some because they do not have access to education or the relationships that command forms of meaning that entitle one to be listened to by others. The user of less pretigious and complex codes is particularly disadvantaged because he or she accepts a standard ideology that includes respect for "accomplishment," "fairness," "equality," "justice," and "competition." But all of these are disproportionately available to, and weighted in favor of, the dominant classes to the disadvantage of the working class (Bourdieu, 1986).

These codes must be understood in relation to one another; in fact, we are required to do so. They are not simply different, but are formed in relation to other codes and sustained and reproduced by their users. The dominant mode of speech is not simply a standard with universal meanings, but requires an "other," an "opposition." The dominant middle-class code gains strength and identity as a counterpoint to restricted codes, street dialects, antilanguages, and all manner of variations. Huspek's (1989) study of working-class speakers' use of the construction "you know" is a good example of how a discourse feature typically understood as weak, resistant to logical development, and deferent to others (Bernstein, 1971) can be understood as a skillful strategy rather than a clumsy circumlocution. He explains how a regular use of "you know" in certain employment situations (as in "You just talk to them y'know, and then go get some help y'know ...") signifies the strain on working-class speakers to incorporate their own class code with that of the dominant code. It is not, in Bernstein's language, restricted, but a skillful navigation of competing ideas and worlds of meaning.

CLASS CULTURES

With the previously mentioned issues in mind, let's overview class cultures with an eye toward the axes that distinguish the classes. The idea here is not to simply describe standard class categories, because such descriptions are available (e.g., Crompton, 1993), but to describe class cultures more in terms of the process of social stratification rather than just mapping tastes and classifications. This is consistent with the theoretical orientation of this book, and recent work by Bourdieu (1987, 1991). The focus is on class cultures with all their economic, power, status, and occupational implications, but also on the more microprocesses of structuring that have resulted in new factors and class arrangements. These result from the postindustrial era, technology, and Bourdieu's important contribution of capital—economic, cultural, social, and symbolic—that empowers (or not) people within social spaces. This approach is also a response to the most common criticism of class analysis, which is that the categories are too rigid and static because they are based on simple "in" or "out" decisions. In other words, all plumbers are put in the same social class, and no distinctions are made between owning a plumbing company and working as a journeyman plumber. I realize that the terminology of upper class, upper middle class, and so forth is hierarchic and implies closed categories, but I use them because they represent terminology that has some semantic standing for most people.

Goldthorpe and Marshall (1992), Wright (1985), and Clark and Lipset (1991) all criticized class analysis for failing to capture the underlying dynamics. Classes should be defined in terms of social relations, not technical ones, even though notions of control, exploitation, cosmopolitanism, and capital remain central to definition and membership in classes. As is seen here, conversation is an integral part of social relationships and responsible for the points of agreement that exist around social settings. These points of agreement sustain values and become the ingredients for the class structures.

Current analyses of class are more concerned with the fragmentation of classes and the increasing complexity and importance of status, identity, and lifestyles on class membership. Traditional class analysis was more "objectivist" in that it was determined by tangible assets with precise definitional require-ments. Groups were then sorted into vertical categories. Newer analyses of class focus on the process of constructing a class status and consciousness. It is con-cerned with the linguistic, social, and communication processes that foster class membership and consciousness. This is not to say that more objective measures of class are ignored, just that cultural changes and postmodernist sensibilities have altered modern capitalism (Bell, 1976). This includes Bourdieu's intro-duction of the capital metaphor, which emphasizes the various ideological con-ditions of existence, and how individuals and groups use their capital to compete for position and resources. So, one individual or group may possess economic capital—money and property—and another group may own cultural capital in the form of education and high-level cognitive abilities. One form of capital can lead to another and redefine the class structure.

We all occupy a social space that carries capital or the lack thereof. Cultural capital, for example, is acquired through the state or social institutions. It is the resources that one can marshal because of their standing or experiences in the culture. Some capital is in the form of inherited understandings and cultural po-sitions. We inherit meanings and discourses associated with class, ethnicity, re-ligion, and so forth, that can be transformed into cultural capital and power, or these inheritances can be disabling. Certain physical embodiments carry capital within cultural contexts (Bourdieu, 1986). Being White and male are overval-ued in our culture and afford one cultural capital. Social mobility is one of the bedrock concepts in stratification theory. It means that people can move up and down the status and class scale. It is an indicator that rewards are distributed ac-cording to talent and personal qualities rather than birthright, personal connec-tions, or inheritance. Having Whiteness and masculinity as cultural capital increases the opportunity for movement. Given an ideological culture that val-ues maleness and Whiteness, it becomes easier for members of these groups to access institutions (e.g., educational institutions) and opportunities.

The young working-class boys observed by Willis (1977), in his often-cited study had only macho physicality as a cultural capital. Their inherited dis-courses did not prepare them to succeed in school and they developed oppositional attitudes about teachers and educational authorities. These young men suffered when it came time to trade on their physicality, which was their only form of cultural capital, and of little use or desirability in a postindustrial service economy.

In July 1995 *Newsweek* magazine ("Rise of the Overclass," 1995) devoted its cover to a story on what they termed *the overclass,* a new elite of wealthy, high-tech strivers who are characterized mostly by brains and hard work. The traditional U.S. class system has probably been most reorganized by these indi-viduals and the idea of a meritocracy, an idea that values expertise, information, professionalism, and ambitious maneuvering ahead of family ties. There was an old established upper class defined by long-term family wealth, ties to the best universities and law firms, Wall Street, charitable foundations, and finance. And although I do not want to overstate the point because this establishment still exists in certain configurations, it did begin to break up and reorganize after World War II. The GI Bill that made education possible for millions who heretofore would not have had education available to them, the civil rights movement, feminism, the Vietnam War, affirmative action, economic affluence, and more open access to elite educational institutions all contributed to a bloodless revolution in the class system. This change was at the more microlevel. Class has traditionally been studied as a macrostructure, but the aforementioned changes in society reflect political coalitions in advanced market economies that make class more politically relevant. The more abstract macrolevel of class does not provide the language for exploring ideas about class that are both suitable for microanalysis and sensitive to political realities.

Class and the Micro–Macro Dialectic

Class, like ethnicity, is a social structure that can be distinguished by micro- or macrolevels of abstraction, or "types" and "tokens." In other words, class structures and their terminology (e.g., upper class, middle class, etc.) are types, and the empirical manifestations of these types are the tokens that point to and indicate membership in the category. In a strict Marxist tradition, the class structure is a "type" that is analytically linked to a mode of production (token). An individual, for example, who controlled capital, privately owned production, and collected surplus capital (profits) would be immersed in a set of everyday behaviors and attitudes that placed him in the aristocracy or capitalist class.

But industrialization, labor movements, and changing definitions of citizenship have altered class conflict such that the traditional Marxist classes of aristocracy, bourgeoisie, and proletariat have given way to new class structures that remain capitalist, but reflect an economy based on technology. Our highly technologized capitalist culture has replaced the production of material goods necessary for life with consumable commodities that must be consumed in order to produce more of them. This has produced a culture of consumers concerned more with objects that confer status (Frankfurt, 1973). The modern technologized capitalist culture is more affluent, which creates a more comfortable nondissenting labor force. Moreover, it seeks to satisfy common consumption patterns and thereby creates mass culture and popular taste.

Critique of industrialized capitalism is not important for my concerns here. Needless to say, these trends have been the subject of much discussion and analysis (cf. Bell, 1973; Held, 1980; Marcuse, 1964). But one of the most discussed changes in the class systems has been the growth of the middle class and the creation of "taste" classes (Bourdieu, 1986). As class identity and consciousness becomes more associated with consumption and tastes, it becomes more reliant on microchoices and behaviors, and more changing and unstable because mobility is so much more a possibility. Rather than a Marxian clash of class titans, there is an expanding stable middle class that continues to absorb the proletariat.

From a micro–macro standpoint, these are new levels of aggregation of social phenomena. One way to conceptualize the micro–macro levels of class is to assume that class macrostructures define a set of micropositions filled by individuals. To fill one of these positions means that the individual is subject to experiences and constraints on how individuals act in the world. Language and communication are the most salient of the micromechanisms because of their role in determining material interests of individuals and shaping subjective understandings. Language and communication are also basic resources that individuals use to pursue their interests. The broadening middle class, and the movement from manual or "blue-collar" work to nonmanual or "white-collar" work begs the question about what these classes are like and how an individual moves from one subjective reality to the other. It is important to at least address these things because class does not exist in ready-made reality. It must be constituted through material and symbolic means, which leaves its borders continually shifting and disputed as they transform themselves.

Focusing more on the micro–macro dialectic produces a more fine-grained analysis without suggesting that class structures are reducible to either structure or action. Integrating the micro and the macro into a logic is one goal. This logic helps us understand how micro level language, communication, and subjective experiences influence macroarrangements. The notions of various types of capital help explain various seeming contradictions and differences in the class system. How, for example, an individual can have easy access to economic capital in the form of wealth and affluence, but lack cultural capital, such as in the case of the modern professional athlete who is very wealthy but is poorly educated (Bourdieu, 1986). This creates new patterns of consumption and communication, and alters the traditionally polarized macro Marxist classes. This more microlevel concentration moves from the abstract to the concrete.

Wright (1985) filled these microclass locations with "jobs" because they are the empty spaces that individuals fill. He categorized jobs as either worker, managerial, supervisory, capitalist, and various levels of skill, and creates a matrix of locations that represent types of work. The cells in these matrices are further influenced by culture, gender, and other ideological factors, and then form coalitions of different sorts that represent the class formations in various cultures. But we should fill these micro locations with interaction and conversational patterns. Wright was correct that jobs are the spaces that individuals fill, but these work patterns are a series of relationships, conversations, and types of talk. People in various types of jobs differ with respect to deference, order giving, cultural capital they can donate to an interaction, and the general network or "culture" of the people who are shaped by similar patterns and experiences, including their social world. This task can be quite arduous, but worth an effort, because it renders class more empirical and helps untie the conceptual knots of the structure–action dichotomy.

CLASSES, COMMUNICATION, AND REPRODUCTION

The section in chapter 4 on interaction ritual chains and conversations explained the theoretical centrality of interaction in determining social experience. One's class placement is not only determined by occupational position, but by class consciousness as well. This consciousness is a reality enacted primarily by the language and communication patterns that pass between individuals. The various types of capital are circulated, and they aggregate into macroclass patterns. High finance, Wall Street, and international economics are real and regular topics of conversation to the upper class, but are rare and foggy for the lower classes. Each of these "jobs" described by Wright are talked about and composed of interaction patterns that take place within an interactional milieu. This milieu is stratified and contains the history of interactions that have led to the present, and are setting one on a trajectory toward the future.

"Classes" are collections of people shaped by interactive experiences. Membership in a social class increases or decreases the probability that one had certain experiences with respect to relationships and interaction. Classes pursue common interests that are economic, aesthetic, and communicative, and then become status groups. They uphold a common culture and attach value to it. Status is ascribed on the basis of one's position in the conversational market. This position can improve or decline in spurts as one achieves or fails in the arenas of occupation, education, and social success. Most individuals develop specialized and repetitive patterns of interaction that have the advantage of increasing confidence and skill, but the disadvantage of too much narrow specialization that places the person within a highly circumscribed enclave. It is possible to think of each individual as the center of a galaxy of relationships. Each is bound to all others and shares an orbit of common discourse. These orbits are interactional situations that are hypostatized into what we call an individual's personality or consciousness.

The *upper classes* interact in an environment where they maintain control and defer very little. Wealth is the most obvious way that one achieves this class status, but politics and the military have also been historically desirable routes. In both the United States and Great Britain, wealth is highly concentrated in a small percentage of the population. The postindustrial society has great concentrations of corporate power in large companies that have tremendous control over their markets and related products. Propertied families, along with a managerial class, continue to hold positions of control in modern economies through an interlocking network of ownership, directorships, and management positions (Scott, 1982). These interaction networks are very cohesive and held together by kinship connections and educational experiences. This upper class forms a status group that works hard to reproduce itself. This class group is like the others, in that it is produced and reproduced by education, leisure, and discourse. These correspond closely to Bourdieu's cultural capital. Money alone does not define these classes. Style, taste, manners, and traditions are equally as important as economic capital for class consciousness.

Certainly the educational experiences of the upper classes are exemplified by private schools and elite universities. Striving parents and students are aware of this, as evidenced by the regular increase in applications to these institutions, known colloquially as "applying up." The integration into social networks is equally as important as the educational "state of mind" that results from university attendance. The relationship between the class system and college attendance is clear. Comparing college attendance to family income quartiles indicates a persistent class gap. Students from higher income classes are almost twice as likely to attend college (U.S. Census, 1990). Crompton (1993) pointed out that even after Thatcherite conservatism and a supposed shift from old-style conservative praticianism in Great Britain, it remained the case that in 1987 not a single conservative member of parliament was from a working-class background, and 44% of them had Oxbridge educations.

This educational experience creates a strong ideology about politics, aesthetics, and language that permeates the upper classes. It results in the acceptance of a common symbol system used to interpret material existence. Even the articulatory style of the upper classes that Bourdieu (1991) explained as a "life style 'made flesh'" (p. 86) betrays class ideology and discourse form. Overly articulate speech that carries "airs and graces" conveys the physical features of tension, distance, and conservatism. Attitudes about speaking, and food for that matter, are characterized by a haughtiness and slight evaluative distance, an analytical turn of mind that directs attention more to judgment than unreflective pleasure. The dominated classes, on the other hand, engage a verbal style that rejects docility and the subordination of emotions that accompany upper class sensibilities. The educational system is the most important institution in society that invades the consciousness of all classes. It alone is responsible for cultural capital. The cultural capital of education, fine arts, sophisticated technical knowledge, and readership are not equally distributed across the classes. These systems of discourse are a code that require a key. Only families and educational institutions have the keys.

Upper class attitudes and perspectives are the result of experiencing control and linguistic distinction and precision. Having others defer to you is related to control of material resources, but is also a matter of bearing. One must expect others to behave in a polite and subordinate manner and treat anything otherwise as unthinkable. The confidence and composure of the upper class is the result of this attitude about deference. The individual reaps so many rewards from financial, social, political, and religious institutions that he becomes the embodiment of their values, and expects others to comply. Educated discourse is distinct and thereby afforded more value.

The educational system is such an integral part of the class system that it is the primary mechanism of a reproduction circuit for the classes. Bourdieu (1991) referred to this process by explaining how the educational system works unequally in the culture. It expends differential time and intensity on different groups and creates knowledge, skill, and competence with educated discourse forms for one group (upper classes), but only recognition of these things for another group (lower classes). This distinct group—the one with cultural capital—contains valued discourse to which others aspire. It is the middle class and professional groups (an intermediate class region) that work hardest to change their language and be accepted into the upper regions of class spheres. As highly capitalized usage increases, and is appropriated by the middle and lower classes, it creates a tendency for new forms of linguistic distinction. Thus, academicians and public intellectuals find new ways to distinguish themselves from more common forms of discourse, as in the discursive gymnastics of postmodernist texts and arguments. It is clear that anything (e.g., linguistic resources) is only considered "capital" if it rare enough and desirable enough to be valued and sought after. So regularly creating rarity and demand is a driving force of a culture, which makes for the continuous reproduction of "differences" in the form of classes.

The fact that the classes have different tastes and lifestyles would be profoundly uninteresting if this were intended as a simple observation. It is trivial, but perhaps amusing, to know that the upper class house sits on stately property with high ceilings, has curved moldings and baseboards, hardwood floors with a threadbare oriental rug, flowers arranged on a table, and that the occupant of the house enjoys oriental drawings, and has the *Hudson Review* and the *Times Literary Supplement* on the coffee table. What is important is to know is that a dominant class demonstrates its superiority by creating aesthetic distinctiveness for these objects and thereby reproducing social and cultural differences in the form of classes. This class of people use their cultural and economic capital to demonstrate superiority, which is impossible to do unless someone else is subordinate and inferior. If a subordinate class is constrained culturally and economically, then it is less valued and the differences among people and classes are sustained and legitimated.

This micro–macro circuit that reproduces distinction for the maintenance of the classes is very apparent in upper-class forms of sociability. Socialization is certainly more formalized in the upper classes: musical events, balls, charity shows, philanthropic activities, as well as entertaining guests take up most of the time allocated to socializing. The "junior committees" in New York are one example of a micro relational structure that helps reproduce the class system (see Yazigi, 1998). These committees are composed of young people from wealthy and distinguished families who are members of committees that organize social and charitable events. Although the committees do some organizational work, they are really much more: a floating cocktail party and a mixer for young people from the right schools and families. The committee members occupy a similar social space, so they form groups and thereby constitute themselves. In doing so, they construct a certain vision of the social world and place themselves in it. All of the committee activities and symbolic representations reinforce a propensity to favor a certain view of the world and devalue other views. Thus, classes and their nature become sociologically objectified, and this macro objectification becomes even more powerful to the extent that it is rooted in reality, and hence corresponds to real divisions in society.

The middle class is a broad continuum of functionaries that covers a variety of situations. At the upper end is the upper-middle class, who are functionaries who deal mainly with other functionaries. They are independent larger businessmen and businesswomen and professionals who have relationships with financial, government, and military institutions. They have considerable mobility, power, and cultural capital. At the other end is the lower middle class, who are respectable and hardworking artisans, and shopkeepers, and hold lower level service jobs. The middle class continuum is quite broad and the structuring processes produce considerable differences between the two ends of the continuum. The micro discursive experiences, as well the taste cultures of the two, are quite distinct. The middle class is particularly organized by the various positions in the communication network of larger society.

The *upper middle class* possesses considerable wealth. The primary difference between it and an upper or capitalist class is that the wealth is earned in medicine, law, or finance. It has a complacent gentility and is organizationally conscious, cosmopolitan, and reasonably formal with respect to social and community affairs. In contemporary society it is what *Newsweek* called the "overclass" ("Rise of the Overclass," 1995) who are publishers, media people, and technology and finance people, all of whom are preoccupied with striving and achievement. The upper middle class has progressively more expensive taste and demands "quality" food, clothing, houses, cigars, and champagne as it borrows from the even more elite. The upper middle class is highly desirable for the lower rungs of the middle class because it is more obtainable: it is a familiar and credible fantasy.

A sense of cosmopolitanism and abstract rhetoric characterizes the upper middle class, and this is often distrusted by those in more constrained classes. This cosmopolitanism is a form of cultural capital that clearly distinguishes the upper middle class from the middle class and below. The abstract rhetoric is one of the objective properties of the class that affirms its existence. Thus, the upper middle class has a broader communication network and a more diverse set of social relationships than typical members of a working-class community. Their work easily spills over into the social world of professional conferences, conventions, and parties composed mainly of people in the same or similar professions.

The topical interaction at these things contains much politicking, shop talk, and work-related gossip. But the cultural capital of the upper middle class—in the form of linguistic prowess and intellectual expertise—makes for interaction infused with intellectual hierarchies; hence, there is cultivated and knowledgeable talk about public affairs, media, technology, and the arts. The upper middle class is skilled at manipulating conversation because of their control in many affairs. Their conversation is less formalistic and more differentiated.

Education and cultural capital (along with symbolic capital) are the prime structuring forces of the upper middle class. Comfort and skill in a syntactic code (Ellis, 1992b) and an orientation toward language that is elaborated, complex, theoretical, and free of rigid contextuality confers the power of representation and signification on its users. Controversial and as complex as these issues are, the discursive forms of education are marked by richer vocabulary, more differentiated meaning, and a structural complexity that is necessary to carry information about persons, events, and ideas (Haslett, 1990). Giddens (Cassell, 1993) spoke to this point when he wrote about class structuration as accomplished in part by the division of labor. And within modern society, the most significant proximate (micro) structuration of labor is between manual labor and highly skilled and technical intellectual nonmanual labor. The cultural capital (in the form of linguistic qualification acquired through education) that is necessary to perform more cognitive nonmanual labor (e.g., law, medicine, finance) separates these individuals from manual and service workers and reinforces the authority system. This physical and emotional separation reinforces the structuring of the classes at the upper levels because it confers control and command on the top levels. Very large corporations that own many small offices and outlets such as medical offices, insurance agents, undertakers, or mortgage institutions create work environments very distant from management and control, often "corporate headquarters" are not in the same state.

Within the upper strands of the middle class, there is a distinction drawn between those groups high in economic capital but low in cultural capital, and intellectual groups that are high in cultural capital but lower in economic capital. These intellectual groups do not have the power and finances of the overclass element of the upper middle class, but they are, in Weber's terms, a different status group. They differ significantly with respect to taste. The nouveau riche, professional athletes, and media performers are good contemporary examples of groups that can be very high in economic capital but poor in education and taste (cultural capital). Their taste, in the Bourdieu (1986, 1987) sense, is characterized by simple culinary preferences, flamboyant clothes or activities, and larger, spectacle entertainment preferences. The more intellectual group is politically active, and more preoccupied with literature, ideas, politics, and interesting and enlightening cultural experiences pertaining to food and travel. These different lifestyles construct and affirm their social position.

The middle of the middle class continuum is increasingly defined by nonmanual service work. This service work shares many things in common with more traditional manual labor such as close supervision, routinization, and low pay. It is quite differentiated from higher level nonmanual labor, which is associated with the dominant structures of wealth and power, and requires more cultural capital. Examples of lower level service work would be the hotel and restaurant trade or "hospitality industry," and other service positions would include midlevel state employees, librarians, physiotherapists, and social workers. Middle-class employment, and the people who occupy these employment positions, are quite heterogeneous, and classifying all these people is difficult. But this is less true of middle-class social practices. Middle-class interaction patterns are affable and carried out mostly during the day in community groups. There is more emphasis on family activities and children participating in sports and community activities than there is in entertaining friends and associates. There is a flow of talk that avoids more serious issues in the interest of avoiding a disruptive and potentially fractionated social life. This is one reason that "intellectuals" denounce the "conformity" of the middle class. The middle class is, of course, the largest, most common, and most diffuse class. The problem of its status, composition, and description has frustrated social theorists for a long time (Wacquant, 1991).

The transformation of the labor process is the key middle-class structuring device in the United States. This is coupled with a recognition of culture, ideology, and interaction as additional structuring devices. The growth of the service sector reflects a significant change in the middle-class experience, and cultural ideology about work. First, many of the occupants of these positions might have been considered working class, but these new jobs require more "social skills" than traditional working-class jobs. That is, they need to communicate more with others. They need to sell, welcome, discuss in groups, coordinate with other people, and so on. Thus, low-level service employees receive training in "communication," where they learn about things like "customer service" and general "people" skills. Because these jobs are typically routine and uninteresting, management devotes considerable time to managing employees by generating commitment to the company and a paternalistic sense of organizational well being. Employers increasingly hire counselors, communication specialists, assertiveness trainers, and so forth to help satisfy the needs and feelings of employees. This represents a significant change in middle-class consciousness that incorporates many more aspects of the human condition. Habermas (1989) and Featherstone (1991) have equated this shift with "postmodernism," or a turn to a discourse that is more humanistic and totalizing than the hard rationality of early theories of work and class.

It is consumption and the continual re-creation of the experience of consumption that structures the middle class. The middle class has only moderate levels of cultural capital, but technology and the increased size and pace of the

American economy have created a vast array of goods and services that are easily consumed and then reproduced for additional consumption. This is all sustained and reinforced by a discourse of pleasure and personal entitlement.
Consumption and the satisfaction of personal desires in food, clothing, family,
and emotional needs is considered real and life affirming. Some, such as Bell
(1973, 1976), have turned this into a symbol of moral decline, but such interpretations are not my concern here. Bourdieu, on the other hand, is more concerned with how the middle class positions itself in social space. Middle-class
consciousness is positioned mostly by a discourse that produces needs and symbols. When a young male demands expensive tennis shoes made by Nike, he is
consuming a sign, not a commodity. He has been symbolically constructed by a
system of meanings informed by an ideology of needs, and the tennis shoes satisfy these needs. These ideologies are always consistent with dominant class interests, and they succeed by taking particular interests and presenting them as
universal. Power groups in the culture such as the upper classes, use communication and symbol systems (e.g., media, persuasive messages, linguistic prowess)
as instruments to create cultural needs, and then satisfy them. This structuring
maintains the differences between the classes. Symbolic power—the power to
constitute meanings and make people believe and confirm a reality—has an almost magical effect with the same impact of physical force.

The lower middle class has even more restrictive social contacts and communication patterns. Time spent with the family, and various ceremonial occasions are the most common situations for social talk. The lower-middle class is
structured by its precarious and restrictive work situation. Occupants of these
positions receive more orders than they give, and defer to others with regularity.
They realize that discipline and order are the skills and dispositions that best
guarantee their success. Individuals in these lower-level service and labor jobs
carry out menial and repetitive tasks, but maintain an identification with the
values of the organization and the rights of authority because they have a stake
in the system, however insubstantial. Giddens explained how "mobility closure"
is an important structuring device for the lower-middle classes. This is a term
from Weber that refers to the relationship between members of a class group and
the market with respect to the possibility of movement between classes. That is,
groups protect their privileges by making it difficult to acquire membership. Social mobility is facilitated by education, skills, inherited consciousness, and
training, all of which are necessary for class mobility. The lower middle class is
particularly restrained by this. They work within a very narrow range of options,
and are therefore vulnerable to market and technological changes that can easily disrupt their economic viability.

From an occupational standpoint, the lower middle class is formed by semi-
skilled workers and uncredentialed service people. However, they are still able
to participate in the economic system and maintain a level of subsistence. This
is an important difference between the lower middle class and the underclass.

The old distinction between manual and non-manual labor that distinguished the "working class" from the middle class has now been superseded. In the postindustrial society working class now includes lower level clerical and service occupations. And some working-class occupations are economically and culturally in the middle classes, but others are lower middle class. The movement of women into the workforce has had a significant impact on the this level of the middle class (Skeggs, 1997). This has fragmented the traditional working-class structure, but added a second income, and the concomitant increase in power and aspiration, to many other households.

This level of the middle class can still organize to protect its own interests, and these organizational activities are a microprocess that structures this class categorization. Old-fashioned trade unions are now less important than informal interpersonal structures that protect interests, even if only defensively. But the most important ideology to develop in the past decades, which has helped maintain the viability of the lower-middle class and the underclass, is the concept of citizenship. Citizenship is the notion, as Polanyi (1957) pointed out, that market forces are not and should not be the only mechanism that decides the fate of human beings. Family, kinship, religion, arts, and moral doctrines are also part of the individual nature and act as a check on cruel market forces. The notion that a society should work to include everyone as a participating member, and ensure political and social rights, has become a regulatory ideology that has furthered the interests—primarily the economic ones—of the lower rungs of the class ladder.

The underclass is a more distinct group from the various levels of the middle class. This is a relatively new term and refers to (a) individuals who experience long-term unemployment, (b) family households with only one parent, usually the mother; (c) a concentration of the poorest members of a society, usually in a deprived inner city; and (d) economic dependence on the state. The underclass is closely related to ethnicity in the United States. It becomes very difficult to escape these circumstances, and a culture of dependency is created that perpetuates these conditions for generations. These people are, to state the matter bluntly, the losers in a market-based economy. This class lacks market capacities, and often they lack full citizenship opportunities which is why many members of the underclass are minorities or immigrants. Moreover, in recent years, a strong ideology about the centrality of market forces, and conservative political trends, have increased the size of the underclass. Citizenship rights that once made for welfare provisions have now been redefined as undermining individual freedoms and creating the culture of dependency and debilitating individual capacities.

An interesting structuring issue with respect to the underclass, is the fact that it does not have a relationship with the dominant means of cultural and material production. It is not part of the normal mechanisms of cultural and capital production. It is not on the middle-class continuum and has very little to do with the upper classes. For this reason, it is typically explained as an individual deficiency. There is a tendency to simply assume that some people are better than others, and those at the bottom are intellectually and even morally inadequate. This is quite different than the rather rigid morality of the middle class, and is a microexplanation for what some believe to be a macro problem. But of course there is a micro–macro dialectic. The argument is that the underclass develops moral and communicative stances that essentially remove efforts at personal improvement and hard work. But the macroside of the dialectic is that skills, values, and communication patterns emerge from social circumstances and reflect class and ethnic positions. This has been called the *structuralist* versus *culturalist* argument in sociology (Wilson, 1991) and is conceptually akin to the macro–micro distinction.

Underclass culture, finally, is built on few attachments to major organizations. Indeed, it is possible to argue that the underclass is not a culture at all because it lacks strong personal ties and stable groups. There are very few, if any, organized gatherings because the culture of the underclass is highly individualistic, with little or no coherent groups. Interaction contexts are relatively unstructured and occur in public places where there is little privacy. Consequently, norms of politeness do not develop in the same way and personal matters are discussed in public. It is an unsure, frustrated, and distrustful world, so relational bonds and emotional personal narrations are rare. Much of the interaction is joking and bantering, which is suited for atmospheres of distrust. These forms of communication allow for emotional release, but guard against ego blows. These forms of communication are a major structuring device for the underclass that is essentially sealed off from the more powerful networks of interaction in standard organized society.

This analysis suggests that an analysis of class, communication, and structuration is a useful area of investigation. Societies remain stratified and theories of class continue to provide us with insights into the nature and distribution of established inequities associated with material and symbolic markets, and access to educational and organizational resources. These inequities are reproduced and perpetuated over time by various structuring processes. Culture is also deeply implicated in class reproduction and maintenance. And culture is carried by communication processes.

In closing, I would underscore the relevance of communication and discourse-analytic processes for understanding social categories such as ethnicity and class. Differences, inequality, and asymmetrical relationships are embedded in communication practices. These are not structures in the traditional sociological sense. And the reformulation of structure by Giddens has emphasized its dual nature and the devices that individuals use to reproduce relationships and meanings. Many writers, although not all, have ignored the discursive and linguistic devices that produce ethnic differences and class conflicts. They examine legal issues, social policy, legislative histories, and economic experiences, but often ignore the symbolic, linguistic, and discursive structures that powerfully and creatively reproduce ethnic and class systems.Power, conflict, and social problems are never a simple reflex of structure. They are always worked at, ground out, negotiated, and produced in the micro moments of human experience. I offer this volume as an effort to redirect our attention to these matters.

References

Abrahams, R. D. (1976). *Talking black*. Rowley, MA: Newbury House.

Adorno, T., & Horkheimer, M. (1944). *The dialectics of enlightenment*. New York: Herder & Herder.

Alba, R. (1990). *Ethnic identity: The transformation of White America*. New Haven, CT: Yale University Press.

Alba, R., & Chaplin, M. B. (1983). A preliminary examination of ethnic identification among whites. *American Sociological Review, 48*, 240–247.

Alexander, J., Giesen, B., Munch, R., & Smelser, N. (Eds.). (1987). *The micro-macro link*. Berkeley: University of California Press.

Alexander, J. C. (1984). Structural analysis: Some notes on its history and prospects. *Sociological Quarterly, 25*, 5–26.

Alexander, J. C., & Giesen, B. (1987). From reduction to linkage: The long view of the micro-macro link. In J. C. Alexander, B. Giesen, R. Munch, & N. J. Smelser (Eds.), *The micro-macro link* (pp. 1–42). Berkeley, CA: University of California Press.

Altheide, D. L., & Snow, R. P. (1991). *Media worlds in the postjournalism era*. New York: Aldine de Gruyter.

Anderson, C. (1994). *Black labor and White wealth: The search for power and economic justice*. Edgewood, MD: Duncan & Duncan.

Anderson, J. A., Birkhead, D., Eason, D. L., & Strine, M. S. (1988). The caravan of communication and its multiple histories. In R. P. Hawkins, J. M. Wiesman, & S. Pingree (Eds.), *Advancing communication science: Merging mass and interpersonal processes* (pp. 276–307). Newbury Park, CA: Sage.

Anderson, J. A., & Meyer, T. P. (1988). *Mediated communication*. Newbury Park, CA: Sage.

Anthias, F. (1992). Connecting "race" and ethnic phenomena. *Sociology, 26, 421–438*.

Antonelli, C. (Ed.).(1991). *The economics of information networks*. Amsterdam: Elsevier.

Arnold, C. C., & Frandsen, K. D. (1984). Conceptions of rhetoric and communication. In C. C. Arnold, & J. W. Bowers (Eds.), *Handbook of rhetorical and communication theory* (pp. 3–50). Boston, MA: Allyn and Bacon.

Asante, M. K. (1987). *The Afrocentric idea*. Philadelphia: Temple University Press.

Atkinson, J. M., & Heritage, J. (Eds.). (1984). *Structures of social action*. Cambridge: Cambridge University Press.

Banks, J. (1996). *Monopoly television: MTV's quest to control the music*. Boulder, CO: Westview Press.

Banton, M. (1987). *Racial theories*. Cambridge: Cambridge University Press.

Baugh, J. (1983). *Black street speech: Its history, structure and survival*. Austin: University of Texas Press.

Beck, E. T. (1992). From "kike" to "jap": How misogyny, anti-semitism, and racism constructure the "Jewish American princess." In M. L. Andersen & P. H. Collins (Eds.), *Race, class, and gender* (pp. 88–95). Belmont, CA: Wadsworth.

Bell, D. (1973). *The coming of post-industrial society*. New York: Basic Books.
Bell, D. (1976). *The cultural contradictions of capitalism*. London: Heinemann.
Bell, D. A. (1987). *And we are not saved: the elusive quest for racial justice*. New York: Basic Books.
Beniger, J. R. (1986). *The control revolution*. Cambridge, MA: Harvard University Press.
Beniger, J. R. (1993). Communication—embrace the subject, not the field. *Journal of Communication, 43,* 18–25.
Benveniste, E. (1971). *Problems in general linguistics*. Miami, FL: University of Miami Press.
Berger, C. R. (1986). Uncertain outcome values in predicted relationships: Uncertainty reduction theory then and now. *Human Communication Research, 13,* 34–38.
Berger, C. R., & Calabrese, R. J. (1975). Some explorations in initial interaction and beyond: Toward a developmental theory of interpersonal communication. *Human Communication Research, 1,* 99–112.
Bernstein, B. (1971). *Class, codes and control* (Vol. 1). London: Routledge & Kegan Paul.
Berreman, G. D. (1987). Caste in India and the United States. In C. S. Heller (Ed.), *Structured social inequality* (pp. 81–88). New York: Macmillan.
Biocca, F. A. (1988). Opposing conceptions of the audience. In J. Anderson (Ed.), *Communication yearbook 11* (pp. 51–80). Newbury Park, CA: Sage Publications.
Bochner, A. P. (1985). Perspectives on inquiry: Representation, conversation, and reflection. In M. L. Knapp & G. R. Miller (Eds.), *Handbook of interpersonal communication* (pp. 27–58). Newbury Park, CA: Sage.
Boden, D., & Zimmerman, D. H. (Eds.). (1991). *Talk and social structure: Studies in ethnomethodology and conversation*. Cambridge: Polity Press.
Boorstin, D. J. (1978). *The republic of technology: Reflections on our future community*. New York: Harper & Row.
Bordewijk, J. L., & van Kaam, B. (1986). Towards a new classification of tele-information services. *Intermedia, 14,* 16–21.
Bourdieu, P. (1977). *Outline of a theory of practice*. Cambridge: Cambridge University Press.
Bourdieu, P. (1978/1993). How can one be a sports fan? In S. During (Ed.), *The cultural studies reader* (pp. 339–356). New York: Routledge & Kegan Paul.
Bourdieu, P. (1986). *Distinction: A social critique of the judgement of taste*. London: Routledge & Kegan Paul.
Bourdieu, P. (1987). What makes a social class? *Berkeley Journal of Sociology, 22,* 1–18.
Bourdieu, P. (1990). *The logic of practice* (R. Nice, Trans.). Cambridge: Polity Press.
Bourdieu, P. (1991). *Language and symbolic power* (G. Raymond & M. Adamson, Trans.). Cambridge, MA: Harvard University Press.
Brockriede, W. (1983). The contemporary renaissance in the study of argument. In D. Zarefsky, M. O. Sillars, & J. Rhodes (Eds.), *Argument in transition: Proceedings of the third summer conference on argumentation* (pp. 3–35). Annandale, VA: Speech Communication Association.
Bross, M. (1992). McLuhan's theory of sensory functions: A critique and analysis. *Journal of Communication Inquiry, 16,* 91–107.
Brown, G., & Yule, G. (1983). *Discourse analysis*. Cambridge: Cambridge University Press.
Bruess, C. J. S., & Pearson, J. C. (1997). Interpersonal rituals in marriage and adult friendship. *Communication Monographs, 64,* 25–46.
Brummett, B., & Duncan, M. C. (1992). Toward a discursive ontology of media. *Critical Studies in Mass Communication, 2,* 229–249.
Burke, K. (1966). *Language as symbolic action: Essays on life, literature, and method*. Berkeley, CA: University of California Press.
Calhoun, C. (Ed.). (1992). *Habermas and the public sphere*. Cambridge, MA: MIT Press.
Campbell, K. K., & Jamieson, K. H. (1978). Form and genre in rhetorical criticism: An introduction. In K. K. Campbell & K. H. Jamieson (Eds.), *Form and genre: Shaping rhetorical action* (pp. 9–32). Falls Church, VA: Speech Communication Association.
Cappella, J. (1979). The functional prerequisites of intentional communication systems. *Philosophy and Rhetoric, 5,* 231–247.
Cappella, J. (1991). The biological origins of automated patterns of human interaction. *Communication Theory, 1,* 4–35.
Carey, J. (Ed.). (1987). *Media, myths, and narratives*. Newbury Park, CA: Sage.
Cassell, P. (Ed.). (1993). *The Giddens reader*. Stanford, CA: Stanford University Press.

Cathcart, R., & Gumpert, G. (1986). I am a camera: The mediated self. *Communication Quarterly, 34,* 88–107.

Chang, B. G. (1992). Empty intention. *Text and Performance Quarterly, 12,* 212–227.

Chaytor, H. J. (1966). *From script to print: An introduction to medieval vernacular literature.* London: Sidgwick & Jackson.

Chomsky, N. (1957). *Syntactic structures.* The Hague, The Netherlands: Mouton.

Chomsky, N. (1959). Review of Skinner's 'verbal behavior'. *Language, 35,* 26–58.

Chomsky, N. (1968). *Language and mind.* New York: Harcourt, Brace, and World.

Cicourel, A. V. (1973). *Cognitive sociology.* London: Penguin Books.

Clark, T. N., & Lipset, S. M. (1991). Are social classes dying. *International Sociology, 6,* 397–410.

Clarke, C. (1940). *The conditions of economic progress.* London: Macmillan.

Cogdell, R., & Wilson, S. (1980). *Black communication in white society.* Saratoga, CA: Century-Twenty-One Publishers.

Cohen, A. P. (1985). *The symbolic construction of community.* London: Ellis Harwood/Tavistock.

Cohen, H. (1994). *The history of speech communication: The emergence of a discipline, 1914–1945.* Annandale, VA: Speech Communication Association.

Cohen, I. (1989). *Structuration theory: Anthony Giddens and the constitution of social life.* New York: St. Martin's Press.

Collins, R. (1975). *Conflict sociology.* New York: Academic Press.

Collins, R. (1981). On the microfoundations of macrosociology. *American Journal of Sociology, 86,* 984–1014.

Collins, R. (1987). Interaction ritual chains, power, and property: The micro-macro connection as an empirically based theoretical problem. In J. C. Alexander, B. Giesen, R. Munch, & N. J. Smelser (Eds.), *The micro-macro link* (pp. 193–206). Berkeley, CA: University of California Press.

Collins, R. (1988). The micro-contribution to macro sociology. *Sociological Theory, 6,* 242–253.

Conquergood, D. (1992). Ethnography, rhetoric, and performance. *Quarterly Journal of Speech, 78,* 80–123.

Covin, D. (1990). Afrocentricity in O Movimento Negro Unificado. *Journal of Black Studies, 21,* 126–146.

Croasmun, E., & Cherwitz, R. A. (1982). Beyond rhetorical relativism. *Quarterly Journal of Speech, 68,* 1–16.

Crompton, R. (1993). *Class and stratification.* Cambridge, MA: Blackwell.

Crozier, M., Huntington, S., & Watanuki, J. (1975). *The crisis of democracy.* New York: New York University Press.

Daniel, J., & Smitherman, G. (1976). How I got over: Communication dynamics in the Black community. *Quarterly Journal of Speech, 63,* 26–39.

Davis, F. (1995). *The history of the blues.* New York: Hyperion.

Davis, J. A., & Smith, T. W. (1989). *General society surveys, 1972–1989.* No. National Opinion Research Center: Chicago.

Deetz, S. A. (1994). Future of the discipline: The challenges, the research, and the social contribution. In S. A. Deetz (Ed.), *Communication yearbook/17* (pp. 565–600). Thousand Oaks, CA: Sage.

DeFleur, M. L. (1970). *Theories of mass communication.* New York: David McKay.

Delia, J. G. (1987). Communication research: A history. In C. R. Berger & S. H. Chaffee (Eds.), *Handbook of communication science* (pp. 20–98). Newbury Park, CA: Sage.

Dennis, R. M. (1991). Dual marginality and discontent among Black middletown youth. In R. M. Dennis (Ed.), *Research in race and ethnic relations* (pp. 3–25). Greenwich, CT: JAI Press.

DeParle, J. (1996, March 17). Class is no longer a four-letter word. *The New York Times Magazine,* 40–43.

Derrida, J. (1976). *Of Grammatology* (G. C. Spivak, Trans.). Baltimore, MD: Johns Hopkins University Press.

Derrida, J. (1981). *Dissemination* (B. Johnson, Trans.). Baltimore, MD: Johns Hopkins University Press.

Desmond, R. (1996). TV viewing, reading and media literacy. In M. Flood (Ed.), *Handbook for literacy educators* (pp. 23–30). Palo Alto, CA: Stanford University Press.

Dillard, J. L. (1972). *Black English: Its history and usage in the United States.* New York: Random House.

Doob, L. (1961). *Communication in Africa.* New Haven, CT: Yale University Press.

DuBoff, R. (1983). The telegraph and the structure of markets in the United States, 1845–1890. *Research in Economic History, 8,* 253–277.

Dundes, A. (Ed.). (1965). *The study of folklore.* Englewood Cliffs, NJ: Prentice Hall.

Durkheim, E. (1938). *The rules of sociological method* (1895). New York: Free Press.

Durkheim, E. (1954). *The elementary forms of the religious life*. Glencoe, IL: Free Press. (Original work published 1915)

Eco, U. (1979). *A theory of semiotics*. Bloomington: Indiana University Press.

Edwards, V., & Sienkewicz, T. J. (1990). *Oral cultures past and present*. Cambridge: Basil Blackwell.

Eisenstein, E. (1979). *The printing press as an agent of change: Communications and cultural transformations in early-modern Europe*. Cambridge: Cambridge University Press.

Ellis, D. G. (1992a). *From language to communication*. Hillsdale, NJ: Lawrence Erlbaum Associates.

Ellis, D. G. (1992b). Syntactic and pragmatic codes in communication. *Communication Theory, 2,* 1–23.

Ellis, D. G. (1994). Codes and pragmatic comprehension. In S. A. Deetz (Ed.), *Communication yearbook 17* (pp. 333–343). Thousand Oaks, CA: Sage.

Ellis, D. G. (1995). Fixing meaning: A coherentist theory. *Communication Research, 22,* 515–544.

Ervin-Tripp, S. (1969). Sociolinguistics. In L. Berkowitz (Ed.), *Advances in experimental social psychology* (pp. 91–165). New York: Academic Press.

Farr, R. M., & Moscovici, S. (Eds.). (1984). *Social representation*. Cambridge: Cambridge University Press.

Fave, R. D. (1980). The meek shall not inherit the earth: Self-evaluation and the legitimacy of stratification. *American Sociological Review, 45,* 955–971.

Featherstone, M. (1991). *Consumer culture and post modernism*. London: Sage.

Ferment in the field. (1983). *Journal of Communication, 33* (3).

Fisher, W. R. (1984). Narration as a human communication paradigm: The case of public moral argument. *Communication Monographs, 51,* 1–22.

Fiske, J. (1987). *Television culture*. New York: Methuen.

Fitch, K. (1994). Culture, ideology, and interpersonal communication research. In S. A. Deetz (Ed.), *Communication yearbook/17* (pp. 104–135). Thousand Oaks, CA: Sage.

Fitzpatrick, M. A. (1988). *Between husbands and wives*. New Park, CA: Sage.

Fitzpatrick, M. A., Marshall, L. J., Leutwiler, T. J., & Krcmar, M. (1996). The effect of family communication environments on children's social behavior during middle childhood. *Communication Research, 23,* 379–406.

Fortner, R. S. (1995). Excommunication in the information society. *Critical Studies in Mass Communication, 12,* 133–154.

Foss, S. K., Foss, K. A., & Trapp, R. (Eds.). (1985). *Contemporary perspectives on rhetoric*. Prospect Heights, IL: Waveland Press.

Foucault, M. (1984). *The Foucault Reader* (P. Rabinow, Ed.). New York: Pantheon.

Fowler, A. (1982). *Kinds of literature: An introduction to the theory of genres and modes*. Cambridge, MA: Harvard University Press.

Frankfurt Institute for Social Research. (1973). *Aspects of sociology*. London: Heinemann.

Franklin, J. H. (1988). A historical note on Black families. In H. P. McAdoo (Ed.), *Black families* (2nd ed.; pp. 23–26). Newbury Park, CA: Sage.

Frederick, H. H. (1992). *Global communications and international relations*. Belmont, CA: Wadsworth.

Friedan, B. (1963). *The feminine mystique*. New York: Norton.

Future of the field 1. (1993a). *Journal of Communication, 43*(3).

Future of the field II. (1993b). *Journal of Communication, 43*(4).

Gadamer, H. G. (1989). *Truth and method* (2nd rev. ed.; J. Weinsheimer & D. G. Marshall, Trans.). New York: Crossroad.

Gamson, W., & Modigliani, A. (1989). Media discourse and public opinion on nuclear power: A constructivist approach. *American Journal of Sociology, 95,* 1–37.

Gans, H. J. (1979). *Deciding what's news*. New York: Vintage Books.

Garfinkel, H. (1967). *Studies in ethnomethodology*. Englewood, Cliffs, NJ: Prentice-Hall.

Garnham, N. (1986). The media and the public sphere. In P. Golding & G. Murdock (Eds.), *Communicating politics* (pp. 37–54). Leicester: Leicester University Press.

Gates, H. L. (1992). TV's Black world turns—but stays unreal. In M. L. Andersen & P. H. Collins (Eds.), *Race, class, and gender* (pp. 310–317). Belmont, CA: Wadsworth.

Gergen, K. J., & Davis, K. E. (1985). *The social construction of the person*. New York: Springer.

Gerstein, D. R. (1987). To unpack micro and macro: Link small with large and part with whole. In J. C. Alexander, B. Giesen, R. Munch, & N. J. Smelser (Eds.), *The micro-macro link* (pp. 86–111). Berkeley, CA: University of California Press.

Gibson, W. (1984). *Neuromancer.* New York: Ace.

Giddens, A. (1976). *New rules for sociological method.* New York: Basic.

Giddens, A. (1979). *Central problems in social theory.* Berkeley, CA: University of California Press.

Giddens, A. (1981). Agency, institution, and time-space analysis. In K. Knorr-Cetina & A. Cicourel (Eds.), *Advances in social theory and methodology* (pp. 161–174). London: Routledge and Kegan Paul.

Giddens, A. (1984). *The constitution of society.* Berkeley, CA: University of California Press.

Giles, H., & Johnson, P. (1987). Ethnolinguistic identity theory: A social psychological approach to language maintenance. *International Journal of the Sociology of Language, 68,* 69–91.

Giles, H., Mulac, A., Bradac, J., & Johnson, P. (1987). Speech accommodation theory: The first decade and beyond. In M. McLaughlin (Ed.), *Communication yearbook 10.* Newbury Park, CA: Sage.

Gilligan, C. (1982). *In a different voice.* Cambridge, MA: Harvard University Press.

Gitlin, T. (1978). Media sociology: The dominant paradigm. *Theory and Society, 6,* 205–253. Reprinted in G. C. Wilhoit and H. de Bock (1981)(Eds.), *Mass communication review yearbook,* Vol. 2, (pp. 73–122). Beverly Hills, CA. Sage.

Givón, T. (1989). *Mind, code and context.* Hillsdale, NJ: Lawrence Erlbaum Associates.

Givón, T. (1995). Coherence in text vs. coherence in mind. In M. A. Gernsbacher & T. Givón (Eds.), *Coherence in spontaneous text* (pp. 59–115). Amsterdam: John Benjamins.

Glaser, B. G., & Strauss, A. L. (1967). *The discovery of grounded theory.* Chicago: Aldine–Atheron.

Goffman, E. (1959). *The presentation of self in everyday life.* New York: Anchor.

Goffman, E. (1967). *Interaction ritual: Essays on face-to-face behavior.* Garden City, NJ: Anchor.

Goffman, E. (1971). *Relations in public.* New York: Basic Books.

Goffman, E. (1974). *Frame analysis.* New York: Harper & Row.

Goffman, E. (1981). *Forms of talk.* Philadelphia: University of Pennsylvania Press.

Goldhagen, D. (1996). *Hitler's willing executioners: Ordinary germans and the holocaust.* New York: Knopf.

Golding, P., & Murdock, G. (1991). Culture, communications, and political economy. In J. Curren & M. Gurevitch (Eds.), *Mass Media and Society* (pp. 15–32). London: Edward Arnold.

Goldthorpe, J. H., & Marshall, G. (1992). The promising future of class analysis: A response to recent critiques. *Sociology, 26,* 381–400.

Goody, J., & Watt, I. (1963). The consequences of literacy. *Comparative Studies in Society and History, 5,* 304–345.

Gozzi, R., & Haynes, W. L. (1992). Electric media and electric epistemology: Empathy at a distance. *Critical Studies in Mass Communication, 9,* 217–228.

Greatbatch, D. (1988). A turn taking system for British news interviews. *Language in Society, 17,* 401–430.

Grice, H. P. (1975). Logic and conversation. In P. Cole & J. Morgan (Eds.), *Syntax and semantics 3: Speech acts* (pp. 41–58). New York: Academic Press.

Groeben, N. (1990). Subjective theories and the explanation of human interaction. In G. R. Semin & K. J. Gergen (Eds.), *Everyday understanding: Social and scientific implications.* London: Sage.

Grossberg, L. (1984). "I'd rather feel bad than not feel anything at all": rock and roll, pleasure and power. *Enclitic, 8,* 96–112.

Gudykunst, W. B., & Ting-Toomey, S. (1990). Ethnic identity, language and communication breakdowns. In H. Giles & W. P. Robinson, (Eds.), *Handbook of language and social psychology* (pp. 309–327). New York: John Wiley & Sons.

Habermas, J. (1989). *The structural transformation of the public sphere: An inquiry into a category of bourgeois society* (T. Burger, Trans.). Cambridge: Polity Press.

Habermas, J. (1995). Institutions of the public sphere. In O. Boyd-Barret & C. Newbold (Eds.), *Approaches to media* (pp. 235–244). New York: Arnold.

Halliday, M. A. K. (1978). *Language as social semiotic: The social interpretation of language and meaning.* London: Edward Arnold.

Hardt, H. (1979). *Social theories of the press.* Beverly Hills, CA: Sage.

Harrison, T. M. (1994). Communication and interdependence in democratic organizations. In S. A. Deetz (Ed.), *Communication yearbook 17* (pp. 247–274). Thousand Oaks, CA: Sage.

Hart, R. P. (1994). *Seducing America: How television charms the modern voter.* New York: Oxford University Press.

Haslett, B. (1990). Social class, social status, and communicative behavior. In H. Giles and W. P. Robinson (Eds.), *Handbook of language and social psychology* (pp. 329–344). Chichester: John Wiley and Sons.

Hauser, M. D. (1996). *The evolution of communication.* Cambridge, MA: MIT Press.

Havelock, E. A. (1963). *Preface to Plato.* Cambridge, MA: Harvard University Press.

Hawes, L. C. (1974). Social collectivities as organizations. *Quarterly Journal of Speech, 60,* 497–502.

Heath, C. (1986). *Body movement and speech in medical interaction.* New York: Cambridge University Press.

Heath, S. B. (1983). *Ways with words.* London: Cambridge University Press.

Hecht, M. L., Collier, M. J., & Ribeau, S. A. (1993). *African American communication: Ethnic identity and cultural interpretation.* Newbury Park, CA: Sage.

Held, D. (1980). *Introduction to critical theory.* London: Hutchinson.

Heller, C. S. (Ed.). (1987). *Structured social inequality.* New York: Macmillan.

Heritage, J. (1984). A change of state token and aspects of its sequential placement. In J. M. Atkinson & J. Heritage (Eds.), *Structures of Social Action: Studies in Conversation Analysis* (pp. 299–345). Cambridge: Cambridge University Press.

Heritage, J. (1990/1991). Intention, meaning and strategy: Observations on constraints on interaction analysis. *Research on Language and Social Interaction, 24,* 311–332.

Herrnstein, R. J., & Murray, C. (1994). *The bell curve: Intelligence and class structure in American life.* New York: Free Press.

Hirsch, E. D. (1967). *Validity in Interpretation.* New Haven, CT: Yale University Press.

Homans, G. (1958). Social behavior as exchange. *American Sociological Review, 63,* 597–603.

Horton, D. & Wohl, R. R. (1956). Mass communication and para-social interaction. *Psychiatry, 19,* 215–229.

Hout, M., Brooks, C., & Manza, J. (1993). The persistence of classes in post-industrial societies. *International Sociology, 8,* 259–277.

Hurlbert, J. S. (1989). The southern region: A test of the hypothesis of cultural distinctiveness. *The Sociological Quarterly, 30,* 245–266.

Hurst, C. E. (1992). *Social inequality.* Boston, MA: Allyn and Bacon.

Huspek, M. (1986). Linguistic variation, context and meaning: A case of -ing/-in variation in North American workers' speech. *Language in Society, 15,* 149–163.

Huspek, M. (1989). Linguistic variability and power: An analysis of YOU KNOW/I THINK variaton in working-class speech. *Journal of Pragmatics, 13,* 661–683.

Huspek, M., & Kendall, K. (1991). On withholding political voice: An analysis of the political vocabulary of a "nonpolitical" speech community. *Quarterly Journal of Speech, 77,* 1–19.

Hutchins, R. (1947). *A free and responsible press: Commission on freedom of the press.* Chicago: University of Chicago Press.

Hymes, D. H. (1974). Ways of speaking. In R. Bauman & J. Sherzer (Eds.), *Explorations in the ethnography of speaking* (pp. 431–451). Cambridge: Cambridge University Press.

Innis, H. A. (1964). *The bias of communication.* Toronto: University of Toronto Press.

Innis, H. A. (1972). *Empire and communications.* Toronto: University of Toronto Press.

Jamieson, K. H. (1988). *Eloquence in an electronic age: The transformation of political speechmaking.* New York: Oxford University Press.

Jaynes, G. D., & Williams, R. M., Jr. (Eds.). (1989). *A common destiny: Blacks and American society.* Washington, DC: National Academy Press.

Jayyusi, L. (1984). *Categorization and the oral order.* Boston, MA: Routledge and Kegan Paul.

Jenkins, A. H. (1982). *The psychology of the Afro-American: A humanistic approach.* Elmsford, NY: Pergamon.

Jenkins, R. (1997). *Rethinking ethnicity.* Thousand Oaks, CA: Sage.

Jensen, A. R. (1969). How much can we boost IQ and scholastic achievement? *Harvard Educational Review, 39,* 1–123.

Jensen, K. B., & Rosengren, K. E. (1990). Five traditions in search of the audience. *European Journal of Communication, 5,* 207–238.

Kellermann, K. (1992). Communication: Inherently strategic and primarily automatic. *Communication Monograph, 59,* 288–300.

Kellner, D. (1990). *Television and the crisis of democracy.* Boulder, CO: Westview Press.

Kerbo, H. R. (1991). *Social stratification and inequality.* New York: McGraw-Hill.

Kinder, M. (1990). *Playing with power in movies, television, and video games.* Berkeley, CA: University of California Press.

Kirby, A. (1988). Context, common sense and the reality of place: A critical reading of Meyrowitz. *Journal for the Theory of Social Behavior, 18,* 239–250.

Kluegel, J. R., & Smith, E. R. (1986). *Beliefs about inequality: Americans' views of what is and what ought to be.* New York: Aldine de Gruyter.

Kochman, T. (1981). *Black and white styles in conflict.* Chicago: University of Chicago Press.

Kochman, T. (1990a). Force fields in black and white communication. In D. Carbaugh (Ed.), *Cultural communication and intercultural contact* (pp. 193–217). Hillsdale, NJ: Lawrence Erlbaum Associates.

Kochman, T. (1990b). Cultural pluralism: Black and white styles. In D. Carbaugh (Ed.), *Cultural communication and intercultural contact* (pp. 219–224). Hillsdale, NJ: Lawrence Erlbaum Associates.

Krauze, T., & Slomczynski, K. M. (1985). How far to meritocracy? Empirical tests of a controversial thesis. *Social Forces, 63,* 623–642.

Kreckel, M. (1981). *Communicative acts and shared knowledge in natural discourse.* New York: Academic Press.

Kress, G., & Hodge, R. (1979). *Language as ideology.* London: Routledge & Kegan Paul.

Kristeva, J. (1986). *The Kristeva Reader.* Toril Moi (Ed.), Oxford, UK: Blackwell.

Labov, W. (1970). *The study of nonstandard English.* New York: Columbia University Press.

Labov, W. (1972). *Sociolinguistic patterns.* Philadelphia: University of Pennsylvania Press.

Langer, E. (1992). Interpersonal mindlessness and language. *Communication Monograph, 59,* 324–327.

Lannamann, J. W. (1991). Interpersonal communication research as ideological practice. *Communication Theory, 1,* 179–203.

Lasswell, H. (1948). The structure and function of communication in society. In S. Bryson (Ed.), *The communication of ideas* (pp. 32–51). New York: Harper.

Lazarsfeld, P. F. (1941). Remarks on critical and administrative communication research. *Studies in Philosophy and Social Science, 9,* 2–16.

Leech, G. (1983). *Principles of pragmatics.* London: Longman.

LeMasters, E. E. (1975). *Blue-collar aristocrats: Life styles at a working-class tavern.* Madison, WI: University of Wisconsin Press.

Lemke, J. L. (1994). *Textual politics: Discourse and social dynamics.* London: Taylor and Francis.

Lorber, J. (1994). *Paradoxes of gender.* New Haven, CT: Yale University Press.

Lorenz, K. (1966). *On aggression.* New York: Harcourt.

Lowery, S. A., & DeFleur, M. L. (1988). *Milestones in mass communication research.* New York: Longman.

Luria, A. R. (1967). *Cognitive development: Its cultural and social foundations.* In M. Cole (Ed.). (M. Lopez-Morillas & L. Solotaroff, Trans.). Cambridge: Harvard University Press.

Machlup, F. (1980–1984). *Knowledge: Its creation, distribution and economic significance* (Vols. 1–3). Princeton, NJ: Princeton University Press.

MacKinnon, C. (1989). *Toward a feminist theory of the state.* Cambridge: Harvard University Press.

Major, C. (1994). *Juba to jive: A dictionary of African-American slang.* New York: Penguin.

Marable, M. (1983). *How capitalism underdeveloped Black America.* Boston: South End Press.

Marcuse, H. (1964). *One dimensional man.* London: Paladin.

Martin, J. R. (1989). *Factual writing: Exploring and challenging social reality.* London: Oxford University Press.

Matoesian, G. M. (1993). *Reproducing rape: Domination through talk in the courtroom.* Chicago: University of Chicago Press.

Maynard, D. W., & Wilson, T. P. (1980). On the reification of social structure. *Current Perspectives in Social Theory, 1,* 287–322.

McCombs, M. E., & Shaw, D. L. (1993). The evolution of agenda-setting theory: 25 years in the marketplace of ideas. *Journal of Communication, 43,* 58–66.

McLaurin, P. (1995). An examination of the effect of culture on pro-social messages directed at African-American at-risk youth. *Communication Monographs, 62,* 301–326.

McLuhan, M. (1962). *The Gutenberg galaxy: The making of typographic man.* Toronto: University of Toronto Press.

McLuhan, M. (1964). *Understanding media: The extensions of man.* New York: McGraw-Hill.

McQuail, D. (1994). *Mass communication theory.* Thousand Oaks, CA: Sage.

Mead, G. H. (1934). *Mind, self and society.* Chicago: University of Chicago Press.

Mehan, H. (1979). *Learning lessons.* Cambridge: Harvard University Press.

Melody, W. (1994). Electronic networks, social relations and the changing structure of knowledge. In D. Crowley & D. Mitchell (Eds.), *Communication theory today* (pp. 254–273). Cambridge, UK: Polity Press.

Merleau-Ponty, M. (1962). *The phenomenology of perception*. London: Routledge and Kegan Paul.

Merton, R. (1957). *Social theory and social structure*. New York: Free Press.

Meyrowitz, J. (1985). *No sense of place: The impact of electronic media on social behavior*. New York: Oxford University Press.

Meyrowitz, J. (1989). The generalized elsewhere. *Critical Studies in Mass Communication, 6,* 326–334.

Meyrowitz, J. (1994). Medium theory. In D. Crowley & D. Mitchell (Eds.), *Communication theory today* (pp. 50–77). Cambridge, UK: Polity Press.

Miller, G., & Holstein, J. (Eds.). (1993). *Constructionist controversies*. Hawthorne, NY: Aldine de Gruyter.

Miller, G. R. (1966). *Speech communication: A behavioral approach*. Indianapolis: Bobbs-Merrill.

Mufwene, S. (1991). Ideology and facts on African-American English. *Pragmatics, 2,* 141–166.

Murdock, G., & Golding, P. (1995). For a political economy of mass communications. In O. Boyd-Barrett and C. Newbold (Eds.), *Approaches to media* (pp. 201–215). London: Arnold Press.

Murphy, J. (1971). The metaphorics of Plato, Augustine, and McLuhan: A pointing essay. *Philosophy and Rhetoric, 4,* 201–214.

Nehamas, A. (1987). Writer, text, work, author. In A. Cascardi (Ed.), *Literature and the question of philosophy*. Bloomington, IN: Indiana University Press.

Ochs, E. (1992). Indexing gender. In A. Duranti & C. Goodwin (Eds.), *Rethinking context: Language as an interactive phenomenon* (pp. 335–358). Cambridge: Cambridge University Press.

Ong, W. J. (1962). Voice as summons for belief: Literature, faith, and the divided self. In W. J. Ong (Ed.), *The barbarian within and other fugitive essays* (pp. 1–76). New York: Macmillan.

Ong, W. J. (1971). *Rhetoric, romance, and technology*. Ithaca, NY: Cornell University Press.

Ong, W. J. (1977). *Interfaces of the word*. Ithaca, NY: Cornell University Press.

Ong, W. J. (1982). *Orality and literacy: The technologizing of the word*. Ithaca, NY: Cornell University Press.

Padilla, A. M., & Lindholm, K. J. (1995). Quantitative educational research with ethnic minorities. In J. A. Banks & C. A. McGee Banks (Eds.), *Handbook of research on multicultural education* (pp. 97–113). New York: Macmillan.

Parsons, T. (1963). *Social structure and personality*. New York: Free Press.

Pearce, W. B. (1994). Recovering agency. In S. A. Deetz (Ed.), *Communication yearbook/17* (pp. 34–41). Thousand Oaks, CA: Sage.

Peters, J. D. (1986). Institutional sources of intellectual poverty in communication research. *Communication Research, 13,* 527–559.

Peters, J. D. (1994). The gaps of which communication is made. *Critical Studies in Mass Communication, 11,* 117–140.

Pinker, S. (1994). *The Language instinct: How the mind creates language*. New York: Harper Collins.

Polanyi, K. (1957). *The great transformation*. Boston, MA: Beacon Press.

Poole, M. S., & DeSanctis, G. (1992). Microlevel structuration in computer-supported group decision making. *Human Communication Research, 19,* 5–49.

Porpora, D. (1989). Four concepts of social structure. *Journal for the Theory of Social Behavior, 19,* 195–211.

Postman, N. (1985). *Amusing ourselves to death: Public discourse in the age of show business*. New York: Viking/Penguin.

Railsback, C. C. (1983). Beyond rhetorical relativism: A structural-material model of truth and objective reality. *Quarterly Journal of Speech, 69,* 351–363.

Rescher, N. (1973). *The coherence theory of truth*. Oxford, UK: Clarendon.

Rescher, N. (1979). *Cognitive systematization*. Ottawa, Canada: Rowman & Littlefield.

Rescher, N. (1987). *Scientific realism*. Dordrecht: Reidel Publishing.

Ricoeur, P. (1976). *Interpretation theory*. Fort Worth: Texas Christian University Press.

Rise of the overclass. (1995, July 31). *Newsweek*, pp. 31–46.

Rogers, E. M. (1962). *Diffusion of innovations*. Glencoe, IL: Free Press.

Rogers, E. M. (1986). *Communication technology*. New York: Free Press.

Rorty, R. (1979). *Philosophy and the mirror of nature*. Princeton, NJ: Princeton University Press.

Rorty, R. (1982). *Consequences of pragmatism*. Minneapolis: University of Minnesota Press.

Rorty, R. (1983). Postmodern bourgeois liberalism. *Journal of Philosophy, 80,* 583–589.

Rorty, R. (1989). *Contingency, irony, and solidarity*. New York: Cambridge University Press.

Rosch, E. (1975). Cognitive representation of semantic categories. *The Journal of Experiental Psychology*, *104*, 192–233.

Rose, L. F. R. (1982/1983). Theoretical and methodological issues in the study of Black culture and personality. *Humboldt Journal of Social Relations*, *10*, 320–338.

Rosenberg, B. A. (1987). *Can these bones live? The art of the American folk preacher*. Chicago, IL: University of Illinois Press.

Sacks, H., Schegloff, E., & Jefferson, G. (1974). A simplest systematics for the organization of turn-taking in conversation. *Language*, *50*, 696–735.

Sanders, B. (1994). *A is for ox: The decline of literacy and the rise of violence in the electronic age*. New York: Vantage.

Scheff, T. (1990). *Microsociology: Discourse, emotion, and social structure*. Chicago: University of Chicago Press.

Schegloff, E. A. (1997). Whose text? Whose context? *Discourse and Society*, *8*, 165–188.

Schiffrin, D. (1990). Conversation analysis. *Annual Review of Applied Linguistics*, *11*, 3–19.

Schiffrin, D. (1994). *Approaches to discourse*. Cambridge, MA: Blackwell Publishers.

Schiller, H. I. (1981). *Who knows: Information in the age of the Fortune 500*. Norwood, NJ: Ablex Publishing.

Schiller, H. I. (1985). *Information and the crisis economy*. Norwood, NJ: Ablex Publishing.

Schneider, J. W. (1985). Social problems theory. *Annual Review of Sociology*, *11*, 209–229.

Schramm, W. (Ed.).(1948). *Communications in modern society*. Urbana: University of Illinois Press.

Schramm, W. (Ed.).(1949). *Mass communications*. Urbana: University of Illinois Press.

Schramm, W. (1964). *Mass media and national development*. Stanford, CA: Stanford University Press.

Schudson, M. (1997). Why conversation is not the soul of democracy. *Critical Studies in Mass Communication*, *14*, 297–309.

Schutz, A. (1967) *Collected papers*. The Hague, The Netherlands: Mouton.

Schutz, A., & Luckmann, T. (1973). *The Structures of the lifeworld*. Evanston, IL: Northwestern University Press.

Scollon, R., & Scollon, S. W. (1995). *Intercultural communication*. Cambridge, MA: Blackwell.

Scott, R. L. (1967). On viewing rhetoric as epistemic. *Central States Speech Journal*, *18*, 9–17.

Scott, J. (1982). *The upper classes*. London: Macmillan.

Searle, J. (1969). *Speech acts: An essay in the philosophy of language*. New York: Cambridge University Press.

Searle, J. (1979). *Expression and meaning: Studies in the theory of speech act*. London: Cambridge University Press.

Searle, J. (1983). *Intentionality*. Cambridge: Cambridge University Press.

Searle, J. (1995). *The construction of social reality*. New York: Free Press.

Semin, G., & Gergen, K. (1990). *Everyday understanding*. Newbury Park, CA: Sage.

Shah, H., & Thornton, M. C. (1994). Racial ideology in U.S. mainstream news magazine coverage of Black-Latino interaction, 1980–1992. *Critical Studies in Mass Communication*, *11*, 141–161.

Shannon, C., & Weaver, W. (Eds.). (1949). *The mathematical theory of communication*. Urbana, IL: University of Illinois Press.

Shoemaker, P. J., & Reese, S. D. (1991). *Mediating the message*. New York: Longman.

Sholle, D. (1995). Resisting disciplines: Repositioning media studies in the university. *Communication Theory*, *5*, 130–143.

Shotter, J. (1993). *Conversational realities: Constructing life through language*. London: Sage.

Shotter, J., & Gergen, K. J. (1994). Social construction: knowledge, self, others, and continuing the conversation. In S. A. Deetz (Ed.), *Communication yearbook/17* (pp. 3–33). Thousand Oaks, CA: Sage.

Siebert, F. S., Paterson, T., & Schramm, W. (1956). *Four theories of the press*. Urbana: University of Illinois Press.

Signorielli, N., & Morgan, M. (Eds.).(1990). *Cultivation analysis*. Newbury Park, CA: Sage.

Singer, D. G., & Singer, J. L. (1992). *Creating critical viewers*. Denver, CO: Pacific Mountain Network.

Skeggs, B. (1997). *Formations of class and gender*. Thousand Oaks, CA: Sage.

Skinner, B. F. (1957). *Verbal behavior*. New York: Appleton-Century-Crofts.

Slack, J. D., & Fejes, F. (Eds.).(1987). *The ideology of the information age*. Norwood, NJ: Ablex Publishing.

Smelser, N. (1986). From structure to order. In J. F. Short (Ed.), *The social fabric* (pp. 33–38). Beverly Hills, CA: Sage.

Smith, D. E. (1987). *The everyday world as problematic: A feminist sociology.* Boston: Northeastern University Press.

Smitherman, G. (1994). *Black talk: Words and phrases from the hood to the amen corner.* New York: Houghton Mifflin.

Spector, M., & Kitsuse, J. (1987). *Constructing social problems.* Hawthorne, NY: Aldine de Gruyter.

Stamp, G. H., & Knapp, M. L. (1990). The construct of intent in interpersonal communication. *Quarterly Journal of Speech, 76,* 282–299.

Stenger, N. (1991). Mind is a leaking rainbow. In M. Benedikt (Ed.), *Cyberspace: First steps* (pp. 49–58). Cambridge, MA: MIT Press.

Stephenson, W. (1967). *The play theory of mass communication.* Chicago: University of Chicago Press.

Streeter, T. (1995). Introduction: For the study of communication and against the discipline of communication. *Communication Theory, 5,* 117–129.

Sum, A., Harrington, P., & Goedicke, W. (1987). One-fifth of the nation's teenagers: Employment problems of poor youth in America, 1981–1985. *Youth and Society, 18,* 195–237.

Swales, J. M. (1990). *Genre analysis: English in academic and research settings.* Cambridge: Cambridge University Press.

Swanson, D. L. (1993). Fragmentation, the field, and the future. *Journal of Communication, 43,* 163–172.

Takaki, R. (1993). *A different mirror: A history of multicultural America.* Boston: Little, Brown.

Tannen, D. (1979). What's in a frame? Surface evidence for underlying expectations. In R. Freedle (Ed.), *New directions in discourse processing* (pp. 137–181). Norwood, NJ: Ablex.

Tannen, D. (Ed.). (1982). *Spoken and written language.* Norwood, NJ: Ablex.

Tannen, D., & Wallat, C. (1993). Interactive frames and knowledge schemas in interaction. Examples from a medical examination/interview. In D. Tannen (Ed.), *Framing in discourse* (pp. 57–76). New York: Oxford University Press.

Tate, W. F. (1997). Critical race theory and education: History, theory, and implications. In M. Apple (Ed.), *Review of research in education Vol. 22* (pp. 195–247). Washington, DC: American Educational Research Association.

Taylor, F. W. (1967). *The principles of scientific management.* New York: Norton.

Taylor, J. R. (1993). *Rethinking the theory or organizational communication: How to read an organization.* Norwood, NJ: Ablex.

Taylor, J. R., Cooren, F., Giroux, N., & Robichaud, D. (1996). The communicational basis of organization: Between the conversation and the text. *Communication Theory, 6,* 1–39.

Taylor, T., & Cameron, D. (1987). *Analyzing conversation.* New York: Pergamon Press.

Tehranian, M. (1992). *Technologies of power: Information machines and democratic prospects.* Norwood, NJ: Ablex.

Tehranian, M. (1994). Communication and development. In D. Crowley & D. Mitchell (Eds.), *Communication theory today* (pp. 274–306). Cambridge, UK: Polity Press.

Thompson, J. B. (1990). *Ideology and modern culture: Critical social theory in the era of mass communication.* Cambridge: Polity Press.

Thompson, J. B. (1995). The theory of the public sphere. In O. Boyd-Barrett and C. Newbold (Eds.), *Approaches to media* (pp. 252–259). London: Arnold Press.

Turner, J. (1988). *A theory of social interaction.* Oxford: Polity.

Turner, J., & Collins, R. (1988). Toward a microtheory of structuring. In J. Turner (Ed.), *Theory building in sociology* (pp. 118–130). Newbury Park: Sage.

Turow, J. (1991). A mass communication perspective on entertainment. In J. Curran & M. Gurevitch (Eds.), *Mass media and society* (pp. 160–177). London: Edward Arnold.

U.S. Bureau of Census. (1990). *Statistical abstract of the United States: 1990.*

van den Berghe, P. L. (1986). Ethnicity and the socio-biology debate. In J. Rex, & D. Mason (Eds.), *Theories of race and ethnic relations* Cambridge: Cambridge University Press.

van Dijk, T. A. (1990). Social cognition and discourse. In H. Giles & W. P. Robinson (Eds.), *Handbook of language and social psychology* (pp. 163–183). New York: Wiley & Sons.

van Dijk, T. A. (1994). Discourse and cognition in society. In D. Crowley & D. Mitchell (Eds.), *Communication theory today* (pp. 107–126). Cambridge, UK: Polity Press.

Wacquant, L. J. D. (1991). Making class: The middle class(es) in social theory and social structure. In S. G. McNall, R. F. Levine, & R. Fantasia (Eds.), *Bringing class back in* (pp. 39–64). Boulder, CO: Westview Press.

Watson, G., & Seiler, R. M. (Eds.). (1992). *Text in Context.* Thousand Oaks, CA: Sage.

Watson, R. (1987). Doing the organization's work. In S. Fisher & A. Todd (Eds.), *Discourse and institutional authority* (pp. 91–120). Norwood, NJ: Ablex.

Watzlawick, P., Beavin, J., & Jackson, D. D. (1967). *Pragmatics of human communication: A study of interactional patterns, pathologies and paradoxes.* New York: Norton.

Weber, M. (1946). *From Max Weber* (H. H. Gerth & C. W. Mills, Eds). New York: Oxford University Press.

Weber, M. (1947). *The theory of social and economic organization* (T. Parsons, Trans.). New York: Free Press.

Weber, M. (1978). *Economy and society.* Berkeley: University of California Press.

Weedon, C. (1987). *Feminist practice and poststructuralist theory.* Oxford: Basil Blackwell.

Weick, K. E. (1979). *The social psychology of organizing.* Reading, MA: Addison-Wesley.

Weick, K. E. (1985). Sources of order in underorganized systems: Themes in recent organizational theory. In Y. S. Lincoln (Ed.), *Organization theory and inquiry: The paradigm revolution.* Beverley Hills, CA: Sage.

Weick, K. E. (1995). *Sensemaking in organizations.* Thousand Oaks, CA: Sage.

Westrum, R. (1982). Social intelligence about hidden events. *Knowledge, 3,* 381–400.

Whalen, M., & Zimmerman, D. (1987). Sequential and institutional calls for help. *Social Psychology Quarterly, 50,* 172–185.

White, J. L., & Parham, T. A. (1990). *The psychology of blacks: An African-American perspective.* Englewood Cliffs, NJ: Prentice-Hall.

Wiener, N. (1948). *Cybernetics or control and communication in the animal and the machine.* New York: The MIT Press.

Williams, P. (1991). *The alchemy of race and rights.* Cambridge, MA: Harvard University Press.

Williamson, O. E. (1975). *Markets and hierarchies: A study of the economics of internal organizations.* New York: Free Press.

Willis, P. (1977). *Learning to labor: How working class kids get working class jobs.* Farnbrough, Hants: Saxon House.

Wilson, W. J. (1987). *The truly disadvantaged.* Chicago: University of Chicago Press.

Wilson, W. J. (1991). Studying inner-city social dislocation: The challenge of public agenda research. *American Sociological Review, 56,* 1–14.

Wimsatt, W. K., & Beardsley, M. C. (1976). The intentional fallacy. In D. Newton-DeMolina (Ed.), *On literary intention* (pp. 1–13). Edinburgh: Edinburgh University Press.

Winston, B. (1986). *Misunderstanding media.* Cambridge, MA: Harvard University Press.

Wittgenstein, L. (1963). *Philosophical Investigation.* New York: Macmillan.

Wolf, E. (1994). Perilous ideas: Race, culture, people. *Current Anthropology, 35,* 1–12.

Wolin, S. J., & Bennett, L. A. (1984). Family rituals. *Family Process, 23,* 401–420.

Wright, C. R. (1986). *Mass communication: A sociological perspective.* New York: Random House.

Wright, E. O. (1985). *Classes.* London: Verso.

Yazigi, M. P. (1998, February 1). He keeps the blood true blue. *The New York Times,* pp. 9–1, 9–7.

Author Index

Clark, T. N., 194
Clarke, C., 50
Cogdell, R., 167
Cohen, A. P., 142
Cohen, H., 17
Cohen, I., 171
Collier, M. J., 140, 147, 155, 164, 165, 167
Collins, R., 9, 30, 37, 82, 89, 90, 103, 106,
    107, 108, 109, 112, 113, 115,
    128, 189
Conquergood, D., 17
Cooren, F., 23
Covin, D., 164, 165
Croasmun, E., 17
Crompton, R., 194, 199
Crozier, M., 65

D

Daniel, J., 162
Davis, F., 165
Davis, J. A., 185
Davis, K. E., 5, 105
Deetz, S. A., 6, 141
DeFleur, M. L., 19, 25
Delia, J. G., 16, 17
Dennis, R. M., 164
DeParle, J., 176
Derrida, J., 74, 81
DeSanctis, G., 126
Desmond, R., 54, 56
Dillard, J. L., 166
Doob, L., 162
Duboff, R., 66
Duncan, M. C., 32, 35
Dundes, A., 132
Durkheim, E., 9, 30, 104, 106, 122, 142

E

Eason, D. L., 16
Eco, U., 75, 81
Edwards, V., 150, 162, 169, 170
Eisenstein, E., 61
Ellis, D. G., ix, xvi, 3, 21, 81, 85, 110, 123,
    148, 149, 160, 161, 191, 202

Ervin-Tripp, S., 92

F

Farr, R. M., 21
Fave, R. D., 184
Featherstone, M., 203
Fejes, F., 52
Fisher, W. R., 17
Fiske, J., 52
Fitch, K., 12
Fitzpatrick, M. A., 108
Fortner, R. S., 45, 46
Foss, K. A., 17
Foss, S. K., 17
Foucault, M., 69, 74, 121, 129
Fowler, A., 132
Frandsen, K. D., 18
Frankfurt Institute, 196
Franklin, J. H., 164
Frederick, H. H., 62
Friedan, B., xv

G

Gadamer, H. G., 80
Gamson, W., 26
Gans, H. J., 26
Garfinkel, H., 14, 90, 91, 109, 119, 150
Garnham, N., 64
Gates, H. L., 150
Gergen, K. J., 5, 6, 7, 105, 141
Gerstein, D. R., 116, 117
Gibson, W., 28
Giddens, A., xii, xiv, 14, 23, 81, 90, 92,
    93, 101, 103, 104, 106, 110,
    111, 113, 119, 124, 125, 126,
    128, 129, 130, 131, 152, 171,
    173, 202, 204, 206
Giesen, B., 82, 89, 103, 104, 105, 106, 113
Giles, H., 148, 158
Gilligan, C., xv
Giroux, N., 23
Gitlin, T., 20
Givon, T., 11, 38
Glaser, B. G., 8

Subject Index